Continuous Improvement
in Operations

Continuous Improvement in Operations

A Systematic Approach to Waste Reduction

ALAN ROBINSON

Editor

Productivity Press

Portland, Oregon

Productivity, Inc.
P.O. Box 13390
Portland, OR   97213-0390
Telephone: (503) 235-0600
Telefax: (503) 235-0909
E-mail: service@productivityinc.com

Book and cover design by Dick Hannus
Printed and bound by BookCrafters
Printed in the United States of America

Library of Congress Cataloging-in-Publication Data

Continuous improvement in operations: a systematic approach to waste reduction/Alan Robinson, ed.
    p. cm.
  Includes index.
  ISBN 0-915299-51-8
  1. Waste minimization.   2. Production management — Quality control.
3. Factory and trade waste. I. Robinson, Alan (Alan G.)
TS169.C66   1991   658.5 — dc20   90-21651
                                         CIP

02 01 00 99 98   12 11 10 9 8

Contents

Foreword

We hear a lot about the "Silo Syndrome" these days and how the walls of these silos are the physical, mental, and organizational barriers that preclude the kind of revolutionary improvement that is required to remain competitive in the marketplace. To effectively implement the value-adding management process as a strategy for continuous improvement, we should have an understanding of the silo syndrome and, more importantly, how these silos were created. With this understanding, the dismantling of the silos can become a strategic part of a continuous improvement process.

First, ask a few questions about your management structure to trigger your thought process. Before you answer them think about your management process or structure, beginning with a customer inquiry and ending when a check is deposited in the bank.

1. Is your management process vertically or horizontally integrated, or, to ask that question another way, do you manage vertically or horizontally?
2. How and where does your customer fit into your management structure?
3. Does your management structure allow you to focus on the customer or simply on elements within the structure?

The answers to these questions will show you how deeply you are embedded in the silo syndrome. Before continuing, let's shift gears for a moment and look at the value-adding management process as a strategy and then come back to this subject.

The value-adding management process of Just-In-Time Manufacturing, Total Quality Control, and Total Employee Involvement is a simple, uncomplicated management strategy that directs focus on the customer and emphasis on cycle-time reduction through the total elimination of waste in the factory and in the non-factory workplace. Although simplistic in nature, it is complex to understand and even more complex to implement. Essentially, it requires that we think completely differently about how we manage our business. Managing differently means significant and revolutionary change from the top to the bottom of the corporation. Only through revolutionary change can we experience revolutionary improvement. Change of this magnitude requires extraordinary leadership, a knowledge base to provide the understanding, and an uncompromising commitment. With increasing competition in the 1990s and into the 21st century, from all corners of the globe, Western-world industry recognizes that change is essential not only for continued growth and prosperity but in fact, in most cases, to survive. Additionally, the expectations of our customers are continuing to rise at an unprecedented rate as they feel the competitive pressure to continuously improve. The decade of the 1990s will certainly be one of total customer satisfaction or beyond to total customer delight. Do we really understand the magnitude of change that must take place, what that change represents, how to refocus our energies? Do we have the leadership, the knowledge, and the courage to address and manage the process of change? First, we should understand the change that has taken place that got us to where we are today.

These thoughts take me back 30 plus years and help me understand the transition from a small company to a large corporation, from simplicity to complexity, and from a horizontal to a vertical management structure. Additionally, they help me understand the challenges we must face, beginning today and every day in the future.

In the late 'fifties and early 'sixties, when many of today's Fortune 500 companies were much smaller and on a high growth-rate curve, the management structure seemed more horizontal. The management was close to the factory floor and more focused on the customer. The management, manufacturing, and support personnel were more aligned with the product being produced. Essentially, most of the processes producing that product were in the same factory, or, as we know it today, were integrated.

The quality and service were good, the cycle times were much shorter and the P&L looked much brighter. Most of the human resources were relentlessly focused on moving both the product and the information towards the customer. There were few conflicting priorities and few conflicting goals. The morale was good, and you could watch teamwork in action. There was a clear sense of direction. We were truly focused on the customer, we were in a horizontal management structure.

As companies began to grow more rapidly, expansion of their resource base was inevitable. It was thought to be more cost effective to specialize by process and to move like processes into factories of their own. Some refer to them as focused factories, but in fact we changed the concept of manufacturing from a product to a process focus. As this expansion continued and picked up speed and as more and more factories were put into operation, something significant began to happen with the management process. It began to move away from the factory floor. As the business continued to expand, management continued to move further and further away.

As this transition evolved, more and more information was needed to manage the business. This process grew larger and larger like a snowball rolling down the side of a mountain. Concurrent with this transitional period the computer industry, which was in its infancy, gained sufficient justification and motivation to move ahead. The computer manufacturers shifted into high gear and the computer age as we know it today was well on its way. During this time many new departments of just about every discipline were added to the organizational structure, more information was necessary and more employees were required to properly organize, manage, and disperse that information.

By this time the management process had moved out of that horizontal position, away from the product process into what seemed to be the beginning of a transition to a vertical management process. This transitional period can now be documented as a significant management milestone of negative impact, and one that we would long pay a heavy price for. We were now process focused with the management aligned in a vertical direction. But during this transitional period, the product process continued to flow in a horizontal direction, always toward the customer.

In the vertical structure the management process is functionally oriented and is managing the information up and down through departments, functions, divisions, and groups. This is characterized as the typical silo syndrome, and today it is alive and thriving. The silo syndrome encourages employee containment in separate work entities. Therefore, each has priorities and goals that are focused within that work entity, which most times are in conflict with the priorities and goals of the neighboring silos and the corporate silo. In this work setting we are most concerned with operating our silos or work entities efficiently, without regard for the next silo or what happens between the silos or in the remaining part of the company.

The silo syndrome introduces enormous waste into the management process. Waste is characterized as activities that do not add value to the product or service that we sell to the customer: waste such as poor communications, waiting time, transportation of products and information or non-essential information, lost motion, inventory of products and information, defective products, over production, and, most importantly, the waste of unused employee creativity.

When the management process is vertical and the product process is flowing horizontally, the result is many crossroads. Each crossroad is characterized as a silo and enormous quantities of waste are introduced into the process at each one. Therefore, in corporations where organizational structures employ the concept of a department, function, division, or group, there could be hundreds or perhaps thousands of crossroads and silos. Companies have reported that as much as 15% to 25% of their human resources are either managing or working waste. The value-adding management concept employed as a corporate strategy quickly leads the corporation to discover what these wastes are and how to eliminate them. Implementation of the concepts and techniques of this strategy begin a journey of continuous improvement through the elimination of waste. As the journey progresses many benefits begin to accrue. Most obvious is an improvement in the quality of work, cycle time reduction, quicker response to the customer, increased inventory turns, cost reduction, and improved employee morale. The list of benefits seems to be never ending. The goals of increasing market share and improving profits through total customer satisfaction certainly become more realistic and, in fact, within grasp.

Let's now go back to the subject of the silo syndrome and think about our challenge for the future. If you fundamentally agree with what was discussed, then our challenge is clear: we must dismantle the silos. The first step in doing that is turning the management process 90 degrees, back to a horizontal position, to once again realign it with the product process. With this accomplished, all of our energies can be relentlessly focused on moving both the information and the product toward the customer.

It sounds easy, but how do we turn this giant process called management 90 degrees? We begin by forming product focused teams into small business units. The small business unit will include a structure that begins at the top of the organization and ends on the factory floor. This structure will require participants of every engineering and administrative discipline to effectively lead and manage the business unit.

The next step is to empower the team to be self managed. In a self-managed team environment, all participants are associates of equal stature; that includes the factory floor workers. All participants take part in the decision-making processes and are expected and encouraged to contribute to the process of continuous improvement. This change in the management structure immediately dismantles the silos. Next is to integrate the team and the manufacturing of the products as closely as is possible in the same work area. As a result there are no conflicting goals or priorities. There is only one mission; focusing all energy to move information and products to the customer in the shortest time, at the least cost and with the best quality.

As we continue to improve in these areas we also will continually improve our value to our customers. This will lead to total customer satisfaction or perhaps even beyond, to total customer delight.

This brings us full circle. Can we move from complexity back to simplicity? From the large corporation syndrome back to the small company mentality? Do only the essential things, recognize and eliminate waste, bring management back to the factory floor? Sure we can, and it is essential that we do so to continue to stay in front of our competition, to create additional wealth for our companies, and most importantly, to secure our future.

I believe history repeats itself. I also know that all of the things that we need to do and become, we already have done and have been.

The Introduction by Alan Robinson and the subsequent chapters of this book provide the understanding that is essential to effectively organize and implement a journey of continuous improvement. This journey is without a road map and is certainly without an end.

You can begin by committing yourself to a journey of continuous improvement. The value-adding management process as a strategy will provide the tools and techniques to start you on the way. The journey of continuous improvement requires that we set goals and objective for ourselves, the teams, and the business unit. Then select measures that will drive the process and measure the improvement. The last and perhaps the most important prerequisite is that the unit head and members of the management team make an unyielding commitment to provide leadership. It is essential that management demonstrate that commitment and support for the strategy of continuous improvement with an education and training process that provides a fundamental understanding of the value-adding management concepts, tools, and techniques.

Education and training are most effective when they are integrated with the implementation process. In addition to formal education and training, self study should be encouraged and motivated by fostering creative dissatisfaction with what we know. Education in these two forms leads to aggressive improvement of both the individual and the organization.

With the silos dismantled, the teams formed to pursue common goals, armed with the education and training for continuous improvement and with excelling leadership, your organization will see results that will show a continual increase in your market share and achievement of your financial objectives.

This book is highly recommended to managers as well as to academia; all will greatly benefit by understanding what is provided herein. As new graduates infuse the work place in what I believe to be the "Modern Industry of Tomorrow," they will be better equipped to more aggressively contribute and to significantly enhance both their work life and their personal life accordingly.

G. Richard Earhart
Director of Manufacturing Development
AMP Incorporated

Publisher's Message

Ninety-five percent of lead time is estimated in many manufacturing processes to be non-value adding activity. At least thirty percent of the cost of defense contracts is estimated to be spent on waste. Some estimate that eighty percent of hospital administrative and clinical procedures is redo work. Waste reduction is the single most critical focus managers need to have. It is the key to Japanese manufacturing methods and the cornerstone of continuous improvement.

Alan Robinson has once again made a superb reader for us. *Continuous Improvement in Operations: A Systematic Approach to Waste Reduction* introduces business and engineering students as well as managers to the processes of Just-In-Time, *kaizen*, and Total Employee Involvement. This well-structured text offers a compendium of selections from Productivity Press's best works to combine the principles of such industry leaders as Henry Ford, Taiichi Ohno (creator of JIT), Shigeo Shingo (creator of Single-Minute-Exchange-of-Die), and Seiichi Nakajima (creator of TPM).

Robinson's introduction integrates the developments of these manufacturing gurus within a two-fold theme — elimination of invisible waste in the work place and the creation of an adaptable work environment that welcomes and fosters employees' ideas. He provides an historical and global perspective on the development of the management systems that employ these methods. In demonstrating that much of Japanese management philosophy was originated by Americans such as Deming, Juran, and Ford, Robinson underscores that there really are no cultural barriers to these systems.

G. Richard Earhart's Foreword offers the manager's perspective on these systems for reducing waste and fostering employee involvement. His contribution adds the valuable insight into organizational structure that is needed to succeed in carrying out one's commitment to continuous improvement. He demonstrates the drawbacks of the traditional vertical management hierarchies. This "silo structure" distances manager's from the process and creates an overwhelming obstacle to identifying and eliminating waste in the system. Earhart offers a cross-functional management structure that brings manager's back in direct contact with the process and disperses responsibility for quality outcomes to everyone in the organization.

We are proud of this volume and grateful to all those who contributed to its concept and completion. To Alan G. Robinson, associate professor of operations management at the University of Massachusetts School of Management, Amherst, for editing the volume and for his introduction and first chapter. To G. Richard Earhart, Director of Manufacturing Development of AMP Incorporated, Harrisburg, Pennsylvania, one of the world's leading manufacturers of electrical and electronic connection devices, for his Foreword. To Dick Hannus for the cover design; to Elizabeth Mokas and Paul Obringer for marketing insight; David Lennon and Beverly Ream and the production team at Rudra Press for book design and layout; and to Diane Asay, Marie Cantlon, and Barry Shulak for managing the editorial process.

Norman Bodek
Chairman, Productivity, Inc.

Introduction

Manpower is something that is beyond measurement.
Capabilities can be extended indefinitely
when everyone begins to think.

Taiichi Ohno

In 1989, the MIT Commission on Industrial Productivity published a book entitled *Made in America*, which contained the results of a three-year study of the competitiveness of American industry. One of the study's findings was that:

> *Another area in which U.S. firms have often lagged behind their overseas competitors is in exploiting the potential for continuous improvement in the quality and reliability of their products and processes. The cumulative effect of successive incremental improvements and modifications to established products and processes can be very large and may outpace efforts to achieve technological breakthroughs.*[1]

"Continuous improvement," for which the Japanese term is *kaizen*, has become a distinctive and successful feature of the Japanese management style. One easily identifiable reason for this is Mr. Taiichi Ohno, who pioneered the Toyota Production System, the first Just-in-Time (JIT) system, at Toyota Motor Corporation. Unfortunately, many people still misunderstand

---

[1] M.L. Dertouzos, R.K. Lester, R.M. Solow and the MIT Commission on Industrial Productivity, *Made in America*, MIT Press, Cambridge, MA, 1989, p. 74.

Mr. Ohno's system, seeing it merely as a set of tools that allows inventory to be lowered further than was usual before Mr. Ohno came along. But that view is flawed, as Mr. Ohno and his colleagues will tell you in the pages that follow, for the real goal of JIT is *to eliminate all waste*, namely, to get rid of anything that adds to *cost* without adding to *value*. To eliminate each particular case of waste, an improvement must be made. A true JIT system, therefore, is also a system of managing *kaizen*.

Implementing *kaizen* requires three things. First, operating practices must expose new opportunities for improvement. Second, every employee should be made to *want* overall improvement rather than to *fear* it, as is often the case. Third, workers should be trained in practical problem-solving techniques so they are *able* to make improvements. The success stories coming from many manufacturing sectors in Japan, and increasingly from other countries as well, reflect the efforts of people like Mr. Ohno who have thought seriously about the management of *kaizen*, have put their ideas into action, and made them work.

There have probably been more books written about what people refer to as "Japanese production techniques" than about impending depressions, or quick ways to become a millionaire. Only in the last few years, however, have the writings of those Japanese who were or are *directly involved* been translated into English. All but two chapters included here are selected from their books and represent the wisdom and experience that is unique to the developers and inventors themselves. As you will see, the selections deal directly with the problem of how constantly to improve — through good operating practices, employee involvement, and rigorous training — and they aim always for the ultimate goal: the total elimination of waste.

THE LUDDITE REBELLION

The Luddite Rebellion of 1812, which took place in northern England, has come to represent the often difficult problem of introducing new technology or methods into the workplace. Every manager should know the story of the Luddites, as it is an interesting one and contains some valuable lessons.

Some thirty years before the actual uprising, an apprentice called Ned Ludd was beaten, although by whom, or for what, is not known. Ludd so resented this treatment that he destroyed the equipment he was learning to use by smashing it with a hammer. Even though motivated by anger at his punishment rather than at his equipment, the destruction of his machinery became a powerful symbol. When the rebellion started, one of its leaders took the name "General Ludd" as his *nom de guerre*, and his followers became known as "Luddites." Since then the word "Luddite" has come to have the looser meaning of "one who opposes improvements in production methods or technology."

The revolt began when some textile mill owners introduced a new machine to perform a cloth-finishing operation called "cropping." The process of manufacturing cloth at that time involved first weaving, then stretching the cloth on a frame, and finally brushing it with wire brushes to give it a smooth surface and texture. This last procedure, while indeed smoothing the cloth, also left a layer of fluff that had to be skillfully removed, or "cropped," to obtain a good final finish. Croppers used huge shears that sometimes weighed more than fifty pounds, for the heavier the blade was, the smoother the finish. They were tough people, with huge arm and chest muscles, since working with fifty pound blades developed great strength and endurance. The average cropper earned almost *four times* the pay of an ordinary worker. In short, they were the elite of the textile workers and were not about to stand back to let machines take their places.

The croppers' fight against the new machines might have remained an historical footnote if their cause had not also spread to involve ordinary workers. Because Britain was then at war with both France and the United States, and all exports of textiles had been banned for the duration, the industry had fallen on hard times. Textile workers were having difficulty; they were getting less work, or losing their jobs. Trouble was to be expected when the mill owners, who were also struggling, tried to cut costs by introducing machines that could crop in one hour what had previously taken a skilled cropper five hours. Since the textile industry was a major employer, accounting in one area of north England for an estimated 97 percent of the workforce, one sees how this grave threat to a group like the croppers might act as the spark for the serious disturbance that it did. Masked Luddites attacked mill after mill, murdered owners, and smashed machinery; soldiers and workers were killed.

By the end of the revolt, tens of thousands of regular troops and local militia had been involved in subduing the workers. Although several hundred people had died, the cropping machinery was nevertheless successfully installed and operating. The power of the cloth croppers had been broken, and their livelihood was gone.

RESISTANCE TO CHANGE = WASTE

The Luddite Revolt was, admittedly, an extreme circumstance, but its message is even more true today. Resistance to new technology or improved work methods is both futile and costly. It can, therefore, be very depressing to observe the operations of an organization whose employees, for whatever reason, are not constantly improving products and processes. Consumers today are increasingly cost-conscious and better-informed — the magazine *Consumer Reports,* for example, has a circulation exceeding 5 million — and quickly move to the best products. How can a company without a program of continuous improvement compete against a company with one? Organizations that resist appropriate change abound with examples of inexcusable waste — waste for which someone has to pay.

In February of 1982, President Reagan formed a presidential commission, known as the *President's Private Sector Survey on Cost Control* (PPSSCC), chaired by Mr. J. Peter Grace, a Democrat. The bipartisan commission's mandate was to identify *pure waste* in the Federal Government, that is, waste that all could agree was waste and which, in theory at least, could be eliminated easily.

Some of the findings of the study were quite shocking. For example, 50 percent of federal travel in 1982 occurred at *full fare,* even though government business was large enough to be eligible for big discounts. If the government had paid the same low rates as an average corporation, the savings would have been one billion dollars over three years. In 1982, it cost the Army $4.20 to issue each paycheck — the average private sector cost was one dollar. The Postal Service used a Treasury account to issue 22.4 million checks in that year, at a cost of slightly over a dollar each. If an ordinary commercial bank had been used where the Postal Service could have negotiated a rate as low as ten cents per check, the annual savings would have exceeded $20 million. In 1982, the cost of processing (not paying) each medical claim at the Veteran's Administration (VA) was about $120, and rose as high as $200 at the Indian Health Service (IHS). In the private insurance industry, the cost to process one claim was between three and six dollars. In addition, 15-20 percent of the payments by the VA and the IHS were made in error — either more than once or for an uncovered service. The possible annual savings from less expensive and more accurate processing were estimated at $1.1 billion. As the commission pointed out, this sum would have paid the medical costs of one million retired couples in 1981.

All in all, the study[2] documented $140 billion per year in pure governmental waste. Ironically, the complete report was more than one and a half million pages long, a total wordage that may account for its quick disappearance from the political scene. Additionally, in my opinion, the report showed a somewhat naive attitude towards public-sector waste, for much of the 'pure' waste was not, in fact, so pure. Special interest groups often stood to gain by it, and could be counted upon to fight change.

Inertia, of course, always impedes change, and sometimes with amusing results. In the Second World War, the British Army Operational Research Group (AORG) was asked to study the operations of the Royal Artillery, to see if more efficient methods of operation could be found. Mr. Omond Solandt, then the director of AORG, explains what happened when the experts showed up:

> *In this case we took movies of the gun unit going into action. Everything looked quite good, except that there was one man who spent a long time just standing still doing*

---

2 Partial findings of the study were published in two interesting books, *Burning Money*, by J. Peter Grace, and *War on Waste*, by the PPSSCC; both books were published in 1984 by Macmillan Co., New York.

nothing. When we looked back over the drill to discover what he was supposed to be doing, we found out he was in fact holding the horses! The horses, of course, had disappeared about twenty years earlier, but this task had not been eliminated when the gun drill had been rewritten.[3]

Force of habit is indeed strong. Quite recently, while visiting a large toy-manufacturing plant, I found myself standing next to a machine designed to count a selection of small parts into a plastic bag, and then seal and weigh it. If the weight was incorrect, that is, if the bag did not contain the right number of parts, a jet of air would blow it into a "defects" bin, with a sharp and noticeable *pssst*. If all was in order, it would instead be dropped into a container of bags that had passed inspection.

Interestingly, the defects bin seemed to contain the majority of the machine's output. The plant's Manufacturing Systems Manager, standing next to me, explained that the bin of defects was full only because it was emptied every five or six shifts, thus the defects we were looking at represented several days' worth. *Pssst!* A rejected bag dropped into the defects bin. "What about that one?" I asked. The manager said that the operator had probably just set up the machine, and was still debugging and adjusting it. But no, the operator was sitting next to the machine filling out some paperwork and was plainly uninterested in the latest defective output his machine had generated. *Pssst!* Another bag was rejected. As we stood there watching, the machine misfilled more bags than it filled correctly. The operator, however, remained unconcerned throughout — as did his manager, who didn't so much as step over to ask his subordinate what the matter was. As we walked away, he commented that the defects really were not a big problem, for at the end of the shift these bags would simply be torn open and the contents reloaded into the machine. At this point, it might be worth mentioning that the machine was not a particularly complicated one and was, in fact, quite commonplace. Identical, but properly operated, equipment in other firms might misfill only one or two bags in every thousand.

---

[3] Ormond Solandt, "Observation, Experiment, and Measurement in Operations Research," *Operations Research*, 3, 1955, p. 3.

Henry Ford and Taiichi Ohno would have had something to say about this plant, as will you, no doubt, after reading the selections in this book. Why do some organizations tolerate waste, while others operate in an atmosphere of constant change and improvement? "Efficiency" should not be something to fear, for it should never mean "working harder or less safely." In fact, the most difficult and hazardous work is usually done in the *least efficient* work environments.

WHO IS RESPONSIBLE FOR WASTE

The Scientific Management movement of the early part of this century was sharply divided over the answer to one question that is very pertinent here: if there is waste and sloppiness, who is responsible for it: poor management or a Luddite workforce? The aim of Scientific Management was an admirable one: to develop methods that would enable managers to study and solve production problems "scientifically," and to set proper piece-rates and labor standards based on tightly controlled time-trials. Interestingly, the two major founders of the movement disagreed over the question of responsibility.

To Frederick Taylor (1856-1915) the main purpose of the new discipline was to eliminate "soldiering" — the practice of workers deliberately not working as fast as they were able to. A new employee would be warned by his associates to work slowly. A fast worker, or "ratebuster," was shunned by his co-workers. During his years in the steel industry, then rife with conflict between union and management, Taylor had witnessed countless instances of soldiering. He deplored, and sought to eliminate, this practice. He proposed that a scientific analysis, involving stopwatch studies of the very fastest workers, could be used to set an *absolute* standard for each job, so that management would know whenever a worker slacked off.

Since the standard times set were based on the work rate of the speediest workers, they were brutal. In fact, Taylor expected that only one worker out of *eight* would be able to meet them. To the delight of the labor unions, he even stressed this last point in the famous Congressional hearings, which had been called at union instigation in order to try to ban Scientific Management from all workplaces receiving federal funds. Prior to the hearings, Taylor, certainly no diplomat, had unfortunately likened workers to oxen. His comments, widely disseminated in the newspapers at the time, did great damage to the reputation of the fledgling field and resulted in legislation that outlawed stopwatch studies on federally-funded jobs. Taylor had already formed a strong dislike for labor unions which, he claimed, worked against the interests of the best workers because

> *labor organizations meant the lowering of their wages*
> *so that inferior men might earn more.*[4]

Taylor also claimed that his methods had weakened and would eventually eliminate the unions completely. In summary, his view of how "science" should be applied to work methods was that it should be used mainly as a disciplinary tool against lazy workers. To Frederick Taylor, the root of inefficiency lay mostly in the *worker*.

To Frank Gilbreth (1868-1924), on the other hand, the problem lay less with the worker and more with *management*, whose job it was to find the simplest and easiest way to do the work. When he entered a plant, he asked to see not the *fastest* worker, but the *slowest*:

> *"The kind of fellow I want,"* he'd say, *"is the fellow who*
> *is so lazy he won't even scratch himself. You must have one of*
> *those around someplace. Every factory has them."*[5]

He believed that by studying the laziest his own work would be made simpler and easier, for such a person would not waste any motions at all.

Frank Gilbreth began his career as an apprentice bricklayer, having opted not to go to college. Throughout his apprenticeship, he was assigned to work under many different master-bricklayers, each of whom told him to lay the bricks in a different way. Natur-

---

[4] Edna Yost, *Frank and Lillian Gilbreth: Partners for Life*, Rutgers University Press, New Brunswick, NJ, 1949, p. 49.

[5] Frank B. Gilbreth Jr. and E. G. Carey, *Cheaper by the Dozen*, Bantam Books, New York, NY, 1988, p. 94.

ally, this set him to thinking about the best way to do the job. He rapidly worked his way up in the construction business until he broke away to start his own firm in 1895, when he was twenty-seven years old. His new company specialized in "speed building" (i.e., building *fast*, but *well*) and rapidly became one of the largest construction enterprises on the East Coast. One example of this speed building was his firm's construction of the Lowell Laboratory at the Massachusetts Institute of Technology, completed less than three months after he signed the contract, even though the start of the project was delayed by rain for ten days. The *Boston Evening Transcript* reported that

> *thirteen hundred piles had been driven, a million bricks laid, iron beams placed and concrete foundations strong enough to support heavy engines and dynamos, and an adequate heating and ventilating system installed — forty thousand square feet laid out in forty-seven rooms, and a powerhouse besides.*[6]

Gilbreth's speed was achieved in a very different way than Taylor's. He studied each job very carefully to make the work simpler and easier. He invented the Gilbreth Scaffold to eliminate the stooping and lifting that made bricklaying so tiring. His studies reduced the number of motions required to lay bricks from eighteen to six. Bricklayers using his methods could lay 2,600 bricks in a day, a far better figure than the industry average of about 500. Not surprisingly, he was able to pay his workers considerably more than they would be able to earn elsewhere, for work that was no harder. His point was: "Work smarter, not harder."

Owing to his background, Frank Gilbreth had a natural sympathy with workers, and favored union labor over non-union labor. He believed that motion studies could find the Gilbreth One Best Way to do any job and applied his methods everywhere he could: hospitals, work design for the handicapped, typing — and even to one kind of work that he observed at the Japanese-British Exposition in London during the summer of 1910:

---

[6] Op. cit. Edna Yost, p. 13.

One of the points of interest at the Exposition was a young Japanese woman who put papers on boxes of shoe polish at so wonderful a speed that she constantly attracted a crowd. An acquaintance who thought Gilbreth was a little too hipped on the efficiency of motion studies, arranged to take him as though quite casually to see the young woman whose work would refute Gilbreth's claim that, unless a job had already been properly motion studied, he could shorten the time it consumed.

They stood watching her for a brief period, then Frank took out his stop watch to time the work. She finished 24 boxes in 40 seconds. He stepped up to her and told her she was not working in the best way. She was irritated, then incensed. But she was working at piece rates and Frank had a way with him when he wanted to win a person over, so she was soon willing to try something better. He made rearrangements, showed her exactly how to do the work in the new way. On her first try she completed twenty-four boxes in twenty-six seconds, on her second try the same number in twenty seconds. When the friend readily admitted the result was accomplished with fewer motions, not harder work, Frank gave the girl a shilling and a smile and walked away. [7]

In short, Frank Gilbreth's version of Scientific Management treated workers with more respect than did Taylor's. Far from *resenting* change, workers who benefited from their increased productivity *appreciated* the improvement. Under the Taylor paradigm, the reaction was precisely the opposite.

Many of the ideas contained in this book have their roots in the Gilbreth version of Scientific Management. There is a good reason for this. The next chapter, entitled "Origins of the Modern Japanese Management Style," tells how vast numbers of Japanese managers first learned about Gilbreth's ideas after the Second World War. But since that time, much more has been added to the understanding of how to manage systems so that their productivity constantly increases. Technology issues aside, there are two main

---

[7] Ibid., p. 181.

points that eluded Frank Gilbreth. First, it is much better if everyone in the company, not just management, is actively involved in seeking improvements. Second, quite often when the One Best Way is thought to have been found, there turns out to be an *even better* way.

THE MANAGEMENT OF KAIZEN

According to Masaaki Imai, one of Japan's foremost improvement experts:

> Kaizen *is everybody's business. The* kaizen *concept is crucial to understanding the differences between the Japanese and Western approaches to management. If asked to name the most important difference between Japanese and Western management concepts, I would unhesitatingly say, "Japanese* kaizen *and its process-oriented way of thinking versus the West's innovation-and results-oriented thinking."* . . . *Basically, there are only two kinds of companies: those that subscribe to* kaizen *and those that do not.*[8]

Interestingly, formal kaizen programs are a relatively recent development in Japan. Indeed, in the period of the Kansei Reforms (1789-93: these reforms followed a period of natural disaster and governmental misrule, and endeavored to get the country back on a civilized footing), one law had declared that "You must never invent anything new."[9] As will also be discussed in the next chapter, a rudimentary form of kaizen was introduced into Japan after the Second World War by the Allied occupation forces under General Douglas MacArthur. Later chapters describe the level of sophistication that the management of kaizen has reached since that time.

Three things are required for a successful *kaizen* program. First, operating practices must expose new improvement oppor-

---

[8] Masaaki Imai, *Kaizen: The Key to Japan's Competitive Success*, Random House, New York, 1986, p. xxix and xxxiii.

[9] Shoichi Watanabe, *The Peasant Soul of Japan*, St. Martin's Press, New York, 1989, p. 177.

tunities; second, *every* employee should be made to *want* overall improvement; and third, workers should be trained in practical problem-solving techniques so they are *able* to make the improvements.

Operating Practices Must Expose New Improvement Opportunities.

It is often asserted that the first JIT system was in fact developed at Henry Ford's River Rouge plant in the early 1900s. Indeed, as the selection written by Henry Ford will show, his goal was, like Mr. Ohno's, the total elimination of waste. For this and other reasons, Mr. Ohno has said frequently that, despite some significant differences between the two, his JIT system is a logical development of Henry Ford's. Henry Ford used minimal inventory, exercised "visual control," and installed foolproofing mechanisms, just as Taiichi Ohno did, though the Toyota Production System is far more advanced. In the selection taken from *Just-in-Time for Today and Tomorrow*, Mr. Ohno discusses the types of waste that the Ford system ignored.

Waste, you will recall, is *that which adds cost without adding value.* It is not always easy to eliminate. Dr. Shigeo Shingo, who worked with Mr. Ohno on the development of the Toyota Production System, explains:

> *Eliminate waste! This slogan is often shouted by management, yet we won't find much of what we imagine as waste lying around in the workplace. Unfortunately, real waste lurks in forms that do not look like waste. . . . We must always keep in mind that* the greatest waste is waste we don't see.[10]

The purpose of the JIT production control system is to expose and eliminate invisible waste. Interestingly, Taiichi Ohno cleverly uses one particular kind of waste, that of the inventory associated with overproduction, to discover the other kinds. Mr. Ohno explains the philosophy of his system with an effective analogy.

---

[10] Shigeo Shingo, *The Sayings of Shigeo Shingo*, Productivity Press, Cambridge, MA, 1987, p. 18.

We are asked to think of the company as a *ship*, and its inventory as the *water* upon which the ship floats. Rocks, hidden under the surface of the water, represent production problems such as unreliable vendors, high absenteeism, poor quality of raw materials or output, machine breakdowns, long setup times or leadtimes, and unbalanced processes. If the water level is high enough, the ship will not hit a rock, that is, the company will not encounter any problems, because they are concealed by inventory. But the problems are there, nevertheless, and together with the inventory required to cover them up, they constitute waste. The tactic of JIT is to lower the inventory water level until a problem rock appears. The rock is then leveled off, so that the water can be lowered further until another problem appears, and so on. In this way, bit by bit, waste that was previously invisible is exposed. A true JIT system is a *kaizen* program, for it never stops trying to make improvements.

Every Employee Should Be Made to Want Overall Improvement.

Many companies that practice *kaizen* use some form of suggestion system to encourage their employees to seek improvements and to collect their ideas. The rate of participation in these systems is a good indicator of the attitude of the workforce. In 1988, Toyota Motor Corporation, for example, received an average of over thirty-three suggestions from each employee. Also in that year, workers at Canon Inc., whose system is described in one of the selections of this book, submitted an average of over forty-six ideas each. The Japanese company with the highest annual suggestion rate in 1988 was Tohoku Oki Electric, which received an amazing average of 1035 ideas from each worker. During a recent visit to the Saiyama plant of Honda Motor (located near Tokyo), I was told that one woman there had submitted 1500 suggestions in 1989. A National Association of Suggestion Systems survey in the same year estimated that U.S. companies received an average of *one* suggestion from every *nine* workers.

John Patterson of National Cash Register Co. (NCR), who founded one of the world's earliest corporate suggestion systems in 1894, called it the company's "hundred-headed brain." When,

early in that year, he learned that his workers were sabotaging the
cash registers by pouring acid in them, he moved his desk onto the
factory floor to find the reason why. He quickly discovered the
sources of the trouble — poor working conditions and bad labor
relations — and took action to eliminate them. His suggestion system, later to be a model for many Japanese companies, was just
one component of the resulting company-wide *kaizen* program.
Earlier, I described a toy-manufacturing plant in which the manufacturing manager unconcernedly watched one of his machines
produce more defects than good output. Later in the day, he was
asked if top management had thought about installing a suggestion system, so that many of the process problems observed on the
production floor could be addressed by those who knew best how
to solve them. The answer came back as a question, "Do you have
any idea what kinds of problems of authority suggestion systems
raise between workers and their managers?"

The selection from *The Idea Book*, written by the Japan
Human Relations Association, discusses what is needed to implement an effective suggestion system. It will indeed cause many
hitherto unnoticed problems to surface, including those involving
human relations and issues of authority. Every suggestion, whether
accepted or not, is an opportunity. If accepted, it leads to an
improvement. If it is not accepted, then the worker learns when
the reason for its rejection is explained. Some other points are
important to remember too.

A Suggestion Is Worth Much More Than the Monetary Savings It Offers.

Matsushita Electric has consistently had one of the strongest
suggestion systems in Japan:

> *At one of Matsushita's plants, the waitresses in the cafe-
> teria formed QC [quality control] circles and studied the tea
> consumption during the lunch period. When large tea pots
> were placed on the tables with no restrictions on use, the wait-
> resses noticed, tea consumption differed greatly from table to
> table. Therefore, they collected data on the tea-drinking
> behavior of employees during lunch. For one thing, they found*

that the same people tended to sit at the same table. After tak-
ing and analyzing data for days, they were able to establish
an expected consumption level for each table. Using their
findings, they started putting out different amounts of tea
for each table, with the result that they were able to reduce
tea-leaf consumption to half. How much were their activities
worth in terms of the actual amount of money saved?
Probably very little. However, they were awarded the
Presidential Gold Medal for the year.[11]

More important than money, apparently, was the attitude of
pride and the sense of participation the QC circle demonstrated.
While it is possible to calculate the value of the direct benefits of a
kaizen program, who can put a worth on the "hundred-headed
brain" — a workforce alert for opportunities to eliminate waste
and improve operations?

Performance Measurement Systems Should Not Blind People To Opportunities for Improvement.

Recently, in a large food processing plant, it was noticed that
one packing line was sealing products into boxes that were then
carried fifty yards to another packaging line where they were being
torn open and emptied. Upon being asked if it were possible, by
not packing in boxes products intended for immediate use by the
second line, to eliminate this waste of labor and materials, the production manager said "no," because the first line had to "sell" its
finished output (the packed boxes) to the second line, for accounting reasons. Each line, it turned out, was a separate profit unit
within the plant. It was a shame, he admitted, but the extra labor,
wasted boxes, tape, labels, and glue were necessary.

Mr. Ohno and his disciples are not the most ardent fans of the
discipline of cost accounting. Since employees tailor their behavior
to whichever performance measurement scheme is used, and since
these schemes often measure only a small part of the full picture,
waste can be created. In the case of the food processing plant, the
accounting scheme encouraged the production managers to move

---

[11] Op. cit. Masaaki Imai, p. 19.

in an expensive and common-sense-defying direction, causing them to run up a huge bill through the destruction of hundreds of new boxes per day, without noticing anything wrong. Information that results from an accounting exercise can give a distorted picture of the situation and should be used with care. A manager must be willing on occasion to disregard such flawed signals. That is what Mr. Ohno did, and suffered for, during the development of the Toyota Production System. His admiration for the accounting profession presumably did not increase when, in 1978, he was passed over in favor of an accountant for promotion to chairman at the company which owed much of its success to him.

Do Not Cash In On Improvements In a Way That Penalizes Workers.

I came across a good example of *kaizen* during a case study of DTL Ltd., a joint venture between Toyota Motor Corporation and DCM Ltd, an Indian company. The DTL plant, located about twenty miles south of Delhi, India, manufactures light trucks and uses the Toyota Production System. One operation involved the adjustment of the windshield washer jets to make them aim at the correct part of the windshield. The job required two workers, one inside the cab to squirt the jets at the command of the other, who was on the outside to make the adjustments. The *kaizen* suggestion was for a simple extension cord, easily attachable to the wiper button on the dashboard, so that someone *outside* the cab could activate the jets. The idea was accepted and, as the Toyota Production System dictated, the extra worker was reassigned to more productive work elsewhere in the plant. Would the worker who suggested the improvement have done so if he had thought the company would lay off either him or his colleague?

James Abegglen and George Stalk, of the Boston Consulting Group's Tokyo office, estimate in their book *Kaisha: the Japanese Corporation*, that in a plant operating under Just-in-Time the productivity of labor is almost three times higher than in an equivalent plant without this system. Since the workers themselves are expected to strive for the total elimination of waste, Mr. Ohno and his colleagues must have a good answer to the following question: what should be done when enough waste is eliminated so that fewer workers are needed? The answer has to be: don't fire the excess workers; use them more productively elsewhere. A foolproof way to prevent improvement, of course, is to lay off employees for improving.

Good Suggestions and Improvements Should Be Well Rewarded.

A job at the Lincoln Electric Company of Cleveland, Ohio, is a highly desirable one and it is not very difficult to see why. Its employees are generously rewarded for their improvement efforts. In 1946, because of his employees' high productivity, James Lincoln, brother of the company's founder and then general manager, was able to boast that his workers were the highest paid in manufacturing anywhere in the world. This might well be true even today: in 1988, the top paid line worker, whose job was to put equipment in boxes, took home $107,000. The compensation of several of his co-workers also exceeded $100,000. The company has never laid off a worker, even during several severe business downturns when another firm might well have done so. James Lincoln articulated the importance of employee involvement when, in 1946, he wrote:

> *Management, if it is to be the best obtainable, must be the collective intelligence of the whole organization. No one man, or even a small group of men, can have sufficient knowledge, experience, and wisdom to make decisions that can be as sound as they would be if these decisions represented the collective intelligence and experience of the group. The problem is to get this collective intelligence and experience to bear on decisions as they are made.*[12]

It is true, though, that the standard suggestion system described in these readings has some limitations. Because suggestion-making is worker-initiated and voluntary, it is undirected. Management has little control over the pace or direction of the change that comes through the suggestion box. Additionally, com-

---

[12] J.F. Lincoln, *Lincoln's Incentive System*, McGraw-Hill, New York, 1946, p. 105.

munication and consideration of improvement proposals require a considerable overhead of paperwork and evaluation committees.

The QC circle, a group of employees gathered to solve specific problems, can be a useful mechanism to impose more order on the process of change. QC circles often operate in conjunction with suggestion systems. They submit solutions to problems as a group and share the reward. One division of General Electric has an enterprising way to cut the overhead of a written suggestion system. Managers reward good ideas *instantly* with prizes they carry on their person, such as cash and tickets to sports events, concerts, or baseball games.

Ironically, NCR, whose suggestion system (mentioned earlier) has been a model for many companies in Japan, dropped its program in 1972, because of the very difficulties mentioned above. Under its current system, each employee "owns" his or her process, and can make the changes to it he or she wishes, as long as assigned performance levels are met. A bonus system provides incentive.

Employees Should Be Trained In Practical Problem-solving Techniques So That They Are Able To Make Improvements.

The selection taken from *Introduction to Total Productive Maintenance* (TPM) by Seiichi Nakajima, is about one useful 'rock leveling' tool. Since *preventive* maintenance is often confused with *productive* maintenance, many plants practice the former without the latter. Much is lost when this happens, for there are higher goals than breakdown prevention, and *all* workers, not just maintenance personnel, can be reaching to attain them. Some companies — including the two discussed at length in this book, Toyota Motor and Canon Inc. — go even further than TPM. They make very nearly all their own manufacturing equipment, for three reasons. First, it is often cheaper to *make* special-purpose equipment than to *buy* powerful general purpose machines of which only a few features will be used. Second, processes are kept more proprietary. Third, and perhaps most important, the resulting in-house engineering know-how gives the company's *kaizen* efforts a strong backbone. At the opposite extreme are firms at the mercy of their equipment; indeed, one Western Massachusetts company has to fly in an engineer from Switzerland each time its Swiss-made machines need servicing.

Another important 'rock,' addressed by Dr. Shingo in the excerpt from *Zero Quality Control*, is poor quality. The concept of *poka-yoke* is at the heart of zero-defect manufacturing. A *poka-yoke* is a device or practice that sees to it that an error, once its cause is known, does not recur. Many companies still use methods of *monitoring* or *controlling* quality (such as Statistical Quality Control), even when it is possible for them to use simple tools like *poka-yoke* that *assure* quality. The distinction between *control* and *assurance* is one that Dr. Shingo makes clear in the selection taken from his book. As can be readily seen, he is not the world's most avid fan of Statistical Quality Control.

A problem-solving tool often associated with the JIT system is Single Minute Exchange of Die (SMED), briefly discussed in the selection taken from the Japan Management Association's *Kanban: Just-in-Time at Toyota*, which reduces setup times.

In the end, however, tools like TPM, *poka-yoke*, and SMED amount to a set of principles, distilled from experience, that can only *guide* the problem-solving process. Only rarely can a specific resolution be found by consulting a book. A creative step is needed. Such a step might be provided by *brainstorming*, a formal procedure for group problem-solving that is briefly touched on in the selection taken from *The Idea Book*. Brainstorming is often attributed to Alex F. Osborn, a Madison Avenue advertising executive who championed its effectiveness in the 1950s and 1960s. The method, however, predates Mr. Osborn. It was known as "Prai-Barshana" to the Hindu teachers who practiced it over 400 years ago. Roughly speaking, the procedure is as follows: the leader poses the problem to the group members, who respond with any answers which occur to them, no matter how farfetched. At this point, quantity of ideas is more important than their quality. So that the fear of criticism will not inhibit the group's creativity, negative reaction to any idea is not expressed until the second stage, when ideas are judged.

All this is not to say that individuals cannot be creative on their own. Obviously, a creative person does better with a well-stocked mind. However, as many authors (certainly Mr. Osborn is included) point out, *willpower* is also a critical determinant of a person's ability to find an effective solution to a tricky problem. Some people not only lack the necessary drive but try to deprive others of it as well. Dr. Shingo has a word for such people: "Nyet engineers."

> Nyet *is the Russian word for "no." A Soviet ambassador to the United Nations was once nicknamed "Mr. Nyet" because he invariably said* nyet *to proposals put forward by Western nations. There are many people like that ambassador who say "No, that's impossible," "No, that's too difficult," or "No, that won't work" to almost all proposed improvements without giving them any real thought.*
>
> *In any plant there are usually several of these nyet-sayers who always have their reasons for claiming that things will not work.* Nyet *engineers tend to be well educated and to hold relatively high positions, which makes the problem all the thornier. Any proposed improvement is bound to entail problems, some minor, some major. But saying "this won't work" all the time will never lead to progress.*[13]

Separation of idea generation from adverse criticism, as employed in the method of brainstorming, is one way to neutralize *Nyet* engineers. Henry Ford, as you will read, had another: simply never assign a difficult job to anyone with experience. John Patterson of NCR practiced the most drastic solution of all: he just fired anyone who said, "It can't be done."

McDonald's somewhat amusing entry into Japan was certainly not led by a *Nyet* engineer. Mr. Fujita, CEO of the new McDonald's Japan, insisted that the first store be in the Ginza, the famous shopping district in Tokyo. His reason? One million people, including many American tourists, walk through the Ginza each day. He felt that if the Japanese saw the Americans eating the hamburgers from McDonald's, they would try the food too. But Mr. Fujita had a small problem. After considerable effort, for retail spots on the Ginza were (and still are) in much demand, not

---

[13] Shigeo Shingo, *Non-Stock Production*, Productivity Press, Cambridge, MA, 1988, p. 193.)

to mention outrageously expensive, he managed to persuade the Mitsukoshi department store to lease him five hundred square feet of space, an area the size of a large living room, and about one-fifth the size of a normal McDonald's restaurant. Since the store did not want its operations disrupted by construction, however, it insisted that the whole restaurant be constructed in *thirty-nine hours.* Mr. Fujita promptly hired a crew of seventy workers and set them to practice-building mock restaurants in a rented warehouse. After a number of sessions, they were ready. Two days before the opening ceremonies, a contingent of top McDonald's executives arrived from America for the occasion and were horrified when Mr. Fujita proudly showed them where the store *would be built.* But the workers did their job and the new store was ready on time.

CONCLUSION

In 1985, the Harley-Davidson motorcycle company came very close to bankruptcy. At that point, it seemed certain that stronger competitors who produced superior products at lower cost, such as Honda and Yamaha, would drive the company out of business. The situation was bad: over half the Harley-Davidson motorcycles were not working when they came off the assembly line (70 percent of them had parts missing!). Their quality was so poor that many dealers operated their own "reassembly lines" to disassemble and reassemble every incoming new bike, since that way was cheaper than making repairs. At any given time, an average of *seven days'* worth of production was awaiting rework in the company's plant. Some processes within the factory were making parts of which over half were defective. Engines leaked oil so badly that puddles formed underneath the bikes when they were parked. The ride, too, was uncomfortable. People joked that Harley-Davidson owners needed two bikes, so they could ride one while the other was being fixed. The Japanese bikes, on the other hand, were quiet, fast, clean, and dependable — in addition to being less expensive. Even worse, Yamaha introduced the Virago, a motorcycle very like a Harley, that cost some 25 percent less. Harley-Davidson's market share of heavyweight motorcycles, once 80 percent, slipped to below 20 percent.

But the management of Harley-Davidson, not easily defeated, took steps to improve the situation. Among their first actions was a visit to the Honda plant in Marysville, Ohio. Surprisingly, Honda welcomed this. For political reasons, it was not in their interest to see Harley-Davidson fail. The difference between the production operations of the two companies was plain as day.

> *The assembly line was neat and uncluttered with hardly any material at the line — unlike our operation, where the line was always littered with parts and material. There was minimum paperwork, and things flowed very smoothly. . . .*
>
> *Labor relations also seemed excellent — whenever workers looked up from the line and saw Harley's Japanese hosts they would smile broadly, wave, and call them by name.*[14]

The story has a happy ending, for Harley-Davidson went on to implement a *kaizen* program, driven by its own version of JIT, called "Materials-as-Needed." Over a period of several years, the company reduced inventory by 70 percent and eliminated its raw materials warehouse. Scrap dropped 50 percent, warranty claims declined by 70 percent, rework was reduced to 10 percent of its former level, and productivity was raised by 40 percent. Instead of the previous hundred quality control inspectors, the company now has only four. In 1989 alone, the company won back 15 percent market share from Honda Motor.

As Harley-Davidson discovered, *kaizen* can make the difference between success and failure. What is more, it is almost cost-free. As Taiichi Ohno used to say[15], it is important to "use your head, not your money."

---

[14] Peter C. Reid, *Well Made in America*, McGraw-Hill, New York, 1990, p. 14.

[15] Mr. Ohno died on May 28, 1990 in Toyota City, Japan.

1
Origins of the Modern Japanese Management Style
by Alan Robinson

The sophisticated production management techniques you will read about in the selections contained in this book are among the major reasons for modern Japan's strong economic position in the world. Yet many of the ideas underlying "Japanese management" have their roots in American management philosophy and practice; they were introduced into Japan by American management experts. The visits, writings, and lectures of some of these experts, most notably those of Drs. Lillian Gilbreth, W. Edwards Deming, and Joseph Juran, are well known. But other, perhaps more significant, American influences were the massive management training programs initiated after World War II by the United States occupation forces under General Douglas MacArthur. The Civil Communication Section (CCS) seminars were for top management, the Training Within Industry (TWI) courses for lower management, and the Management Training Program (MTP) for middle management.

Surprisingly, few people outside of Japan know about these programs. As technical knowledge developed in Japan after the war, the training programs were revised and kept up to date. Although CCS was dropped in 1974, both MTP and TWI continue to be taught ever more widely each year. Some Japanese observers estimate that over half of all supervisors and managers in Japan have taken MTP or TWI. Interestingly, it now appears that Japan, in its turn, wishes to export these programs to less developed

1

countries. A very reasonable prediction is that the programs will boost national productivity in the Far East, Latin America, and Eastern Europe in the same way that they have done in Japan. Certainly, the programs will continue to play a role in the development of managers around the world for the foreseeable future.

A good way to understand these programs is first to place them in the context of the period of the Occupation of Japan, a time during which changes were imposed on that country at a furious pace. The aim of the Occupation was straightforward: to introduce political and social democracy into Japan so comprehensively that the country could not return to the extreme militarism responsible for the war. The Occupation reforms laid the groundwork for the prosperity and industrial power of modern-day Japan. CCS, TWI, and MTP were part of this general drive for democratization.

BACKGROUND

At the end of World War II in 1945, the United States was faced with the question of how to handle the vanquished Japan. Some Americans felt that harsh punishment was in order, for the wartime propaganda had portrayed all Japanese as evil and repulsive. At that time, few Americans had enough knowledge to distinguish between the Japanese people and the government that ruled them.

According to a Gallup poll taken in November of 1944, thirteen percent of the population of the United States wanted to kill all the Japanese still alive at the end of the war.[1] Ernest Hooton, professor of anthropology at Harvard, thought it would be wise to sterilize all members of the Japanese royal family.[2] Senator Theodore Bilbo of Mississippi went a step further: he wrote to General Douglas MacArthur during the Occupation to urge him

---

[1] Louise Merrick Van Patten, "Japan: An American Problem," *Far Eastern Survey*, May 9, 1945, p. 117.

[2] John C. Perry, *Beneath the Eagle's Wings*, Dodd, Mead & Co., New York, 1980, p. 28.

to sterilize the entire population of Japan.[3] In 1943, Captain Pence, a naval officer attached to the influential State-War-Navy Coordinating Committee, the body which would oversee the Occupation, had pressed for an extensive bombing, so that the Japanese race would be almost totally eliminated.[4] Even President Franklin D. Roosevelt himself had been interested in the possibility of interbreeding the Japanese with other peoples in the Far East, to make them less 'nefarious.'[5]

Some Americans wanted Japanese industry to be completely dismantled after the war, as Treasury Secretary Henry Morgenthau had urged for post-war Germany. Major George Fielding Eliot, a prominent military writer, authored an article in the April 23, 1943 issue of the *New York Herald Tribune* which advocated

> *that not one brick of any Japanese factory shall be left upon another, so that there shall not be in Japan one electric motor or one steam or gasoline engine, nor a chemical laboratory, nor so much as a book which tells how these things are made.*[6]

Fortunately for the Japanese, and probably for the rest of the world as well, cooler heads prevailed:

> *It is certainly true that the Japanese are extremely nationalistic, that they are educated for loyalty and war, and that [the] official [national religion] Shinto promotes support of national aggressiveness. On the other hand, psychological explanations of Japan's actions confuse the picture by obscuring the concrete factors making for aggression. Although the people of Japan hold many*

---

[3] Michael Schaller, *The American Occupation of Japan*, Oxford University Press, Oxford, Great Britain, 1985, p. 3.

[4] Roger Buckley, *Occupation Diplomacy*, Cambridge University Press, Cambridge, Great Britain, 1982, p. 15.

[5] Christopher Thorne, *Allies of a Kind*, Hamish Hamilton Ltd., London, 1978, p. 167.

[6] Lawrence K. Rosinger, "What Future for Japan?" *Foreign Policy Reports*, September 1, 1943, p. 144.

unsound ideas, their shortcomings result not from neuroses or so-called "racial" characteristics, but from economic, social, and political conditions. Their views, like these conditions, are subject to change.[7]

Far from being punitive, the emphasis was to be on positive reform, that is, on instigating change that would eliminate the militarism that had become endemic and deeply rooted in Japan before and during the war. At the time of the surrender, over 320,000 Japanese people were political prisoners, and more than 600,000 had lost their civil rights for political reasons.[8] A system of secret police, of neighborhood associations, of thought control laws, and of employer-controlled labor organizations, allowed the Home Ministry and *zaibatsu* (the huge business combines) to keep tight control. In fact, much of this oppression was directed at labor, specifically for the purpose of keeping it low-paid. It was clear that political and economic reform was urgently needed.

Less than three weeks after Japan surrendered, the country was occupied by the American armed forces. The Occupation period, which lasted from 1945 to 1952, was one of great stress and rapid change for the Japanese people and, of course, left a lasting mark. The central figure in the Allied Occupation was the Supreme Commander for the Allied Powers (SCAP) — General Douglas MacArthur. MacArthur had spent the previous fourteen years in Asia, mostly in the Philippines, without once returning to the continental United States. Nevertheless, his prior experience with Japan was limited to a few visits. Although the Occupation was officially an *Allied* affair, with MacArthur under the orders of the thirteen-member-nation Far Eastern Commission, the truth was that the Occupation was *American-run*, and the general was in command.

The situation he faced upon his arrival in Japan was far from easy. To begin with, the Japanese government had surrendered while it still retained a considerable amount of control over the populace. Many of the people responsible for the war still held

---

[7] Ibid., p. 148.

[8] Joe Moore, *Japanese Workers and the Struggle for Power,* 1945-1947, The University of Wisconsin Press, Madison, Wisconsin, 1983, p. 14.

positions of high authority and hid themselves well by changing jobs and destroying evidence of their complicity in the war. Very few Americans spoke Japanese, so SCAP ('SCAP' was used to denote MacArthur's headquarters organization as well) relied on the Japanese government to enforce its decrees and could not always check that instructions were followed. Almost every reform attempted encountered great resistance. Often records were destroyed or instructions deliberately misconstrued and not followed. For example, undemocratic organizations, such as employer-controlled work councils, that had been ordered abolished were often replaced by similar bodies with different names run by the same people as before. In addition to all this, the economic circumstances of the people were very bad. One quarter of all the housing in Japan had been destroyed; in some of the larger cities, almost half of the housing lay in ruins. Twenty-two million people were homeless. Rampant inflation meant that, for example, one rice ball cost almost ten times the average daily laborer's wage.[9] Unemployment was close to thirty-three percent, and industrial activity was less than ten percent of its 1935-37 level. Compounding this, the *zaibatsu* were hoarding many essential supplies for sale in the highly lucrative black market.

Over the next seven years, some very significant reforms were made, all consistent with the Occupation's overall mission to instill democratic values in Japan. These reforms included:

A new constitution. The best-known provision of the new American-written constitution is Article 9, which renounces the right to make war:

> *Art. 9. Aspiring sincerely to an international peace based on justice and order, the Japanese people forever renounce war as a sovereign right of the nation and the threat or use of force as means of settling international disputes.*
>
> *In order to accomplish the aim of the preceding paragraph, land, sea, and air forces, as well as other war potential, will never be maintained. The right of belligerency of the state will not be recognized.*

---

[9] Ibid., p. 90.

Chapter 3 of the new constitution, entitled "Rights and Duties of the People," gave Japan a more extensive bill of rights than that of the United States. Among other things, it comprised academic freedom, universal free education (free dental care was almost included) the right to work, and the articles emancipating women. One of these was the "Japanese Equal Rights Amendment":

> *Art. 14. All of the people are equal under the law and there shall be no discrimination in political, economic or social relations because of race, creed, sex, social status, or family origin.*

The Constitution mandated that all members of the Cabinet be civilians. Also, it stripped the Emperor of all powers related to government.

The breakup of the zaibatsu. The member companies of the *zaibatsu* were tightly interconnected, for they owned stock in each other, shared managers and directors, and signed contracts which gave each company considerable control over the strategic business decisions of the other members. Japan's economy was dominated by only fifteen *zaibatsu*, some of the more prominent of which were Mitsubishi, Mitsui, Sumitomo, and Yasuda. In her 1948 *Harvard Business Review* article, "Trust Busting in Japan," Eleanor Hadley illustrates the size and power of such *zaibatsu* with the following analogy:

> *A comparable business organization [to Mitsubishi] in the United States might be achieved if, for example, United States Steel, General Motors, Standard Oil of New York, Alcoa, Douglas Aircraft, E.I. duPont de Nemours, Sun Shipbuilding, Allis-Chalmers, Westinghouse Electric, American Telephone and Telegraph, R.C.A., I.B.M., U.S. Rubber, Sea Island Sugar, Dole Pineapple, United States Lines, Grace Lines, National City Bank, Metropolitan Life, the Woolworth Stores, and the Statler Hotels were to be combined into a single enterprise.*[10]

---

[10] Eleanor Hadley, "Trust Busting in Japan," *Harvard Business Review*, July 1948, p. 429.

The attempts to break up the *zaibatsu* were, to the Americans, among the more controversial reforms undertaken by the Occupation authorities, and encountered strong resistance from the Japanese as well. Even though these business combines had employed their own secret police forces to oppress labor, had engaged in various maneuvers to choke off small independent businesses through their executives who controlled the war rationing boards, and had been heavily involved in the Japanese militarization from which they made immense profits, many Americans felt that it would be "un-American" and "communist" to break them up.

However, the *zaibatsu* were largely broken up — although it took some time, and some severe measures that included forced stock sales by the controlling *zaibatsu* families, a ban on companies owning stock in each other, a purge of top executives, and a stringent wealth tax passed in 1946. (The tax rate rose to ninety percent for individual wealth amounting to the then-equivalent of one million dollars.) The new tax was a harsh but effective measure, and made it much more difficult for so few families to control such vast resources.

Labor law reform. Another priority was to promote industrial democracy, that is, the right of workers to bargain collectively and to organize into unions under their own control, with officials elected by secret ballot. For a long time, government and business had conspired to suppress severely labor union activity. Now union activity became a constitutional right:

> *Art. 28. The right of workers to organize and to bar-gain and act collectively is guaranteed.*

It was hoped these reforms would install organized labor as a new power group, whose demands for higher wages and better working conditions would further weaken militarism and the *zaibatsu*.

The resulting boom in union membership and strength brought with it a rather unexpected result, which came to be known as "production control." Production control was a labor action that involved locking out management and continuing to run the company for a profit, as if management did not exist. It was a sensible and effective tactic for unions not allowed to strike by SCAP. Often, the workers ran things *better* without their managers. For example, during one production control campaign at the flagship plant of the Kobe Steel Co. in November 1946, the workers finished in four-and-a-half hours what had customarily taken them eight hours with one hour of overtime to produce, and used the remaining three and a half hours for machine maintenance and recreation.

Several hundred companies were subjected to production control in the first one-and-a-half years of the Occupation. The argument of the unions that this type of action was legal had a certain appeal. It was roughly this: if strikes are within the law, then surely a less harmful action should be legal also. Initially, SCAP often winked at production control, because it usually did increase industrial output, alleviating shortages and giving SCAP a stronger hand in the tough negotiations with the *zaibatsu*. Eventually, however, the law was revised and production control became illegal, in part because of the fear of rising worker communism.

Land reform. In December of 1945, General MacArthur directed the Japanese government to begin a far-reaching program of land reform. At that time, most of the farmers were tenants, who farmed the land of a landlord to whom they turned over half or more of their crop as rent. After expenses for fertilizers, equipment and supplies, the tenant farmer was often left with as little as one third of the crop for his own use. This was not much, for the size of the plots allotted to each farmer was frequently an acre or less, and the landlord could, and often did, terminate the lease on very short notice. As can easily be imagined, the life of the vast majority of farmers was not an easy one, and SCAP, quite rightly, regarded the system as a breeding ground for discontent and instability.

Acting on orders from SCAP, the Japanese government forcibly purchased five million acres, which amounted to eighty percent of the land cultivated by tenants, to whom it was sold on very generous terms with easy payment schedules. On the main island, landlords were permitted to own no more than 2.5 acres, and no one was allowed to own more than 7.5 acres. It is estimated that this huge redistributive effort required approximately 60 million land transactions, and upwards of 300,000 staffers to accomplish. It was finished in March of 1950, slightly over four years after it had been ordered. The new landowners, over three million strong, were instantly better off and became a strong force behind the new social and political order.

It is easy to understand why the Occupation authorities felt that training was needed to redirect Japanese managers away from authoritarian leadership styles. Not only would such training fit with the overall mission of reform, but industry also needed to be restarted, so that the country could feed, clothe, and shelter its own people, as well as pay its way in the world. Better management would carry the country a long way towards this end.

THE SEEDS OF AMERICAN MANAGEMENT ARE PLANTED

The messages imparted by CSS, TWI and MTP were essentially all the same: openness and democracy in the workplace bring better results. In its own way, each course showed trainees the importance of proper leadership and coaching, and taught them the need for employee participation and for getting constructive, and possibly critical, suggestions from their subordinates. Good human relations practices were advocated, as was a scientific "plan/do/see" attitude for decision-making.

As it turned out, each of the three programs was implemented independently by separate groups within the Occupation forces, to solve what were thought to be different problems. For that reason, the American transfer of management know-how was not as tightly planned and organized as were other reforms. Nonetheless, the coincidence of message and subject matter among the three programs meant that the *overall effect* was sufficiently directed to lead to success. Japanese managers were extremely attentive to the content of CCS, MTP, and TWI, since it represented the collective knowledge and wisdom of the country that had overwhelmed them with its industrial power. The devastation and hunger, as well as the lack of any serious commercial activity, undoubtedly served to focus minds as well. In addition, MacArthur had purged all the old-line top executives of the *zaibatsu* and replaced them with younger men open to new ideas. The industrial management of Japan was to get a fresh start.

Civil Communication Section (CCS)

The purpose of the CCS, one of about twenty sections of SCAP, was to help establish a reliable nationwide communications network.[11] In the early days of the Occupation, the system was constantly breaking down, making it difficult for the U.S. forces to administer the country. The malfunctioning network meant that information tended to spread through the Japanese population by rumor which, because it could be sensationalist, was a possible source of civil unrest. CCS quickly determined that the main obstacle to the improvement of the system was the poor quality of products supplied by Japanese manufacturers of communications equipment. Two CCS staffers, Charles Protzman and Homer Sarasohn, were assigned the task of solving this quality problem:

> *I understood my job was to advise the Japanese on rebuilding their communications system. I found, however, that they were very competent engineers and needed little or no technical advice. What I did find was that they did not understand and apply the systems and routines of production management. Within a month of arriving in Japan, I had concluded that rather than try to correct each company individually, we should present a set of seminars on the principles of industrial management for top company executives.*[12]

The resulting course, originally entitled "Fundamentals of Industrial Management," came simply to be called "CCS," and was taught only twice. It was restricted to top executives from large communications equipment manufacturers including Fujitsu, Hitachi, Matsushita, Mitsubishi, NEC, Sanyo, Sharp, Sumitomo Electric, and Toshiba (or their predecessor companies). The course length was 128 hours of classroom time, spread out over eight weeks in four afternoon sessions per week. A large portion of it —

---

[11] The source for this section is "Creating Japan's New Industrial Management: The Americans as Teachers," by Kenneth Hopper, *Human Resource Management*, Summer, 1982, pp. 13-34.

[12] Ibid., Charles Protzman quoted on p. 19.

six sessions — was devoted to the management of quality. (Interestingly, it was another member of the CCS staff, Mr. Magill, who is said to have first suggested to Japanese industry that it adopt Statistical Quality Control.) According to the course manual:

> *The primary objective of the company is to put the quality of the product ahead of any other consideration. A profit or a loss notwithstanding, the emphasis will always be on quality . . . [and, in the words of Andrew Carnegie] The effect of attention to quality, upon every man in the service, from the president of the concern down to the humblest laborer, cannot be overestimated. The surest foundation of a business concern is Quality. And after Quality — a long time after — comes Cost.*[13]

But other subjects were covered in the course as well:

The importance of good leadership. The leader "must himself be the finest example of what he would like to see in his followers . . . . [The leader] earns his people's loyalty by being loyal to them . . . . If one is a good enough leader, one can usually find ways of encouraging subordinates to see what is needed without 'telling' them. When this is done, the subordinate is helped to develop his own ability."

The importance of teamwork. "Teamwork and cooperation must be established by the attitude and example of each executive level from the President down . . . . This concept of teamwork, of working together, should be the basic approach of each supervisor in the analysis of the job of subordinates . . . to make it possible, through teamwork to correct the cause of the trouble — to do a better job."

The importance of good human relations. The course taught that poor human relations, and a rigid management class structure, impeded the upward flow of information within the company and meant that employees would not be highly motivated. Suggestions and friendly criticism were things to be cultivated, not stifled. "If we who are paying these people for working with us

---

[13] Ibid., p. 23.

could foster that desire to participate, what a profitable undertaking it would be."

The importance of good coaching. "Today a company cannot afford the extravagance of managers who are not good teachers."[14]

After the course had been taught twice, once in Tokyo and once in Osaka, it was discontinued by SCAP, because the Occupation was coming to an end. As was true for both TWI and MTP, the course was run by various organizations before being taken over by JITA (the Japan Industrial Training Association) in 1959. JITA continued teaching the course until 1974, by which time it had graduated over 5100 top executives. (The total count of CCS graduates over the years is probably much higher, since other organizations have taught versions of it as well.) The course is still so highly regarded that it is the first one listed in the JITA catalog, and is referred to in the 1990 JITA brochure, although sixteen years have passed since it was discontinued.

Training within Industry (TWI)

The Training Within Industry (TWI) programs were taught to a far greater number of Japanese than were either CCS or MTP. It was clear to the Economic and Scientific Section (ESS) of SCAP, the group charged with supervising economic reform, that the economy would not grow very much without a strong backbone of competent supervisors:

> *Supervision is ordinarily a 'haphazard,' rule-of-thumb process, and . . . in-plant training is characteristically done by putting a new man under an experienced worker to pick up his skills as well as he can. Such practices are incompatible with modern industrial methods and with the achievement of high output per worker. Neither industry nor government has developed a suitable program for the adequate training of supervisors in industrial establishments. The improvement of technology, machinery and raw*

---

[14] Ibid., pp. 24-25.

*materials will not assure a substantial increase in produc-
tion unless the supervisors and the workmen are prepared
to utilize these elements in the most effective manner.*[15]

Unlike CSS and MTP, the TWI programs had been developed and used prior to the Occupation period. For ESS, the
choice of TWI was a natural one, for TWI was designed to boost
quickly industrial output and productivity on a national scale,
specifically through the mass training of supervisors and foremen.
It also came with an excellent track record.[16]

The Beginnings of TWI

After the Fall of France in 1940, it became clear that the
United States, even if it did not become involved as a combatant,
would need to expand and mobilize its industrial capacity very
quickly. Consequently, one of the first emergency services set up
by the government was the Training Within Industry service,
whose job was to help private industry with this expansion,
through consultation and education. TWI was to play a critical
role in boosting wartime production capacity to the levels required
to win the war.

TWI began primarily as a consulting service, and consisted
almost entirely of volunteer experts from industry, assigned to help
individual factories and plants with their specific problems. Very
quickly, though, TWI became heavily backlogged with requests,
many of them for help with the same sorts of issues, and began to
think about how it could reach the most people in the short
amount of time available. Not surprisingly, TWI's aim soon came
to be: *educate* people to solve their own problems. By the time
TWI was deactivated in 1945, 1,750,650 certificates had been
issued to supervisors in 16,511 plants who had, in their turn,

---

[15] 1949 SCAP/ESS memorandum quoted in Sung-Jo Park, U.S. Labor Policy in
Postwar Japan, EXpress Edition, Berlin, 1985, p. 95.

[16] A primary source for this section is "The U.S. Training Within Industries programs and their role in the development of the Japanese management style,"
by Alan G. Robinson, Dean M. Schroeder, and Nalini Dayanand. This paper
was presented at the Academy of Management on August 14, 1990.

trained and supervised over ten million workers. 400,000 supervisors in the government and military had earned TWI certificates as well. This training system deserved much of the credit for the successful wartime boom in industrial production.

TWI taught three courses: Job Instruction Training (JIT), a course designed to teach supervisors the power of proper training; Job Methods Training (JMT), a course in methods improvement; and Job Relations Training (JRT), which taught supervisors about leadership and proper worker-supervisor relationships. The courses, given to groups of ten supervisors at a time, were painstakingly designed to communicate the subject material effectively, and to induce a "multiplier effect." Thus the goal became to:

> *Develop a standard method, then train people who will train other people who will train groups of people to use the method.*[17]

This "multiplier effect" was the inspired principle underlying TWI: by spawning rapidly, it was hoped, the programs would expand their reach quickly, so that the relatively small TWI service would achieve the national impact sought.

The desired explosion was not so easy to induce. The courses had to be designed to be taught by a diverse set of instructors, including both experienced and inexperienced supervisors, minorities, women, and even people who reported to other people attending the same session. A class full of experienced and older supervisors might need to be taught by a younger, less experienced trainer. Before the course could be released nationally, TWI had, therefore, to perform extensive pilot-testing with a wide variety of test teachers in many different industries, and in companies ranging from those that were merely continuing as if the war was not happening, to companies that were expanding dramatically. This phase included as many as seventy test-runs of a particular course and lasted as long as a year.

An early success for the TWI service was its role in eliminating the nation's critical shortage of skilled lens grinders. In late

---

[17] Walter Dietz with Betty W. Bevens, *Learn by Doing: The Story of Training Within Industry*, published by Walter Dietz, Summit, NJ, 1970, p. 14.

1940, a government search for 350 such specialists, urgently needed to make precision lenses for use in bombsights, periscopes, and other optical equipment, had turned up no qualified people. Unfortunately, under the existing system it took five years to train a master lens grinder. TWI was asked to study the problem. It was found that a master lens grinder was expected to be able to perform twenty jobs, of which only a few were highly skilled. The unskilled jobs could be assigned to less skilled workers. When these tasks were reassigned according to TWI recommendations, the problem eased tremendously. What is more, TWI specialists, using the methods from the JIT course, redesigned the program for new lens grinders and managed to reduce the training time from five years down to two months.

The question of how to sustain the multiplier effect was of paramount importance to TWI, which quickly found that tight quality control of its courses was needed, that is, they all had to be taught strictly by the book. In all TWI instructor manuals, the sentence "Work from this outline — don't trust to memory" appears frequently, sometimes on every page. The left hand margin of the manual has notations which tell the instructor to the *minute* where the class should be at any given time. This rigid uniformity sometimes brought another benefit with it, as the following incident at one JMT course shows:

> *The day shift superintendent was "kibitzing" the group. One detail of the [job] breakdown was "Start the machine." The trainer asked, "How do you start the machine?" Before the foreman could answer, the superintendent cut in: "What difference can that possibly make? The man has already made his improvement."*
>
> *"I don't know what difference it might make, because I don't know anything about this machine," said the trainer. "But I do know this program, and we are following the program. To follow the program, we have to have every detail, and we do not have the details of starting the machine." He turned to the foreman and asked him how the girl started the machine.*
>
> *The foreman, who had been through J.I. [Job Instruction], told and showed and explained: "She takes*

two steps to the right, like this, and then she jumps into the air like this, and swats the starting lever. "The trainer got all that down on the blackboard as the man did it, for three or four additional details. Then he checked the "Stop machine" detail. The foreman told him the girl took the same two steps, jumped, and hit the lever again, except that she knocked it the other way. The trainer put all that on the board.

Then he turned to the superintendent and said: "Does this operator have to start and stop this machine for every piece?" "Sure." "And how many pieces a day will this operator slit for you?" "Forty an hour, 320 a day," said the superintendent. "So this girl has to jump and hit that lever twice for each of 320 pieces, making 640 jumps a day," said the trainer. "Now, Mr. Superintendent, will you please go over there in the corner and jump as high as you can 640 times, and swing your arm as far as you can on every jump, and then let us know if it fatigues you at all?"

The result was that, in addition to the initial improvement, 640 jumps per day were eliminated by extending the lever so the girl could reach it easily. The superintendent ordered method breakdowns made on every job over which he had jurisdiction.[18]

The three "J" courses all followed the same format and philosophy: each group of ten to twelve supervisors spent ten hours in the classroom with their instructor. In the first session of the course, a realistic problem was presented and a bad solution was given. The intention was that every supervisor present would feel that in the same situation he or she might well have taken the same action. Once the class was interested in finding a better way to solve the problem, the instructor would present the TWI "Four Step" method. The last six hours of the class were devoted to "learning by doing," that is, practice. Each supervisor would find a problem from his or her workplace, apply TWI's methods to solve it, and present the solution to the class for comment and criticism.

---

[18] Training Within Industry Service, *The Training Within Industry Report: 1940-1945*, Bureau of Training, War Manpower Commission, Washington D.C., 1945, p. 183.)

Job instruction training (JIT). At the outbreak of the war there were still eight million unemployed, most of whom had no industrial experience at all. Without the proper training of these people, the expansion would soon become chaotic:

> *In 1942, approximately 6,000 new workers were reporting for work every day as night shifts and extra day shifts became necessary. Four hundred workers who had no experience in directing the work of other people were being appointed as supervisors every day.*[19]

The JIT course sought, by means of a classroom demonstration using a complicated knot called the "fire underwriter's knot," to convince the assembled supervisors that knowledge of proper training methods would be important to them. The instructor first told the class that about 80 percent of all production problems could be traced to poor training. He or she then asked for a volunteer, and explained to this person carefully and slowly (although without actually demonstrating it) how to tie the knot. The volunteer, unless familiar with the knot (which rarely happened), would invariably fail to tie it correctly. The instructor then said (emphasis as in manual):

> *MUCH OF THE INSTRUCTION IN THE SHOP IS TELLING — THOUSANDS OF WORKERS ARE BEING TOLD AT THIS VERY MOMENT. HOW MANY OF THEM REALLY UNDERSTAND?*
>
> *This kind of instruction is the real cause of some of the [types of production] problems [listed previously] on the problem sheet.*[20]

The instructor picked another volunteer, to whom he or she then *showed* how to tie the underwriter's knot, while making sure that the person saw it *backwards,* as is often the case in practice. Once again, the volunteer was usually unable to tie the knot successfully. The manual then tells the instructor to say:

---

[19] Ibid., p. 36.

[20] Training Within Industry Service, *Training Within Industry Materials,* Bureau of Training, War Manpower Commission, Washington D.C., 1945, JIT Manual, p. 10.

> *COUNTLESS THOUSANDS OF EMPLOYEES*
> *ARE BEING SHOWN HOW TO DO THEIR JOBS AT*
> *THIS VERY MOMENT. HOW MANY OF THEM*
> *UNDERSTAND? . . .*
> *IF THE WORKER HASN'T LEARNED, THE*
> *INSTRUCTOR HASN'T TAUGHT.* [21]

At this point it was expected that the members of the class, many of whom were guilty themselves of training by "telling" or "showing," would be very receptive to the TWI 4-step method of training. It was then introduced, and was as follows: 1) put the trainee at ease and make him or her interested; 2) teach the job, while carefully identifying the "key points" — those which, if not performed correctly, will cause problems; 3) make trial runs and force the trainee to explain the reason for every step; and 4) taper the coaching off and tell the trainee whom to see if he or she has any problems in the future.

By the end of the war over 1,230,000 American supervisors had been JIT-certified.

Job Methods Training (JMT). The aim of this program was to teach supervisors the importance and techniques of continuous methods improvement. A TWI Bulletin introduced the new course in December of 1942:

> *You know materials are growing scarcer. Machines are difficult to get or replace. And manpower is getting to be a critical issue.*
>
> *A big part of the answer is to develop better ways of doing the work you supervise with the manpower, machines, and materials NOW AVAILABLE.*
>
> *Perhaps you worked out a better way to do one of the jobs you supervise today. If so, you made an important contribution to victory. But are you working out better methods every day?*
>
> *Here is a Plan that will help you develop those BET-TER JOB METHODS NOW. It will help you to produce greater quantities, of quality products, in less time . . .*

---

[21] Ibid., JIT Manual, p. 11.

> *Look for the hundreds of small things you can improve.*
> *Don't try to plan a whole new department layout — or*
> *go after a big new installation of new equipment. There*
> *isn't time for these major items. Look for improvements*
> *on existing jobs, with your present equipment.*[22]

The JMT course began with a trainee-operated assembly line constructed in the classroom. It had been carefully designed to *appear* to be efficient. But then the TWI 4-step method was applied: 1) Break the job down into its minute constituent operations; 2) question every detail (why? what? when? where? how?); 3) develop the new method by eliminating, combining, rearranging and simplifying all necessary details; and 4) apply the new method by "selling" it to everyone. The supervisors were surprised to find that their mock workplace was rife with waste and inefficiency, and that its productivity could easily be raised by 300 percent.

The subject of JMT was Scientific Management, particularly, Frank Gilbreth's motion study method. This method consisted of watching or filming the operation to be studied, and breaking it down to its tiny basic motions, which were then scrupulously analyzed for waste that could be eliminated. His way of "selling" the new method to everyone was simple — *order them to do it!*

TWI paid more attention than did Gilbreth to the last point — how a person should "sell" his or her idea to others. TWI taught the supervisors to write up the improvement suggestion for their bosses, and to include a very clear explanation of the expected benefits if the proposal was adopted. This way, the supervisors were taught, the idea would get beyond the "talking" stage.

Job Relations Training (JRT). In 1941, the government asked the National Academy of Sciences to study the following question: "What can be done to increase knowledge and improve understanding of supervision at the work level?"[23] One of the recommendations returned was that efforts should be aimed at

---

[22] Ibid., Bulletin #4-C, p. 1.

[23] Training Within Industry Service, The Training Within Industry Report: 1940-1945, Bureau of Training, War Manpower Commission, Washington D.C., 1945, p. 204.

"improving and accelerating the training of supervisors in handling the human situations under their charge so as to secure maximum cooperation."[24] This advice was forwarded to the TWI service which, after one and a half years of research and development, produced the JRT course.

The course was well-designed and successful. By the end of the war, over 600,000 supervisors were JRT-certified. JRT is not worth detailing here, however, because for a variety of reasons that are beyond the scope of this chapter, JRT was not to catch on later in Japan as its two sister "J" courses did.

TWI Arrives in Japan

It is clear why ESS felt that the TWI programs made sense for Japanese industry in 1949. For example, in order for the shipbuilding industry to survive, cost reductions of about thirty-five percent would be needed. The wartime U.S. experience with TWI suggested that twenty-five percent savings could be achieved after all supervisors had been certified in the TWI "J" courses.

Although SCAP debated whether to send Japanese supervisors to the United States for training or to import American TWI specialists into Japan, it finally decided to bring Americans to Japan. Three "J" program training specialists from Training Within Industry Inc. of Cleveland, Ohio, contracted with ESS to come to Japan for a period of about six months in 1951. They were: Lowell Mellen, President of TWI Inc. and a specialist in JMT; Edward Scott, a specialist in JRT; and Dale Cannon, a specialist in JIT.

Earlier in the Occupation period, the Japanese Labor Ministry had set up a small TWI working group with ten people who acted as TWI Institute Conductors, that is, people who could train TWI instructors. But, according to the newly arrived American specialists, the fledgling Japanese attempts at TWI had so far lacked the strict uniformity and quality control that was needed for them to have a national impact. When the American specialists departed from Japan, they left behind thirty-five "people who could train other people who could train groups of people to use the method,"

---

[24] Ibid.

that is, they had begun the TWI multiplier effect which, according to Lowell Mellen, generated over one million certified Japanese supervisors by the end of 1952.

Readers of *The Wall Street Journal* were reminded of the importance of these programs to the overall mission of the Occupation in an article published on September 23, 1951:

> *The American concept of industrial democracy is being brought to Japanese industry for the first time by employe [sic] training experts from this country . . . . Mr. Mellen's group has been given the task of training Japanese employes [sic] in the well-known "J" programs for many of the most prominent industries in the Japanese economy . . . . [Mr. Mellen said that] the development in industrial foremen . . . . is the logical conclusion of the steady indoctrination in political democracy given so rigorously to all sections of the Japanese population by General Douglas MacArthur and his successors of the American occupying force.*

After the departure of the American trainers, the Japanese Ministry of Labor continued to promote and sponsor the TWI courses throughout the country. In 1990, it remains actively involved in TWI, and currently licenses nineteen organizations to train TWI instructors. Primary among these is the previously mentioned Japan Industrial Training Association (JITA), which has trained over eighteen thousand TWI instructors since 1955. Many companies send employees to JITA for certification, after which they return to their firms and run their own "J" programs. Because of this intramural growth, it is difficult to arrive at hard statistics about the current extent of TWI practice in Japan. It is clear, however, that the programs are very widely used to train workers and low-level supervisors. Canon Inc. offers a good example. It maintains a full-time training staff of about 1,200 for its worldwide workforce of about forty thousand people. All Canon trainers are certified TWI instructors; TWI courses are run every three or four months in each plant. Smaller companies that cannot justify the expense of their own in-house TWI instructors send their employees to outside courses. In 1989, JITA, for example, ran a total of eighty TWI courses for employees of small companies.

TWI did succeed in its aim of helping to introduce a more democratic management style into the workplace. Like CCS and MTP, its teachings helped to break up authoritarian management styles. Before these programs took effect, the average Japanese had no hope of reaching the ranks of top management. He was expected not to speak at meetings until all those senior to him had spoken (a practice that was continued at meetings at Nissan until 1986). Mr. Mellen credited TWI with opening up the promotion system, so that advancement to top positions would be based more on merit than on family connections or on the university that the candidate had attended.

TWI is also given credit for introducing the practices of *kaizen* and suggestion systems into Japan:

> *The forerunner of the modern Japanese-style suggestion system undoubtedly originated in the West . . . TWI (Training Within Industries), introduced to Japanese industry in 1949 by the U.S. occupation forces, had a major effect in expanding the suggestion system to involve all workers rather than just a handful of the elite. Job modification constituted a part of TWI and as foremen and supervisors taught workers how to perform job modification, they learned how to make changes and suggestions.*[25]

Management Training Program (MTP)

The Management Training Program (MTP) was originally developed in 1946 to train Japanese civilian employees of the United States Far East Air Materiel Command (FEAMCOM) air base, located near Tokyo. Many of these people were highly skilled mechanics or machinists who had worked at the same base during the war for the Imperial Air Force, repairing equipment such as airplanes, trucks, jeeps, loaders, and bulldozers. When the United States Air Force (USAF) took over the air base for its own use, it,

---

[25] Japan Human Relations Association, *The Idea Book*, Productivity Press, Cambridge, MA, 1988, p. 202.

too, needed the skills of these workers, and hired them to work on the American equipment. In the period 1945-47, the air base employed over seven thousand Japanese civilians.

Difficulties soon arose owing to differences in language, culture, and management styles, and to the manifest lack of trust between the Americans and their Japanese employees. The USAF felt that the Japanese workers had poor work habits, poor attitudes towards safety, and were ignorant of many of the proper procedures for maintaining and repairing equipment. In addition to teaching English, the Air Force organized classes on subjects like posting, warehousing, and inventory. But it was quickly determined that this kind of training, which aimed to teach specific jobs and practices, would not alleviate all of the problems. The Japanese supervisors needed to be taught the management techniques required for functioning properly in their jobs. The Air Force assigned this task to three of its staff — an American, Dixon Miyauchi, and two Japanese, Shinichi Takezawa and Hitoshi Shimamura.

The Management Training Program they developed drew heavily on the United States Air Force Basic and Primary Management courses, which in turn were based on the management courses of companies such as Ford and General Motors. The content of MTP comprised Scientific Management, the work of Henri Fayol, and miscellaneous other topics. Unlike CCS and TWI, MTP was taught in Japanese almost from the outset. MTP was pitched at *middle* management, that is, those people with responsibility for some 20 to 150 subordinates. The structure of MTP was a little different from that of CCS and TWI. It consisted of twenty two-hour conference discussions, led by the instructor in a Socratic and informal style, and it included many short cases. The subjects of the first part of the course were the four principles of organization — unity of command, span of control, homogeneous assignment, and delegation of authority — and the five functions of management, that is, organizing, planning, commanding, coordinating, and controlling. Later sections offered an advanced and quicker-paced version of the three "J" courses of TWI.

Halfway through the course came an interesting pedagogical device. After one class called "conducting meetings," most of the remaining classes were turned over to the trainees to teach, each of whom was given the appropriate portions of the instructor's manual to use. Topics like safety and morale were covered in these later sessions. As was intended by FEAMCOM, MTP invited an open and democratic "leadership" style of management. Many of the cases and much of the discussion concentrated on why the "boss" approach was poor human relations and bad business practice. In matters of quality, MTP taught the importance of process control, and what was to become known as Total Quality Control:

> *Quality control formerly was carried out by making inspections of the finished product only. This method, however, involves too much waste of manpower and time.*
>
> *By making inspections at each stage of a long process the standards of the finished product as required by the specifica- tions can be assured.*
>
> *Quality control must be examined and studied systematically from all angles — planning, procurement of materials, manufacturing, sales, storage, distribution, and so forth.*[26]

MTP also propounded a more thoughtful attitude towards methods improvements:

> *Businessmen are apt to consider profit against expense in improving job methods. Profit should, however, be considered last . . . . Job method improvement should be made from the viewpoint of hazardousness and essentiality, and immediate profits should not be expected of it. Safety improvement may cost one million yen and yet take a long time before the expense is refunded.*
>
> *You may have an improvement which will cost one million yen and take ten years before profits from it are realized. On the other hand another improvement of a less essential phase may bring about more immediate and larger profits. From the long-range view of the future*

---

[26] 20316 — FEC P&PC — 11/15 — 700 [MTP manual], Conference 7, Worksheet 22.

development of the company, the improvement with higher
essentiality and less profit will probably be selected.[27]

MTP met with such success that it soon came to the attention of the U.S. Army and Navy, and they, too, began to run MTP courses for the Japanese civilians who worked at their bases. The three services combined employed over 24,000 Japanese civilians during the Occupation period.

In May of 1950, MTP was taught for the first time to managers in Japanese private industry and government. As the Occupation began to wind down, the administration of the course was turned over to the Ministry of International Trade and Industry (MITI) which, by July of 1952, had produced 256 MTP instructors who had themselves trained over 26,000 Japanese middle managers in about 900 different institutions. In 1955, MTP was turned over to JITA, which continues to teach it in 1991. Since 1955, JITA has trained almost four thousand MTP instructors, one of whom, I know, has trained over 150,000 middle managers! As with TWI, these newly-trained instructors return to their companies to teach their own MTP courses. Canon Inc. itself has 35 MTP instructors on its staff. Canon candidates for promotion to the rank of manager must take the MTP course.

MTP is also credited with playing a large role in introducing suggestion systems into Japanese industry:

> *Less well known is the fact that the suggestion system*
> *was brought to Japan about the same time by TWI*
> *(Training Within Industries) and the U.S. Air Force.*[28]

Many Japanese managers and academics attribute a deeper influence to MTP than one of mere transfer of techniques. In their opinion, MTP left a legacy of three things: an understanding of the importance of human relations, an appreciation of the rational and scientific approach to management, and a common vocabulary for Japanese managers to talk in.

---

[27] Ibid., Conference 15, Worksheet 72.

[28] Masaaki Imai, *Kaizen*, Random House, New York, 1986, p. 112.

CONCLUSION

Without a doubt, the training programs begun by the United States occupation forces succeeded in what they set out to do. The care and professionalism with which they were developed, and the timelessness of much of the material in them, suggest that other countries might well find them useful today.

As you read the writings of the Japanese production experts included in this book, you may ask yourself how dependent their methods are on Japanese cultural factors, that is, factors which might prevent certain practices from being usefully transferred to other countries. It is a good question. Japanese managers must have asked themselves the corresponding question 40 years ago when American management methods were being introduced into their country at a fast pace, before overcoming their doubts and adopting many of them.

Chapters 2, 3, and 4 are selections from Kanban Just-in-Time at Toyota: Management Begins At the Workplace, *Japan Management Association, editors (Cambridge: Productivity Press, 1985)*

2

The Source of Profit Is In the Manufacturing Process

COMMERCIAL PROFIT AND MANUFACTURING PROFIT

In 1976 and 1977 — shortly after the first oil shock — when Toyota Motors registered profits of ¥182.2 billion ($597.4 million)[1] respectively, the company was criticized for making too much money.

For a company to succeed, making money is actually a precondition or a goal, irrespective of the industry one is in. Now, what do we mean by the phrase "making money"?

In commercial enterprises, the selling price is set by adding a certain margin over the purchase price. To make money means "to buy cheaply and to sell dearly." Thus "making money" usually conveys a negative image, and some newspapers would even write articles condemning companies that make too much money as being engaged in anti-social activities. They reason that the companies make money by buying cheaply and selling dearly, is by making the consumers pay the difference.

In manufacturing, is money made by buying raw materials and parts cheaply and selling finished products at a higher price, as done in the commercial sector?

Does it mean that Toyota can somehow buy steel plates cheaper than any other car maker? Does it mean that there are suppliers who are willing to sell parts at a lower price to Toyota? No,

---

[1] Based on the exchange rates for those two years.

that is not the case. Can Toyota command a higher price by the use of its brand name? The mere fact that the Toyota name is on the car does not mean that it can automatically command a price $1000 higher than any other car.

Toyota buys its raw materials, processed materials, parts, electricity and water at the prevailing market value. The price of its products is also governed by the rules of the same marketplace. If Toyota should put an unreasonably high price on its cars, it would put an end to its sales drive everywhere.

This is not confined to Toyota. All manufacturers share the same marketing consideration. The manufacturing industries derive their profit from the added value obtained through the process of manufacturing. Therefore, manufacturing industries and commercial enterprises cannot make money in the same way.

WE CANNOT BE GUIDED BY COST ALONE

If profit is expressed in terms of a margin obtained by selling at a higher price than the purchase price, or by selling products above the manufacturing cost, it can then be summarized in the following equation:

$$\text{Profit} = \text{Selling price} - \text{Cost}$$

On the other hand, if one wishes to take into account the purchase price and manufacturing cost before adding profit, another equation may be established as follows:

$$\text{Selling price} = \text{Cost} + \text{Profit}$$

When the two equations are expressed in numbers, they may be the same, but at Toyota, we do not use the "selling price = cost + profit" formula.

The so-called cost principle states that inasmuch as it costs so much to manufacture a certain product, a just amount of profit must be added to it to arrive at the selling price. Thus it becomes "selling price = cost + profit." If we were to insist on abiding by this cost principle, we would have to say to ourselves: "Well, we cannot help it if this product costs so much to make. We have to be able to make this much money out of it." This would mean that every cost would have to be borne by the consumer. We cannot afford to take this attitude in this age of intense competition. Even if we wanted to, we could not use this formula.

Returning to the first equation, it is stated that profit is the balance after subtracting cost from the selling price (profit = selling price − cost). As discussed earlier, the price of a car is determined generally by the marketplace. Thus in order to make a profit, the only recourse left to us is to *lower the cost as much as possible*. Herein lies the source of our profit.

SAYINGS OF OHNO

Don't confuse "value" with "price."

When a consumer buys a product, he does so because that product has a certain value to him.

The cost is up, so you raise your price! Don't take such an easy way out. It cannot be done. If you raise your price but the value remains the same, you will quickly lose your customer.

TRUE COST IS THE SIZE OF A PLUM SEED

Cost can be interpreted in many different ways. Cost consists of many elements, such as personnel cost, raw materials cost, cost of oil, cost of electricity, cost of land, cost of buildings and cost of equipment. Some people may add all of these costs and obtain a total and say that it costs this much to manufacture a certain product. But is this the true cost? No, when one considers it carefully, what emerges is that the total just obtained does not seem to reflect the true cost at all.

The expression "true cost" may sound odd. But there is a notion that in making a passenger car the true personnel cost is about this much, and that only a certain amount of the cost of materials is sufficient. That is an approximation of the true cost.

Let us now take the personnel cost as an example. In order to make any given product, a worker must work a requisite number of hours to process a certain amount of material needed for the day. That is close to the true cost. But suppose the worker processes those materials needed for tomorrow and the day after tomorrow?

The excess materials which are manufactured, if kept in the same workplace, will hinder the orderly functioning of the workplace. So they are shipped somewhere. This means that a process called *shipping* has to be created, and a need for a storage place also arises. Furthermore, someone has to count and rearrange these materials in the name of *management*. If the number increases, slips will be needed to show that certain items are placed in storage and certain items are removed from storage. Next comes the need for storage clerks, and then workers monitoring various processes . . . Just because someone has overproduced, there is created a need for an unlimited amount of work and additional personnel.

Those people who are engaged in these newly created tasks must be paid, and that cost is counted as part of the personnel cost. In the end, their salaries and wages become part of the cost of that product.

The same thing can be said about the materials cost. If you have just enough materials for today's work, your day's work can run smoothly. And you may keep a ten-day supply, for the sake of your suppliers. That, of course, is more than sufficient. But in many companies, when inventory is taken, it is often discovered that they have supplies sufficient for one or two months lying idly in storage. It is not uncommon to have a supply for six months, which is not an acceptable condition.

Do not forget that these materials are already paid for. In addition to the materials cost, there is the interest charge. Furthermore, during storage, materials may be rusted, broken or disjoined to become odd pieces that cannot be used. In a more serious case, you may have design changes making the materials in storage obsolete. Then there are instances in which a shift in your sales may obviate the need for some materials. In any event, storage can create waste.

This waste, the cost of unused materials which are discarded, is also entered as the cost of materials by your accounting department, and it becomes part of the cost of that particular product.

In most instances, when people speak of *cost* it is expressed in terms of a hybrid of just and unjust costs, and in the case of the latter, it includes those portions of personnel and materials costs that are not really necessary in manufacturing a product.

In Toyota we have a saying: "The true cost is only the size of a plum seed." The trouble with most managers is that they have a penchant for bloating the plum seed into a huge grapefruit. They then shave off some unevenness from the rind and call it cost reduction. How wrong can they get?

CHANGE YOUR MANUFACTURING METHOD, LOWER YOUR COST

At Toyota, we do not adhere to the so-called cost principle. Behind the cost principle lies the notion that "no matter how differently we manufacture our products, the cost remains the same." If it is proven correct that, regardless of the manufacturing methods, cost remains constant, then all industries must abide by the cost principle.

However, by changing its manufacturing method, a company can eliminate its personnel cost, which does not produce added value, and its materials cost, which pertains to those materials not used. By changing the manufacturing method, cost can be substantially reduced.

There is a Toyota subsidiary that makes metal-stamped parts and is located next to the Toyota headquarters. In 1973, it was at a standstill and all officers were replaced. Starting anew that year, employees did their very best, and two years later, in 1975, the company was completely recovered.

Today that company is a very profitable one. According to its president, one day an inspector from the National Tax Administration Agency came, ready to grill its officers. "Why is it that your company experienced a sizable deficit in 1973 when the economy was at the height of a boom," asked the inspector, "and a good income in 1976 when there was a recession?"

The president's response was typical of Toyota: "That is what we call improvement and effort by the company." The inspector remained incredulous. At any rate, cost is changed by the method of manufacturing. Naturally the profit picture changes along with it, and the above provides a good example.

PRODUCTION TECHNIQUE AND MANUFACTURING TECHNIQUE

Today Toyota produces well over 200,000 units per month. In 1952, it took ten employees one month to produce one truck. In 1961, Toyota's monthly production was 10,000 units. There were 10,000 employees then, and it meant that every month one employee produced one passenger car. In the last couple of years, the monthly production ranged from 230,000 to 250,000 units, and we have 45,000 employees. This means that each employee is credited with making five passenger cars each month.

Toyota has a number of assembly plants overseas. There the number of processes required in assembling the same Corolla or Corona may be five to ten times that of Japan. For the same Toyota, depending on the time and place, there is this much difference.

How is this difference created? In part the difference in the production facility is responsible, but to a large degree, such a difference comes from the difference in the manufacturing methods.

For many years, we have thought about and improved our manufacturing method. That is what we call today the Toyota production system.

Two techniques are utilized in manufacturing. One is the production technique and the other is the manufacturing technique.

Simply stated, *production technique* means the technique needed to produce goods. Normally when the term *technique* is used, it refers to this production technique.

In contrast, *manufacturing technique* means the technique of expertly utilizing equipment, personnel, materials, and parts. If we consider the production technique to be proper technique, conforming to established standards, then the manufacturing technique can be considered management technique, utilizing and synthesizing various methods. What we call the Toyota production system refers to this manufacturing technique.

It is of course important to consider the production technique in order to obtain the effect of changing costs by changing the method of manufacturing. But we must keep in mind that in today's world, the difference in production technique in whatever industry is insignificant. One element that can make a major difference is the manufacturing technique. By effectively utilizing equipment, personnel and raw materials, a substantial change in the cost can result.

WHEN YOU SAY "I CAN'T" YOU ADMIT YOUR OWN IGNORANCE

We often meet a foreman with a neat white cap when we visit the workplace. He may have worked in the assembly line for thirty years, or he may have been in metal stamping for twenty-five years. People like him are living dictionaries for the workplace.

When machines or parts malfunction, the man in the white cap can discover right away what is wrong. Other workers may try to adjust them with unsteady hands, but the foreman comes with a hammer and strikes lightly, making the necessary adjustment.

Even in a process that requires high precision, the man in the white cap can adjust the machine to 1/1000-mm or 1/100-mm accuracy with ease. No one else can equal his expertise.

However, in spite of their great skills, these foremen tend to be unconcerned with the manner in which the work flows. "This line can plane 15,000 units," they will say, "and that has been our best record. Are you saying we must plane 17,000 units? No, we can't do it. Order 2,000 units from an outside source."

There are some metal-stamping mold makers with the same dilemma. Normally they create excellent molds. But once the amount is increased, they manufacture defective molds. Their schedule is disjointed and they do not know when they can deliver the extra molds ordered.

These are common occurrences. They do have excellent production techniques to produce molds, but they lack manufacturing techniques to let the entire work flow smoothly and to utilize effectively their equipment, personnel, and raw materials.

Many people in the workplace will say: "We don't have the capabilities. We don't have enough people to do it." Change the manner in which things flow and change the manner in which you arrange your storage, and you will discover within a month that you can do what you have been saying you cannot do. Not only can you do it, but you will have a little extra change after paying the bill. In fact, you can even eliminate some of the processes!

SAYINGS OF OHNO

A man-hour is something we can always count. But do not come to the conclusion that "we are short of people," or "we can't do it."

Manpower is something that is beyond measurement. Capabilities can be extended indefinitely when everyone begins to think.

TO WORK AND TO MOVE

To engage in a job means to work. In Japanese, the verb *hata raku* means to work. Someone has said that to work is to make people around you (*hata*) happy (*raku*). At Toyota, we define the term *to work* very precisely. It means that we make an advance in the process and enhance the added value.

Therefore, the term *to work* is used only when a certain action is definitely carrying forward a process or enhancing the added value. We do not call it work when someone is engaged in picking up something, putting down something, laying one thing on top of another or looking for something at the workplace. That is merely making a motion.

It is not that the Japanese people are especially diligent in their work habits, but they do feel uncomfortable when they have nothing to do at their place of work. After all, they are paid to do something, and for want of something productive to do, they engage in unnecessary motions. Thus, in work, there are two types of movement. One is the movement necessary for making products, one that moves the manufacturing process forward, and the other is not. The latter, of course, is a wasted motion.

Factories are equipped with chutes and conveyor belts to connect separate manufacturing processes. But what we often see in these factories is a site where workers place parts and materials two or three columns abreast on a chute or a conveyor. If there is only one item, a roller conveyor (or any other type of conveyor) can move with ease. But its movement is hindered when things are placed side by side or are scattered along the conveyor. When the subsequent process tries to pick up the materials it needs, it has to engage in a lot of unnecessary motion to do so.

Figure 2-1. To Work and To Move

When the subsequent process picks up one item, other items may fall off the conveyor. Workers involved may be worried about their fingers being caught. All that tension and work are produced in picking up some items needed. It hardly seems worth the effort.

To pick up something or to replace something means simply that we change the location of certain items. We are merely moving them three centimeters away from the center of the earth or one meter closer to it!

What is important and what is not important, then? When we have this frame of mind, it becomes easier to differentiate the work load in the workplace. We may suddenly discover that only about one half of what we are doing is real work. We may give an appearance of working hard, but half our time is merely making moves without engaging in work. We move about a lot. This is a terrible waste and it must somehow be eliminated.

Reducing man-hours means to lower the waste and increase the amount of actual work. It does not mean that the size of the circle in Figure 2-1 has to be enlarged. And it is totally different from a movement to make the workers work harder.

SAYINGS OF OHNO

Moving about quite a bit does not mean working. To work means to let the process move forward and to complete a job. In work there is very little waste and only high efficiency.

Managers and foremen must endeavor to transform a mere motion (ugoki) *into work* (hataraki).

ENHANCING LABOR DENSITY

Generally people associate man-hour reduction with making the workers work harder. At Toyota, our thinking on labor density and making the workers work harder is as follows:

An example of making the workers work harder occurs when the work load is increased without improving the work process itself. For example, in a place which has been producing ten units per hour, the company orders that henceforth fifteen units be produced, without improving the work process or equipment. If we try to illustrate this, it is like putting a bump on someone's head (or on a circle, as shown in Figure 2-2).

In contrast, rationalization through man-hour reduction changes the wasted motion (*ugoki*) into work (*hataraki*) through improvement.

An act of omission (*tenuki*) occurs when someone does not do what he is supposed to do. For example, a plate must be secured tightly with five bolts, but a worker nonchalantly places four or five bolts without tightening each of them sufficiently. That is an act of omission or *tenuki*.

Toyota's man-hour reduction movement is aimed at reducing the overall number of man-hours by eliminating wasted motions and transforming them into work. All of us have some notion of what our work consists of. This movement eliminates from our work those actions which do not produce profit and which do not advance our process. It is a movement which channels the energy of men into effective and useful work. It is an expression of our respect for humanity.

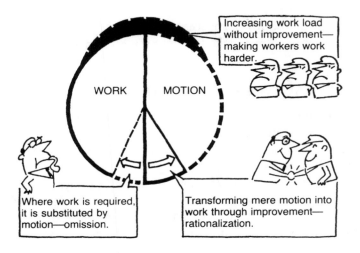

Increasing work load without improvement—making workers work harder.

WORK   MOTION

Where work is required, it is substituted by motion—omission.

Transforming mere motion into work through improvement—rationalization.

Figure 2-2. Enhancing Labor Density

Employees give their valuable energy and time to the company. If they are not given the opportunity to serve the company by working effectively, there can be no joy. For the company to deny that opportunity is to be against the principle of respect for humanity. People's sense of value cannot be satisfied unless they know they are doing something worthwhile.

At times, man-hour reduction has been considered to be merely an imposition of harder work without respect for humanity. This is due in part to misunderstanding and in part to the wrong method of implementation.

Based on what we have discussed so far, we can now define *labor density* as:

$$\frac{\text{Work}}{\text{Motion}} = \text{Labor Density}$$

The denominator is an impersonal motion and the numerator is work with a human touch. The act of intensifying labor density or of raising the labor utility factor means to make the denominator smaller (by eliminating waste) without making the numerator larger. Ideally labor density must be at 100 percent.

$$\frac{\text{Work}}{\text{Motion}} = 100\%$$

Around 1971, Toyota Motors' slogan was: "Eliminating waste to bring about improvement in efficiency." This was another expression of trying to make the denominator smaller.

UTILITY FACTOR AND EFFICIENCY

In manufacturing industries, elimination of waste is tied in with a better utility factor. As a result, if one can manufacture more products and parts than before, then one can say that the efficiency has increased.

Utility factor and *efficiency* are measuring sticks that we use daily. If we misuse these measuring sticks, we will be depriving ourselves of our ability to make the right evaluation. In fact, we can be faced with a situation in which efficiency has risen along with the cost.

The term *utility factor* is defined as the percentage of the energy supplied to a machine relative to that machine's actual capabilities. It can never be expressed in a number larger than 100 percent. When this definition is applied to production, the utility factor in production becomes the percentage of labor expended for producing a given product in relation to the labor required for making that product.

When the utility factor in production is 50 percent, it means that only half of the worker effort is useful in making that particular product. The remaining 50 percent is being wasted. When the utility factor in production is 80 percent, it means that 80 percent of the worker effort is useful, and the utility factor in production is much higher than in the previous example.

Thus any production which has a high utility factor means that most of the labor expended is going into the power to produce a given product.

In contrast, the term *efficiency* is used when one wishes to compare output. That is, within a given time frame, how many people have produced how many pieces? To compare, one needs a set standard (criterion). Normally, the actual performance of the past, such as the past month or year, is the standard. Or a company may set an arbitrary standard and say: "This month we have raised our efficiency by 15 percent (relative to our standard)." Thus, unlike the utility factor, efficiency may exceed 100 percent.

DON'T BE MISLED BY APPARENT EFFICIENCY

At one production line, 10 workers made 100 pieces every day. As a result of improvement, the daily output has increased by 20, to 120 pieces. This has been called a 20 percent improvement in efficiency. But is it?

When efficiency is expressed in an equation, it becomes:

$$\text{Efficiency} = \frac{\text{Output}}{\text{Number of workers}}$$

Generally, when there is talk of raising efficiency, most people think in terms of increasing the output (the numerator in this equation).

It is relatively easy to increase the number of machines or the number of workers in order to increase the output. Also, by sheer determination, all the workers can work together to raise the output. In a period of high economic growth, or in a company that is experiencing an increase in sales, either one of these approaches would, of course, be fine. But in another period and in a different company, can either one of these approaches work?

In a recession, or when the company's sales are declining, can it continue to allow this particular line to produce 100 pieces daily as part of the company's production plan? Can the line insist on producing 120 pieces because of its efficiency, even though the production plan calls for reducing the output to 90 pieces? What can the company do with the 20 to 30 pieces that are overproduced daily? The overproduction forces the company to pay for the costs of unnecessary raw materials and labor. Then there are costs of pallets (for storage and transporting) and of storage areas. For the company, overproduction means a net loss. Improvement in efficiency which does not contribute to the company's overall performance is not an improvement but a change for the worse.

Now, using the same example, but where the output needed does not change or is reduced, how can a company secure an improvement in efficiency that will assure profitability?

In such an instance, the process must be changed in such a way that only 8 instead of 10 workers will be required to produce 100 pieces. (Or if the quantity required is 90 pieces, let 7 workers handle the task.) In this way, efficiency will improve and be accompanied by a reduction in costs.

When we speak of attaining a 20 percent improvement in efficiency, there are two ways of doing it. It is easy to increase the number of machines to raise efficiency. But it is several times more difficult to reduce the number of workers and still raise efficiency. No matter how difficult the latter may be, we must take it up as a challenge. This is especially important in a period of recession, when we must attain efficiency through man-hour reduction.

Toyota does not allow an increase in output to create an appearance of efficiency improvement, when there is a need to reduce production or maintain the same output. We call it *an efficiency improvement for the sake of appearance.*

SAYINGS OF OHNO

When output needed does not change or must be reduced, do not attempt to improve your efficiency by producing more. Do not engage in an efficiency improvement for the sake of appearance.

No matter how difficult it may be, take it up as a challenge to reduce man-hours as a means of improving efficiency.

IT'S A CRIME TO OVERPRODUCE

What the Toyota production system seeks is a total elimination of waste.

We say that "a manufacturer's profit can be found in the way he makes things." It reflects our philosophy of attaining a cost reduction through the elimination of wasteful operations. There are many types of wastes. At Toyota, in order to proceed with our man-hour reduction activities, we divide wastes into the following seven categories:

1. Waste arising from overproducing
2. Waste arising from time on hand (waiting)
3. Waste arising from transporting
4. Waste arising from processing itself
5. Waste arising from unnecessary stock on hand

6. Waste arising from unnecessary motion
7. Waste arising from producing defective goods

The most common sight found in many workplaces is the excessive progression of work. Everything moves too fast. Normally, it must be consigned to waiting, but workers proceed to the next stage of work. Thus the time that is supposed to be waiting time becomes hidden. When this process is repeated, materials or parts produced accumulate in between or at the end of the production line, creating unnecessary stock on hand. To transport this stock or to rearrange it for storage requires creation of another type of work. By the time this process takes its course, it becomes more and more difficult to find where the wastes are.

Under the Toyota production system, we call this phenomenon the *waste arising from overproducing*. Of the many infractions of wastefulness, this is considered by far the worst offense.

The waste arising from overproducing is different from other wastes, because unlike other wastes, it overshadows all others. Other wastes give us clues as to how to correct them. But the waste arising from overproducing provides a blanket cover and prevents us from making corrections and improvements.

Thus, the first step in any man-hour reduction activity is to eliminate the waste arising from overproducing. To do so, production lines must be reorganized, rules must be established to prevent overproduction, and restraints against overproduction must become a built-in feature of any equipment within the workplace.

Once these steps are taken, the flow of things will return to normal. The lines will produce one item at a time as needed. The waste becomes clearly discernible as the waste arising from time on hand. When a production line is reorganized in this fashion, it becomes much easier to engage in the activity consisting of "elimination of waste — reassignment of work — reduction of personnel." *The waste arising from time on hand (waiting)* is created when a worker stands idly by an automated machine to serve as a watchman, or when he cannot do anything constructive manually because the machine is running.

This waste is also created when the preceding process fails to deliver parts needed in the present process, thus preventing workers in the latter from working.

In the illustration below, a worker is assigned to each of the machines designated as *a*, *b* and *c*. In this process, the worker stands by idly while the machine moves. He cannot work, even if he wants to, and there is a waste arising from waiting.

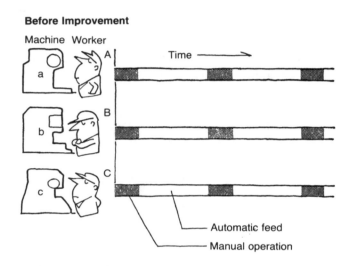

Figure 2-3. Waste Arising from Time on Hand

In order to eliminate this waste, the worker named A is assigned to all three of these machines to operate their automatic feeds sequentially. Under this arrangement, worker A places material in machine *a* and pushes the starter figure, switch and moves to machine *b*. He places material in machine *b* and starts it. He moves on to machine *c*, and repeats the same process he has done with machines *a* and *b*. After *c* is started, he moves back to *a*. By the time worker A returns to machine *a*, the work there is completed, and he can immediately start another round of work on machine *a*.

By eliminating the waste arising from waiting, two workers can be removed from the work process. Similarly, one may also consider eliminating unnecessary motions, which do not contribute to the work itself.

The waste arising from transporting refers to waste caused by an item being moved a distance unnecessarily, being stored

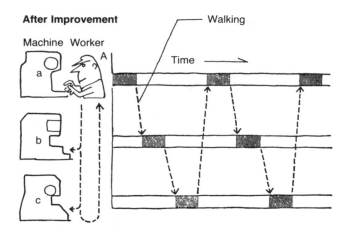

Figure 2-4. Eliminating Waste Arising from Time on Hand

temporarily or being rearranged. For example, traditionally parts are transferred from a large storage pallet to a smaller one and then placed temporarily on a machine several times before they are finally processed. By improving the pallets, we have been able to dispense with these temporary placement procedures and let one worker operate two machines.

Another instance of waste arising from transporting occurs when parts are moved from a warehouse to the factory, from the factory to the machines and from the machines to the hands of workers. At each of these steps, parts have to be rearranged and moved.

The waste arising from processing itself occurs, for example, when a guide pin in the jig does not function properly and the worker has to hold the jig with his left hand. The processing does not go smoothly and time is wasted.

In addition, there are wastes arising from unnecessary stock on hand, from unnecessary motion and from producing defectives. Explanations for each of these are not necessary.

ELIMINATE WASTE THOROUGHLY

There are many foremen and managers who allow their subordinates to work on something they suspect to be wasteful. Many

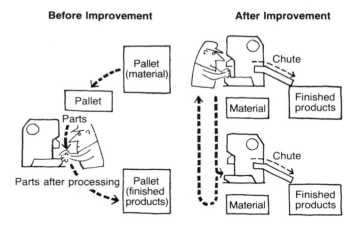

Figure 2-5. Eliminating Waste Arising from Transporting

SAYINGS OF OHNO

A worker or a line with excess capacities inevitably moves forward if left alone. When this happens, wastes are hidden.

In other words, overproduction creates a countless number of wastes, such as over-staffing, pre-emptive use of materials and energy costs, advance payment to workers, interest charges on mechanical devices and products, storage areas needed to accommodate the excess products and the cost of transporting them.

In a period of low economic growth, overproduction is a crime.

of them consider such an act a necessary part of their job, and often they do not understand the nature of the waste.

No matter how determined one may be in the desire to eliminate waste, if one does not know what constitutes waste, then there is no way of eliminating it. Therefore, an important task awaiting each of us is to make sure that waste always appears — distinctly and clearly — as waste to everyone. This is the first step toward attaining an improvement in efficiency.

Among the many types of waste, some are easy to discern and others are difficult. Among them, the easiest to discern is the waste arising from time on hand, or waiting.

For example, if the cycle time is three minutes and there is a one-minute period of waiting before a worker can resume his work, the worker himself, his supervisor and other supervisors certainly will know that this one minute is wasted. However, if the worker moves around to spend this one minute as if he were working, no clear-cut image will emerge (the wastes of transporting and of processing itself). Or if he should use this time to process the next item, no one can tell if a waste has actually occurred (the waste of overproducing). All these three wastes must be translated back into the waste arising from waiting. It can facilitate devising appropriate countermeasures.

In this connection, we may consider taking the following three steps:

1. Let the workers strictly observe the standard operations. Do not allow any deviation.
2. Control excessive forward movements through the production system, which utilizes *kanban*.[2]
3. Clearly indicate on the conveyor line the work area for each worker, thus preventing any worker from moving ahead of the schedule to do excessive work.

An important thing to remember is that to eliminate waste, you must find it first. You must rearrange the workplace in such a

---

[2] A *kanban* is a signboard or card; the work also refers to the system utilizing standard containers, each of which has a card designating what and when to produce.

way that waste can be easily found. Each of the steps you take by themselves seem insignificant. For example, you may even have to worry about a small quantity of goods stored between two processes. But as long as the problem is related to your "efficiency enhancement — cost reduction" movement, you must be prepared to ask this question: "Why has this occurred?" Before long, you may find a clue to the very improvement you are seeking.

Enhancement of efficiency can be attained through elimination of waste. Of course, there are may way of finding different wastes. But the most effective way remains that of *translating such wastes into the waste arising from waiting.* It is one that is easy to detect, and provides the first step toward efficiency enhancement.

This total dedication to the elimination of waste is the heart and soul of the Toyota production system. It also constitutes the very source of its profit.

3

Basic Assumptions Behind the Toyota Production System

TOYOTA PRODUCTION SYSTEM AND KANBAN SYSTEM

Many people may immediately associate the Toyota production system with the *kanban system*. While this is not wrong, it is not exactly accurate.

The kanban system is one of the methods of control utilized within the Toyota production system (the way we make things). One cannot discuss the kanban system out of context. If anyone tries to imitate that system without regard to all the factors contributing to its success, then his or her efforts will be in vain.

The Toyota production system is unique and unparalleled. The thinking behind it and the method of implementation have been perfected after long years of trial and error.

In a nutshell, it is a system of production, based on the philosophy of total elimination of waste, that seeks the utmost in rationality in the way we make things. We call this the Toyota-style production system or the Toyota production system. Hereafter, we shall use the term *Toyota system* to represent it.

Only when the Toyota production system in its totality is satisfactorily conducted, can there be effective utilization of the kanban system. Without changing the method of making things, it is impossible to engage in the kanban system.

Please take note of this fact before proceeding further in this chapter.

AN OUTLINE OF THE TOYOTA SYSTEM

We have prepared a chart to provide a bird's-eye view of the Toyota system. It is reproduced on the following page.

An ideal condition for manufacturing is where there is no waste in machines, equipment and personnel, and where they can work together to raise the added value to produce profit. The most important concern for us is how closely we can approach this ideal.

To make the flow of things as close as possible to this ideal condition — whether they be between operations, between lines, between processes or between factories — we have devised a system in which the materials needed are obtained *just-in-time* — that is, exactly when needed and in the quantity needed.

On the other hand, for this ideal condition to occur in the line operations, including machines and equipment, if there is abnormality, everything must be stopped immediately at the discretion of the worker or workers involved. (Machines must be endowed with the same faculty.) The reasons for the occurrence of abnormality must be investigated from the ground up. This is what we call *automation with a human touch.*

We believe it is best to manufacture everything in a balanced manner. This *load-smoothing production* serves as the base for the two pillars of the Toyota system, namely the just-in-time and automation-with-a-human-touch approaches.

CHARACTERISTICS OF THE TOYOTA SYSTEM

Now that we have a general notion of the structure of the Toyota system, we may proceed to enumerating the characteristics of this system. In this way, we shall be able to discern the basic ideas behind the Toyota system.

A Company-Wide IE Activity Directly Connected with Management

There is no specific formula for a manufacturing method that can apply to all products in all processes. Therefore a product may be manufactured by one worker in one company while at another

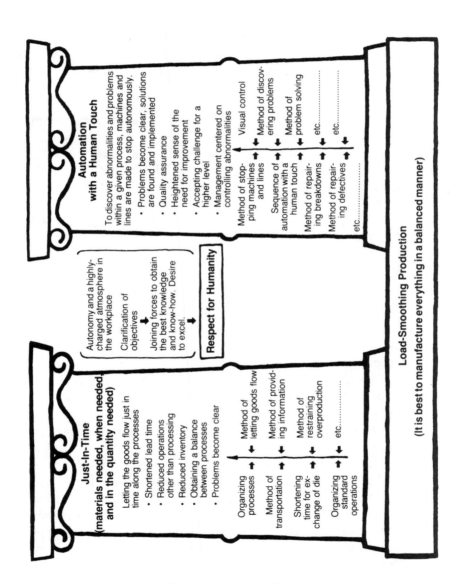

Figure 3-1. The Two Pillars of the Toyota System

it may take two workers to produce the same amount. In a company that is not concerned with the method of production, it may even require three workers to do the same work.

In this instance, the company using three workers must assume a higher cost for its warehouse, transporters, pallets, conveyors and other facilities. Along with this, there will be an increase in the indirect personnel cost. Its total cost is likely to be twice as much as that of other companies, and there will be a significant difference in its profile.

Industrial engineering (IE) plays an extremely important role in managing a company. Companies that are not engaged adequately in IE are very much like houses built on sand. At Toyota we have a saying: "IE makes money." We assign IE a firmly established management role to enhance improvement in production activities.

As to the production system, our basic thinking goes along the following lines. These criteria are adopted in order to permit all divisions related to production to operate more efficiently as a whole.

1. *The production plan must be load smoothed.* If we think only in terms of the final assembly process, it may appear that is more efficient to let the same type of products flow at the same time. But this will create a number of wastes in the preceding process.

2. *Make the lot size as small as possible.* Metal stamping is produced by lot, and its lot size must be made as small as possible. This is to avoid creating a large inventory and increasing the number of processes required for transporting. A mixup in the assignment of priorities has often resulted in shortages, creating an impression that the capabilities of the metal-stamping process are inadequate. As a result, some managers may insist on installing additional lines. Small-lot production avoids these pitfalls. However, to ensure that production in a small lot will not result in the lowering of capabilities, it is recommended that the procedures for the exchange of dies be improved.

3. *Be thorough in your resolve to produce only what is needed, when needed and in the quantity needed.* This is to ensure

that there will be no waste arising from overproduction, and to make it clear to everyone that the process has an excess capacity.

Scientific Attitude Emphasizing Facts

At the workplace, we start from the actual phenomenon, investigate the cause and find a solution. We do not deviate from this approach. In other words, anything related to the workplace is based on facts. No matter how much information is provided through data, it is difficult to see the true picture of the workplace through data. When defects are produced, and we find out only through data, we miss the chance to take appropriate corrective actions. Thus we may not be able to discover the true cause of the defects, resulting in our inability to take effective countermeasures against recurrence. The place where we can accurately capture the true state of the workplace is the workplace itself. We can catch defects on the spot in the workplace and then find the true cause. We can immediately take countermeasures. That is why under the Toyota system, we say that data is important but we emphasize facts even more at the workplace.

When a problem occurs, if the manner of probing into the cause is insufficient, measures taken can become blurry. At Toyota, we have the so-called five W's and one H. The five W's are not the conventional "who, when, where, what and why," but every word is replaced by a "why," and we say "why, why, why, why, and why" five times before we finally say "how?" In this way, we delve into the true cause that is hidden behind the various causes. It is essential that we come face to face with the true cause.

To make this method thoroughly understood by all, we take the following steps:

1. *Make sure that everyone can understand where the problem is.* If we know where the problem is, it is relatively easy to solve. Quite often difficulty arises because we cannot determine what the problem is. Thus we frequently use the *kanban* and *andon*. (The word *kanban* refers to the signboard of a store or shop, but at Toyota it simply means any small sign displayed in front of a worker. The word *andon*

refers of a Japanese paper-covered lamp stand, but at Toyota it simply means a lamp. Hereafter the word *kanban* will be used throughout. The word *andon* may either be used in its original form or translated as a display lamp, as the occasion demands.)

2. *Clarify the purpose behind the task of problem solving.* We probe into the true cause and offer a solution. If we do not probe deeply into the true cause, we may be offering merely a temporary solution, which cannot result in prevention of recurrence.

3. *Even if there is only one defective item, provide a corrective measure.* Even if the defect occurs only once every thousand times, ascertain the facts. With these facts, the true cause can be found and steps can be taken to prevent recurrence of defects. This type of defect is harder to find than those that occur more frequently. Be attentive, and do not overlook it when it occurs.

The Man-Hour Reduction Activity Must Be a Practical One

A step-by-step approach is required in this. The goal may be set high, but its implementation calls for progression in stages. We also place a great deal of emphasis on results. From these two basic assumptions, the following considerations emerge:

1. *Move from work improvement to equipment improvement.* Toyota insists on carrying out the work improvement phase of improvement activities thoroughly before moving on to the equipment improvement phase.

   When good results can be obtained with work improvement, and when such work improvement has not been undertaken sufficiently, there is no justification for investing a huge sum in automation machines. The effect of the introduction of automation machines may roughly equal that of a thoroughly conducted work improvement activity. In such a case, the money spent for equipment investment is wasted.

2. *Differentiate between man-hours and number of workers, and between labor saving and people saving.* In calculating

the number of man-hours required, it is possible to say that a certain process requires 0.1 to 0.5 worker. But in reality, the work requiring only 0.1 worker still needs one person. Thus if the work load of one worker is reduced by 0.9 worker, it still does not result in any cost reduction. True cost reduction can come about only after the number of workers is reduced.

Therefore, when we engage in a man-hour improvement activity, we must focus our attention on reducing the number of workers.

When automation devices are installed, there may be a labor saving of 0.9 worker. But if the process still requires 0.1 worker, the money spent does not result in reducing the number of workers. This is often erroneously looked upon as labor saving. In order to avoid confusion resulting from the use of this term, Toyota refers to a reduction in the number of workers, which can truly bring about cost reduction, as *people saving* to differentiate it from *labor saving.*

3. *To check means to give thought to something.* An improvement activity is completed when the result sought in the initial goal is obtained.

If the result cannot be obtained, it is often because the work has been done without much thought given to it. Confirm the result of implementation at the workplace, adjust all those parts inadequately done and confirm the result again. By repeating this process, a good result can be obtained through improvement.

When we check things, we do not merely look them over. It must be a process through which we rethink and reflect on our own work.

"Economy" Is Everything in the Standard of Judgment

The objective of the man-hour reduction activity is to lower the cost. Therefore, in every thought process must be a yardstick that asks: "Which one is more economical?" In its practical application, there are these considerations:

1. *The ratio of operation for equipment is determined by the quantity required for production.* Some people say that the higher the ratio of operation, the better, and they may overproduce those items that are not needed every day. They must store the excess products, and the loss resulting from overproduction is far greater than if they had produced only what was needed. It is dangerous to establish a standard based on raising the ratio of operation. Do not ignore the fact that the ratio of operation of machines and equipment must be based on the quantity required for production.

2. *When you have time on hand, use that to practice exchange of die.* The wages of workers who have established working hours but have nothing to do remain the same whether they remain idle or engage in the practice of exchange of die. If there is any time left, utilize that time to practice exchange of die, which is relatively complicated, or to train a not-so-skilled worker to become skilled in the standard operations in that particular area.

The Workplace Is the Boss

We consider the workplace to be an organic entity. The hands and legs have not entrusted their brains to the management division. Therefore, engineering must not act as if it were the commander-in-chief of the workplace. On the contrary, the autonomy of the workplace must be emphasized and respected. The engineering division gives support to the workplace and provides services in those areas that need them. It makes certain that the responsibility is not scattered and that the information provided is neither excessive nor deficient.

Emphasize Immediate Response to Change

Once the plan is established, it is often forced to change due to external and internal conditions. If the workplace insists on carrying out the original plan, distortion will occur, and it might adversely affect the rest of the company.

The workplace must establish a system that can respond quickly to changes forced upon it through the interplay of external and internal conditions. The greater the ability to respond to change, the stronger the workplace.

For example, due to an increase or decrease in production or to the stopping of the production line, the plan previously given to the workplace has to be changed. If the workplace can immediately establish the best system possible to solve all the problems quickly, and in the process show no confusion, then it is showing the ideal style of operation. We call such a place a workplace with its own soul.

THE GOAL IS COST REDUCTION

The Toyota system is a series of activities that promote cost reduction through the elimination of waste to achieve enhanced productivity. All companywide improvement activities must directly contribute to the goal of cost reduction.

The various methods for improvement and the thoughts behind them, in the final analysis, must be related to cost reduction. Conversely, cost reduction becomes the basic criterion on which we base our judgement.

If this basic criterion is not clearly understood, some managers may become unthinking advocates of improvement. Overly anxious about improvement after improvement, they may end up creating the waste arising from overproduction.

A company may spend money to improve its equipment and machines and spend time to improve its operations, yet find, in the end, that its only increase is excess inventory. The more they do, the worse off they become. That is an act of improvement contributing to a company's demise.

It is easy to say "cost reduction," but in making a decision there are two avenues, and they must be clearly differentiated. The first is a question of judgment, determining which is more advantageous between A and B. The second is a question of selection, choosing the most economically advantageous plan from among plans A, B, C and others.

ONE GOAL, MANY APPROACHES

Should a product be manufactured by the company or subcontracted? Should a company purchase a machine for the exclusive use of a certain process, or should it concurrently utilize for this particular process a machine it presently owns and uses for other purposes? These are questions of judgment, and the company must decide whether A or B has greater overall merit for the company.

Now, let us consider the question of selection, plan for its economic advantage among the many options.

For example, the goal is to reduce manpower, for which there are many approaches. Automation can reduce manpower, and so can restructuring the work process. Or a robot may be introduced. The company must study carefully all of these options to determine which is most advantageous.

Let us assume that there is a plan which suggests that an electric control device, costing $500, be installed to reduce the number of workers by one. If this is implemented, with a mere $500 Toyota will be able to reduce its workers by one. This represents a considerable saving for the company and sounds like a good idea. But is the device really necessary? On closer examination, we see that by changing the work sequence, one person can still be removed from that particular process. The $500 is therefore actually wasted. It is a premature plan that is a failure. We cannot select a plan simply because it can save some money. We must select a plan that can save more than other plans can save. Often, without thinking, companies choose automation. Beware of the pitfall just mentioned.

In undertaking the task for improvement, as discussed earlier, during the investigation stage there are two alternatives. The important thing to remember is that there are many approaches and methods to reach the same goal. So, carefully study as many plans as possible, take into account the company's overall objectives, and then select a plan best suited for the particular process.

Do not proceed with your improvement activity without full investigation. It can turn into an improvement plan that costs too much. Be sure to keep this fact in mind always.

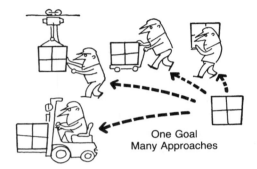

One Goal
Many Approaches

Figure 3-2. One Goal, Many Approaches

SAYINGS OF OHNO

Every decision must be based on these principles:
"Can the cost really be lowered?" and "Can this action
help the company's overall performance?"

EXCESS CAPACITY AND ECONOMIC ADVANTAGE

A decision about economic advantage can be swayed by whether or not a company has excess productive capacity. If there is excess capacity, the company merely uses workers and machines that are not occupied. There is no new expenditure, and the entire process can be free to the company.

Producing within the company or subcontracting

Should a certain part be produced within the company or subcontracted? Often management compares the relative costs. However, if there is excess capacity within the company, the new cost created is merely a fluctuation in the cost of materials and energy. No comparison of costs is necessary in this case. Production within the company is to its advantage.

Using stock on hand

A worker who transports parts from one line to another is waiting until the pallet is filled. To let him engage in the line work or preparatory work does not raise the cost. There is no need to study profit and loss in this situation. Do not add the man-hours spent here as an increase in man-hours.

As these examples demonstrate, when there is excess capacity, cost accounting is not needed to show which action is more advantageous to the company. It is important to make the existence of excess capacity known at all times. If this is not made clear, managers are liable to make a wrong decision and raise the cost for the company.

WHAT IS EFFECTIVE UTILIZATION?

Facilities and personnel are more than adequate, but they remain idle because there is no work. This is a fairly common sight in many companies.

When this type of situation develops, the reaction is often one of "well, we can't do anything about the machines, but it's wasteful to let the workers remain idle." So managers may order the workers to mow the lawn or clean the windows. This is the wrong approach.

These managers may have effective utilization of idle workers in mind. But no matter how meticulously the lawn is mowed or the windows kept clean, it does not produce a dollar of profit. Effective utilization must at least contribute to cost reduction. This is especially important when no work can be found for the workers, and there is no way to increase the added value for the company.

At a certain factory, there was no longer any work available, and workers were left with literally nothing to do. It so happened that at a number of locations there were water leak problems that were left unattended when the factory was in full operation. The company decided to fix the leaks during this period. The following month and thereafter, the water bill was trimmed by $5,000 each month. This is an example of true effective utilization.

IS IT A WASTE IF YOU DO NOT USE
AN EXPENSIVE MACHINE?

Many people have an erroneous notion that an expensive piece of equipment already purchased must be fully operated to get their money's worth. The higher the purchase cost, the greater its depreciation. So there is a feeling that unless the ratio of operation, or machine utilization, is close to 100 percent, money is lost.

However, while it may be true that the higher the ratio of operation the better, the loss resulting from overproduction may become far greater if the factory produces something that is not needed. Therefore, as stated earlier, it is dangerous to set the criterion solely on the basis of raising the ratio of operation. One must not ignore the fact that the ratio of operation of machines and equipment must be based on the required amount of production.

At Toyota, we are thoroughly committed to the idea that we must respect the work of our people at the core, usually hidden behind the many machines. In other words, we are people-centered and not machine-centered. If we become machine-centered, we may overproduce and create an excess of workers. If we develop our work schedule in a people-centered manner, we will be able to adjust the ratio of machine operation and eliminate the waste arising from excess workers. We can achieve this by making our work consistent with the required output or demand, and by operating the machines accordingly.

The money already spent is called *embedded expense*, or *sunk cost*, and cannot be used for future plans. When one is thinking of improvement, do not consider this to be a restraining factor. Many mistakes have arisen because of it.

For example, there may be a feelings that money is lost if a high-priced or high-performance machine is not used. But in principle, as long as a machine is in the workplace, irrespective of its high or low cost, the usage that the workplace has of the machine and its price are not related. If there is an issue arising whether to use a high-priced or a low-priced machine, simply use the one that costs less to operate.

HIGH SPEED AND HIGH
PERFORMANCE CAN BE A NO-NO

Car seats are sewn together by industrial sewing machines. Some lines are straight and some are curved. When one stands by the side of such a machine, he hears the sounds: JA-JA-JA-JA-JA,JA-JA,JA-JA-JA-JA-JA,JA-JA . . . The sound of the sewing machine changes and is interrupted as the worker sews the straight line, curved line or a more complex patch.

Sewing machines used to be foot-pedaled. Today the machine is powered by a motor and its speed is fast. It used a clutch to connect and disconnect power, just as in a car.

Most unskilled workers will not have any problem in guiding a piece of cloth forward when it is sewn straight, and they usually sew that part in one stretch. For curved lines, they cannot move the cloth forward consistently with the speed of the machine. So they slow the speed and their work is represented by the interrupted sounds of JA,JA,JA.

For skilled veteran workers, their rhythm is about the same whether the lines are straight or curved. On the other hand, they do not sew the straight line part in one stretch. Their motion is actually slightly slower than that of the inexperienced workers, but with an even JA-JA-JA-JA sound. With the same pace, they then proceed to sew the curved line part.

This is so because the more experienced workers become, the better is their clutch action. In a sense, they control the machine's mechanical speed with their personal touch, dropping the machine's speed to meet the requirements of their work.

Traditionally, industrial machines had to sew thick and hard materials, and their speeds were not that fast. But thanks to new technology, their speeds have become much faster, and today they have literally become machines of high speed and high performance. However, along with their speed and performance, the price of these machines has also risen.

Yet these expensive machines may stop frequently in the hands of inexperienced workers. And the veterans lower their speed in order to meet their work requirements. Why is it necessary to buy these expensive machines in the first place?

Taking this into account, Toyota asked its cooperating company to manufacture lower speed machines. The cost of these was half that of the higher speed machines.

A LITTLE OVER TIME ADDS UP

The cost that recurs every day look inconspicuous enough every time one sees it, and it is easy to overlook. Conversely, the one-time-only cost often appears to be a very expensive one because the sum for one time is rather substantial. However, if we convert into a one-time expenditure the cost caused by the waste which continuously occurs over a two-year period, we will be unpleasantly surprised by how large a sum it really is. We may feel that the one-time expenditure needed for improvement is too high (aside from the desire to find less expensive alternatives), but if we neglect elimination of waste that continuously occurs, we may incur a greater loss in the end. We cannot be led by a vague feeling. Instead we must count. In setting up lamps and kanban, there will always be an added cost. Or when the improvement is implemented, on a strictly temporary basis, overtime work may increase. Debates over these issues always surface, but we must always remember to count carefully and accurately.

HOW TO USE YARDSTICKS

Some familiar sayings, such as "The x ratio has increased," or "This method yields a higher y ratio and is therefore more advantageous to us," may sound fine. But depending on the goal the company seeks, this type of thinking may actually cause poor judgement. Yardsticks such as the profit ratio of a product or a particular type of investment are useful tools. Yet there are times when these yardsticks cannot be used to select a production or investment plan advantageous to the company.

I have already referred to the ratio of operation a number of times. It is wrong to assume that a decline in the ratio of operation equals a loss. The most profitable way, and at the same time the least wasteful way, is to manufacture products at the time needed in the quantity needed. If a company is too concerned with the ratio of operation and insists on operating all machines at 100 percent capacity, it may be left with surplus finished and semi-finished products piling up here and there. It will probably require two to three times the manpower just to handle these excess products. The company will also be forced to buy several times more materials and parts than required.

When this is seen strictly from the perspectives of expenditure and income, the amount expended is likely to register three to four times above normal, while the amount of income remains constant. In such a case, the term *loss* will sound too moderate.

Therefore it is best to consider that the ratio of operation is determined by the required output. However, the factory must always be ready to operate whenever called to do so. Otherwise, it will result in a loss from lost opportunities — or a necessity for overtime, which is also a loss.

There are several ways of expressing in a ratio the relationship between the results of work and labor. In addition to the commonly used terms such as *utility factor* and *efficiency*, there are phrases such as the *ratio of operation, labor productivity* and *strokes per hour (SPH)*. All of these are yardsticks designed to evaluate how efficiently the work in progressing.

In using these yardsticks to measure the results of work, consider the following:

1. *To raise the ratio of operation or SPH in itself cannot be the goal of the company.* Our goal is to reduce cost. Raising the ratio of operation or SPH without regard to all existing conditions can often result in a higher cost. For example, a line can raise its ratio of operation somewhat by any of the following methods: by allowing each process to have semi-finished products that can cover for equipment failures; by holding all types of parts in abundance, so as not to be affected by the shortage in the preceding process; and by assembling those goods for which all parts are on hand. But the past thirty years of experience in workplace management have shown us that these approaches often raise the cost. Therefore these approaches can be used only when they are consistent with the overall goal of the company. They can be used as yardsticks only when those employing them have a clear picture of all conditions present.

2. *The way you look at "capacity" is very important.* If you are speaking of machines and equipment, the highest capacity for them is generally represented by their *machine cycle* (or the period of continuous stamping). To evaluate properly

the machine presently in use, ascertain its present capacity, and look at it with a view to how far it can be raised when needed. If you are talking about manpower, you must differentiate between mere movement and working. Do not consider it to be a worker's capacity, when he moves about with wasted motions.

3. *It is important to think about the concept of time that "faster" expresses.* To work faster can become meaningful only if more processes and fewer people can do the same job.

   To produce faster means that more products are manufactured within a given time frame. Yes, the efficiency is enhanced. But at times it can also mean a loss for the company.

HIGH EFFICIENCY DOES NOT EQUAL LOWER COST

As discussed earlier, the purpose of enhancing efficiency is to lower the cost. Therefore enhancement of efficiency cannot in itself be considered a goal to be pursued. Only when higher efficiency and lower cost become one can there be meaning to the act of enhancing efficiency.

We often see production lines adopting as their management objective the enhancement of SPH (strokes per hour or per hour productivity). They place behind the line a production control board, which records the amount of finished products every hour on the hour.

When this is continued, one tends to confuse the enhancing of SPH with the objective itself.

To enhance SPH, a foreman or manager may decide to engage in production by a large lot, reducing the number of times the line engages in the exchange of die. After the day's quota is filled, if there is time left, the line may start producing the next day's or even the day after tomorrow's quotas. Indeed, SPH will rise and people who are directly involved may feel that their efficiency is high and they have made money for the company. But in reality what they have created is a mountain of stockpiled materials and parts between themselves and the subsequent process.

In this instance, the first condition for this line to observe is to produce only the amount needed, in as small a lot as possible. If they try to raise SPH within this framework, they can succeed in cost reduction.

Without abiding by this condition, if the line attempts to raise SPH, it only creates a net negative situation for the factory. High efficiency does not always equal low cost.

RATIO OF OPERATION AND RATIO OF MOVABILITY

The *ratio of operation* refers to the ratio of how many hours during a working day a machine is utilized to manufacture. Since the work day is generally defined as eight hours, if a machine is operated only four hours, the ratio of operation of that machine is a mere 50 percent.

In Japanese we use three Chinese characters (*kanji*), *ka-do-ritsu*, to represent the term *ratio of operation*. The character *ka* stands for the word *kasegu*, which means to make a profit, and the character *do* means to move. Therefore when we use the term *ratio of operation*, we literally expect the machine to be operated in order to make a profit. If a machine moves continuously for the entire day without producing anything, the ratio of operation will remain zero. As discussed earlier, we must differentiate very clearly between an act of "moving" and an act of "working." This concept is equally applicable to a machine. If there is wasted motion in a machine, or if hours are spent without producing real work, such waste must clearly be avoided.

Because of this, at Toyota we write the term *ratio of operation* with one extra radical added to the character *do* to signify real work with a human touch.

With all of these in mind, if we are to provide a new definition for the Toyota-style ratio of operation, we mean "the ratio of actual production to the capacity of a machine when it is fully utilized." In other words, if machine A has the capacity for producing 100 pieces per hour of a given part, and if in a particular day only 50 pieces per hour are produced, then the ratio of operation for that day is 50 percent.

The ratio of operation fluctuates from month to month, influenced by the sales figures and the number of cars produced. If sales are down, so is the ratio of operation. Conversely, when orders are up, longer overtime hours and extra shifts may be required. If the normal full eight-hour operation is defined as 100, then the ratio must be raised to 120 or 130 percent.

This is why we say no factory can establish a certain percent ratio of operation as its production goal.

Toyota factories are very much like those of any other car manufacturer in that many machines stand side by side. But what distinguishes Toyota factories from others is that while some of the machines are operating, others are stopped.

Visitors are often heard to say: "How can you make money while keeping this many machines idle?"

Our response is simple. The way in which we organize our work is based on this principle: "Timing is the key to everything we do."

For example, there is a machine which is capable of cutting a piece in 10 seconds. If the machine is forced to cut each piece at a 10-second interval without interruption day and night, it may break down within a year or two. But if we time it so that a piece is cut every four minutes, the actual cutting time remains 10 seconds, but the machine is stopped for the remaining three minutes 50 seconds.

The term *ratio of operation* shares the same sound in Japanese, *ka-do-ritsu*, with another term, *ratio of movability* or *reliability*.

The ratio of movability represents the state in which a given machine functions properly when operated. When the switch is on, the motor turns, the machine moves and the operation proceeds. This is the normal state of the machine's operation.

Ideally, the ratio of movability must be 100 percent, and that must be set as the target.

In order to attain this, preventive maintenance must be done to avoid a breakdown. It is also necessary to shorten the time interval between the exchange of die.

Let us use your car as an example. The ratio of movability is whenever you want to take a ride, the car starts immediately, the engine moves smoothly and you can have a nice drive.

For a pleasure ride on a Sunday afternoon, the ratio of movability may not be a serious consideration. But suppose your child is suddenly taken ill, and you have to go to a doctor. The engine does not start, a tire is flat and there is no gasoline in the tank. There is no end to all the trouble you may have. That is why the ratio of movability must always be kept at 100 percent.

On the other hand, the ratio of operation is the number of hours you operate your car. You have finally bought the car of your dreams. But will you ride in it nonstop day and night? On weekends, you may take your family for a ride. But on an average day, you may take your wife shopping and operate it for an hour or two. And, unless you commute by car, you may not operate it at all on some days.

People drive their cars when needed. Thus, the 100 percent ratio of operation in this case is nonsense. Driving a car unnecessarily means a net loss. Aside from the expense for gas and oil, one must also consider the wear and tear on the car, which can result in an earlier breakdown.

SAYINGS OF OHNO

The ratio of operation is the burden imposed on a machine in relation to its capability when it is fully operated, and is determined by the sales figure. The ratio of movability is the condition of that machine to operate on demand. In this case, the ideal state is 100 percent.

SHORTEN THE LEAD TIME

Whatever the process, be it the way in which machines are aligned or the manner in which materials flow, the longer the lead time for production, the worse it is for the process.

At Toyota, we define *lead time* as the time elapsed from the time we start processing materials into products to the time we receive payment for them.

For example, a certain product is said to take a month to produce. But if we take a closer look at it, we discover that the actual time the production processes take is extremely short. The time spent for manufacturing is far shorter than the time the product lies idle in storage.

Generally speaking, lead time is the sum of the time required for processing and the time the product is in storage. Thus in some quarters, fear is expressed that the ratio between the time required for processing and the time the product is in storage may become as high as 1 : 100.

When the lead time becomes lengthy, it can create a lot of distortion in forecasting.

If the workplace says that the product cannot be manufactured unless information is received three months in advance, the marketing department must receive an order from the customer at least three months in advance. It must, of course, immediately process the order.

In a competitive industry, materials must be purchased even before an order for its products is received. Now, assuming that the order the company is seeking has gone to a competitor, the materials purchased in anticipation of the order will remain in storage to gather dust.

This is an extreme case. But in plain English, to have a lead time of three months means that three months' worth of products are lying idle in the company. Assuming that the company has to initiate a model change quickly, everything bought for the old model has to be discarded. They have been "sleeping" in storage for more than two months, have become useless and must meet an inglorious death in the end.

This is not fair to the workers in the workplace who have been toiling day and night to rationalize the entire process.

There is not a single factor which commends a lengthy lead time. Shortening of the lead time creates the following advantages: decrease in the work not related to processing, decrease in the inventory and ease in the identification of problems. Altogether the workplace becomes more manageable.

A few years back, we tried to measure the lead time with the engine built at our Kamigo plant. Parts were cast in the morning and then assembled to become an engine. By evening, that engine was inside a car which was driven around the Toyota Sales Headquarters. This has been and is the lead time in Toyota.

ZERO INVENTORY AS OUR CHALLENGE

For an industry, the most desirable condition is not to have any inventory. Of course, it is practically impossible to have a zero inventory, but that must be set as a goal. What a company can do is to accept this as a challenge and try to reduce the inventory as much as possible.

Many managers will say that they have successfully eliminated one half of the inventory previously maintained, and they can do no more. This is not good enough. If it has taken so long to reduce the existing inventory by half, obviously not enough effort has been expended.

If these managers accept the challenge of reducing their inventory to zero, they will inevitably continue the following process:

- If you get to the one-half mark,
- Reduce the remainder by half, and
- Again reduce the remainder by half, and
- Again reduce the last remainder by half.

If this is done, the inventory can be significantly reduced. In the end, there may be only one or two pieces remaining.

Ask yourself this question: "Can we do our work without any goods in process in stock?" If your answer is "No, for this process, we do need one piece," then you retain only that one piece. In this way, the workplace will be trained to retain only the very essential inventory for itself.

If the process does not call for a single item of inventory, then zero inventory must be the norm. If the process calls for one piece of inventory, then that must be kept. But it must be clearly understood that the one piece is the absolute necessity. The workplace learns to know the nature of its own work through the process of inventory reduction.

CAN THE WORKPLACE RESPOND TO CHANGE?

We often hear that after an improvement, many lifts and pallets are no longer needed and a lot of new space is created. However, these cannot be accepted as the accomplishments resulting from the improvement. The excess recovered or found still does not contribute a penny's worth of profit for the company. A proper procedure is to give this information to the planning division. After all, those items that have just been removed at one time looked as if they were all needed. The cause of this waste was the improper method of production. With this feedback, the planning division can plan better next time around.

Normally, planning is done with the existing condition as the base. Thus, if the present method is quite wasteful, all types of waste can still be included in the next plan. Once an investment is made, no amount of improvement can later recover it. This is a very serious matter.

Beware of the relationship between planning and the present status. Be on the lookout for eliminating waste in the workplace. Do not neglect to inform the planning division at all times of your discovery of the waste.

The above is a description of the Toyota production system and the basic thoughts behind it. We have paid special attention to the issue of economic judgment, the manner is which we use these criteria to promote our cost reduction activities. There is one final point which requires further elaboration — this is the issue of "economy," which differs from time to time depending on external conditions.

To make a rather harsh statement, what was profitable until yesterday may be a losing proposition for the company today. For example, if the wage contract is changed from an hourly-rate contract to a subcontracting agreement, the issue of profit and loss will take on an entirely different meaning.

An important things to remember is to remain flexible. When trying to reduce waste, conditions always vary. Your way of thinking and implementation plan for improvement must always be based on this consideration.

4

Leveling: Smoothing Out the Production System

PEAKS AND VALLEYS OF WORK

In a normal workplace, the more the flow of things varies, the greater the incidence of creating waste. The capacity of the workplace is often adjusted to the peak work demand and not to its average value. At Toyota, there was a time in which this was the normal occurrence for us also.

Assuming that the amount of work in a day (or a week or a month) varies as shown in the illustration, the capacity of that workplace must be adjusted to the peak demand, and it must have the requisite number of personnel, machines and materials.

However, when capacities are adjusted thus to the peak demand, under-utilization occurs when a smaller amount of work is available. If that is not the case, the worst waste arising from overproduction may result.

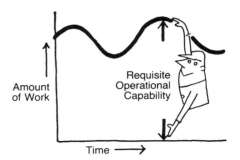

Figure 4-1. Peaks and Valleys of Work

73

The same story can be heard in the accounting division at the time books (or accounts) are closed.

In the accounting division, the peak appears within a one-month unit, or a six-month unit. At the normal workplace, the peak does not appear with such a large cycle. It may appear once every hour or once every ten minutes. We must be prepared to deal with these peaks that come in a piecemeal fashion.

GIFT SHOPS IN TOURIST SPOTS

The peaks and valleys of work can be found in almost any workplace, and many companies insist on having personnel and machines to be able to cope with the peak demand.

Why do they insist on maintaining the capacity to meet the peak demand? Because they are not aware of the waste inherent in it.

Tourist spots illustrate this point clearly. Their appeal is seasonal. When guests arrive in season, there is no more space for parking, the toilet may overflow, and the food served is terribly expensive but not tasty. Coca-Cola, which we buy at 75¢ a can, becomes $1.50 a can. This is something we experience very often.

From the point of view of the guests, this does not make much sense. But from the point of view of gift shops, it is natural that they want to recover the cost incurred during the entire year. They want to do so during the peak season and also add a little profit.

When not in season, many gift shops simply close down. Their proprietors may be engaged in other businesses. In the meantime, the shops, dishes and dinnerware, parking fields, etc. remain idle without raising a penny for the proprietors. At the same time, owners still have to pay taxes, mortgage payments and interest on the operating capital previously borrowed.

Gifts shops and restaurants in tourist spots have no other choice but to do as they do. But manufacturers who sell their products cannot do the same. They cannot say, "We have to charge you this much because our cost has been rising," forgetting that they have wasted a lot of resources. The fierce competition existing in the manufacturing sector prevents them from taking this easy way out.

Even among gift shops in tourist spots, if guests arrive in equal numbers regardless of the season, sales will stabilize. In such an instance, operational efficiency will be good, even without much effort.

The most efficient condition exists when the amount of work is equalized, or when the work itself is performed at an even pace.

ON THE AUTOMOBILE ASSEMBLY LINE

How does the concept of equalizing apply in the case of car manufacturing? We shall now proceed with examples from the assembly line.

If we assemble 20,000 Corona units a month and we operate 20 days, our daily allotment comes to 1,000 units.

It is easy to say 20,000 units. But even within the same Corona, specifications are extremely varied. When styles, tires, options and paint colors are all taken into account, it is possible to design and manufacture 800,000 combinations through these specifications. We manufacture them according to the orders we receive.

In the case of Crown, there are 250,000 possible combinations; in the case of Corolla, there are 16 million.

Of course, in reality we do not have that many varieties of specifications moving through our assembly lines. For Corona, that number is usually at the level of three to four thousand, and the question becomes how to manufacture these three to four thousand varieties. In other words, in this particular example, how do we line up the four thousand varieties when we assemble 20,000 Corona units a month.

A thought that immediately comes to mind is to assemble those that are similar in specifications close to one another. If the exterior paint is white, then we assemble those with white paint specifications together.

For the painting process, the procedure suggested is very convenient. All we have to do is paint everything the same color. We do not have to clean the pipe — the procedure that is required when the paint color is changed. In fact, we do not even have to exchange the paint gun.

For the assembly process, we have to keep in mind that there are five different types of engines that can go into a car that is painted white. If by chance the same type of engine is ordered for successive cars, the work process becomes identical. There will be no mistake committed in installation, and efficiency will certainly improve.

However, in reality this cannot happen. We have experienced that in a given month, with its 20,000-unit production, if we can get 50 units a month with similar specifications, that is as much as we can expect. A more realistic view is that each car has its own specifications, and we must manufacture them accordingly.

PROCESSES ARE LINKED

There are roughly 3,000 different types of parts required to build a car. If we count each bolt and each screw as a separate unit, then we will need 30,000 pieces. Is there a better way of assembling a car using these 30,000 parts?

In the previous example, we talked about using white paint exclusively. This means that the paint manufacturer must make only white paint. Now, assuming that we want to establish manufacturing processes differentiated by color, we will need a manufacturing process for blue and another one for yellow. But if we only utilize the line with white paint, the blue and yellow lines must remain idle. As for the paint manufacturer, there cannot be an even work flow.

When the exterior paint is white, the interior often calls for either black or blue. This means that the seat lines for brown and red must remain idle. Thus the work of those engaged in car seats cannot achieve equalization either.

Behind each of these 30,000 parts, there are manufacturers and processes. We must find a way to equalize these 30,000 parts and move them forward. An assembly method that can respond to this requirement must be created.

LEVELING QUANTITIES AND TYPES

We have discussed the waste in capacity when geared to the peak demand. Even so, when producing only a single item, it is not impossible to rearrange the production plan and personnel to level somehow the peaks and valleys of the work load. For example, a process that has less work can come to the aid of those having excess work. In this way, a single-item manufacturer can reduce waste.

However, to even out production for the automobile industry is an entirely different matter. The industry has multiple types of parts in multiple numbers. The process it must go through is a very complex one.

The only viable solution for most car manufacturers (including Toyota in its earlier days) has been to maintain a certain amount of inventory on hand. They have planned in such a way that every line will have some work to do every day. However, this approach is a costly one, because it requires holding a parts inventory three to four times larger than that required when the assembly line has an equalizing system of production. The waste created is enormous.

What is the solution then?

To have a successful system of equalized production, we must equalize not only the quantities but also the types.

In the case of the Corona already discussed, we have a production schedule of 1,000 units a day. All units are different in their engines, transmissions, axles, bodies, external colors and interiors. We scatter them all, and then do our assembly work.

Many visitors to the Toyota assembly line will ask: "Why do you have a red Corona here and another red Corona there? Why don't you bunch all the red ones together and let them flow in sequence?" The reason is very simple. We want to equalize the types.

If we allow cars with red-colored exteriors to be placed on the assembly line to the exclusion of others, red seats and interior parts will flow very heavily in the morning. In contrast, in the afternoon, there may not be enough work left for those dealing with the red color.

As for the engine, we try to let the 2000-cc and 1800-cc engines flow roughly in proportion to the number used. As for the left steering wheel cars for export and right steering wheel cars for domestic use, the determinant factor in the assembly line is the sales records of that particular time. Or we may make every third car with a left steering wheel.

There must not be peaks and valleys in our work, even in the most minute parts of the process. In so doing, we can then proceed to the equalizing system of production for our entire process.

This equalization of the quantities and the types is called *load smoothing (heijunka)* under the Toyota system. The load-smoothing system of production is the major premise for the elimination of waste.

The kanban system can succeed in a place where the final process is under the load-smoothing system of production. If there is no load-smoothing system of production, the kanban system will fail.

CYCLE TIME

When the factory attempts to equalize not just the quantity but also the type, what can be adopted as the standard to even out variations in the type?

In every work, timing is crucial. If not done adequately, the delivery time may be missed and the order may be canceled. On the other hand, if the product is manufactured too early, there may be a mountain of inventory. In baseball, if a runner reaches the plate just in time, he is safe. But if he is a little late, he is out.

This timing is determined by no one other than the customer.

Let us assume that Corona is sold in the quantity of 20,000 units each month. It means that 1,000 units must be produced each day (assuming that there are 20 work days in a month). In an eight-hour a day operation, 1,000 units must be produced in 480 minutes. Therefore:

$$480 \text{ minutes} = \frac{48 \text{ minutes}}{1,000 \text{ units}}$$

In other words, one unit must be produced every .48 minutes. Otherwise, the company will not be able to meet the demands of the customer.

In this way, for every product or part, it is important to have a notion of the *cycle time*, which is defined as the minutes and seconds required to produce one item.

·The cycle time is a key concept in manufacturing things. It is determined by the customer. In other words, it is determined by the sales record. The waste arising from overproduction can be eliminated through the use of this cycle time. True efficiency — not an apparent one — can result from its application.

AN EXAMPLE OF PROCESSING A GEAR

At one section of a factory within the Toyota headquarters compound, one worker is responsible for 16 machines that process and finish a gear. This phenomenon would not be surprising at all if all the machines did the same work, as is seen in automatic spinning machines. But in the case of these 16 machines, each has a separate function. One may grind, another may cut and shave, and so on.

Let us observe how one worker manages. First, he takes a gear coming from the preceding process and sets it on the first machine. He removes from the same machine a gear already processed and puts it into the chute. The gear is rolled over to the next machine.

The worker then moves from the first machine to the second, and while moving he turns on the switch located between the two machines. At that moment, the first machine starts moving.

The same motion is repeated at the second machine before he moves on to the third. While he walks he turns on the switch, and the second machine starts moving.

As he repeats the same motion over and over again, he can make a round of 16 machines in exactly five minutes. In other words, one gear is completed if a worker makes a round of 16 machines in five minutes.

Now, if we need to mass produce the gear, we can place one worker each at these 16 machines. By simple arithmetic, one gear can be produced in a little over 18 seconds.

However, if the car that uses this type of gear is only sold every five minutes — or, in other words, if the gear's cycle time is five minutes — then there is no need to station 16 workers.

In this instance, it is sufficient to have one gear every five minutes. We do not need to produce more.

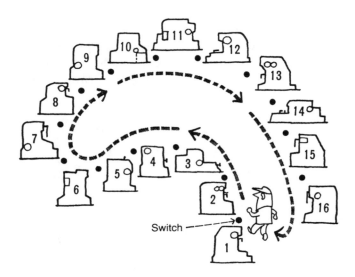

Figure 4-2. Processing a Gear

METHOD OF LOAD-SMOOTHING PRODUCTION

Implementation of the load-smoothing system of production becomes easier when one has a clear notion of what the cycle time is.

We have previously stated that there are 800,000 specifications for Corona. However, in order to make the explanation of the load-smoothing plan simpler, let us assume that Corona has only five types, named A, B, C, D and E.

The required amount (amount of production) and cycle time for the five are given in Figure 4-3.

To obtain the cycle time, the following simplified formula may be used:

$$\text{Cycle time(tact)} = \frac{\text{Daily operating time}}{\text{Required quantity per day (unit)}}$$

Often we see lines making mistakes in obtaining the cycle time. Care must be taken to ensure that this does not happen.

The mistakes occur because these lines calculate everything from the present condition, including equipment capabilities and

	Month	Day (480 minutes, 20 work days)	Cycle Time
A Car	4,800 units	240 units	2 min.
B Car	2,400 units	120 units	4 min.
C Car	1,200 units	60 units	8 min.
D Car	600 units	30 units	16 min.
E Car	600 units	30 units	16 min.
	9,600 units	480 units	1 min.

Figure 4-3. Required Quantities and Cycle Times for Five Auto Models

man-hours. They say: "We have this much equipment capability and this many people. Therefore we can produce this many units. And we can produce one unit in this many minutes."

From the perspective of the Toyota system, this approach is totally wrong. "We need this many units today," however, will give the right start. One must obtain the number of people needed to work from the cycle time, which in turn is obtained from the required amount of production for the day. Toyota's aim is to do the work required with the minimum number of people. If one calculates based on what he can do with the people the line already has, then the result is likely to be having too much capacity, creating the waste arising from overproduction.

HOW TO LET THINGS FLOW

Now that the cycle time has been determined, how does it work out in the actual assembly line?

Let us assume that A through E are all assembled by lines exclusively devoted to each. Thus as seen in the figure below, at Line A, units are moved at a two-minute interval, but at Line E, only one unit is assembled every 16 minutes.

When the separate exclusive lines are merged into one, the flow will take the form indicated at the bottom of the figure. At Toyota's assembly line, the cars may be the same Corona, but

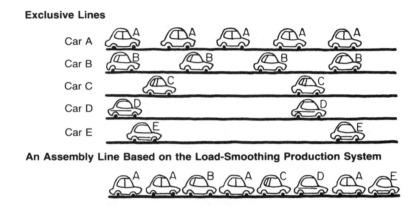

Figure 4-4. Load-Smoothing Auto Production

there are many different colors, two-door and four-door models, left and right steering wheels, all mixed together and interspersed while moving through the assembly line.

With this assembly line in operation, it becomes possible to have load smoothing not just for the quantities but also for the types. The work done in this fashion at the final assembly line guarantees that equalization can occur in all preceding processes.

Now take another look at the upper portion of the figure. These exclusive lines could just as well be processes devoted to parts (or to assembly). When all of these lines are equalized, then every line can have adequate work, and work can also become equalized.

PLAN MUST ALSO BE LOAD-SMOOTHING

The load-smoothing system of production has been created to eliminate peaks and valleys in the work load and to avoid excessive production and excessive progression in a particular process. Its aim has been to equalize the work load. However, there is still another contribution that has not been discussed.

That is, through this system it has become increasingly easier to change the production plan. And the workplace has accepted plan changes more cheerfully.

One line produces 100 units every day. A plan change calls for increasing its output to 105 units daily. The workers do the job without thinking of changing their production capacity or system.

However, if suddenly an order requiring 150 units daily is sent to a line that has been producing 100 units, difficulties will arise. Overtime may become necessary, there are not enough workers, and in an extreme case, a new machine may have to be brought in. If this condition persists, the company may be forced to hire more personnel or to utilize subcontractors. Its ability to respond to change becomes rather limited.

The key to solving this problem is the production plan. But almost every factory and company seem to have poorly managed production plans.

During the month of January, the line in question is producing at the rate of 100 units. In February, it is likely that 120 units must be produced because orders are coming in. This fact is usually known by January 10. However, a common practice is to draft a plan for presentation at monthly production meetings. The workplace receives a written plan after January 20. In an extreme case, a 20-percent increase in February and an additional 20-percent increase in March are the facts already known, but management insists on waiting until the very last minute to hold its monthly planning meetings. Management does not think to change the previously set dates for these conferences.

If management continues to follow this practice, there is no way the workplace can respond to change. It becomes a victim of its own silly rules, resulting in a curious inability to move ahead.

Therefore, when making a change in the production plan, build in the necessary changes gradually. Change the plan when an increase or decrease in the amount of production is known. In this particular example, it was known by January 10 that the demand would be higher by 20 percent in February. The management should have asked the workplace on January 11 to increase its daily output immediately by five to eight units. By taking this gradual approach, the workplace could have handled it well.

To have a load-smoothing system of production, load smoothing must also become part of the production plan.

EASIER TO ESTABLISH STANDARD OPERATIONS

In any work, it is important to establish standards. But unless the work itself is somewhat stabilized, standardization becomes rather difficult. In some instances, standards may be established, but they are worthless for practical purposes.

"The first step toward improvement is standardization." Where there is no standard, there can be no improvement.

When we engage in the load-smoothing system of production, we can establish standard operations throughout the entire process, covering all processes and lines. This is one of the main goals of load-smoothing production.

At Toyota, we manufacture through load smoothing, we figure out the cycle time and we create standard operations. We then promote our improvement activities. These are the basic steps we have consistently followed.

In a nutshell, the Toyota kanban system removes the signboards proportionate to the quantity used, and goes to the preceding process to withdraw exactly the same quantity. The preceding process manufactures the exact quantity just withdrawn. The kanban system is a system that keeps on turning this cycle.

Frequently we hear this comment: "That's a very snappy way of doing things. Even for those parts bought from outside suppliers, all one has to do is send a piece of paper and the parts arrive." But the success of the kanban system is dependent on the thoroughgoing conformance to the load-smoothing system of production at each of the final processes.

Assuming that the final process has not been converted to the load-smoothing system of production, but insists on using the kanban to receive parts — for a party receiving this demand, it is a bolt from the blue.

The workplace cannot use the kanban to order 50 boxes today, none tomorrow and 150 boxes the day after tomorrow. If the preceding process or supplier is treated in this manner, utter confusion will result.

Under the kanban system, the subsequent process withdraws parts and material from the preceding process every day, with consistency — in the same manner, at the same interval and in about the same amount. It is only in this way that the system can succeed.

OBSTRUCTION CALLED EXCHANGE OF DIE

A bottleneck is often created in the load-smoothing system of production by the exchange of die.

Normally the exchange of die is considered a time-consuming process. Why?

The preponderant reason is that where there is no desire to do die exchange quickly, it becomes a self-fulfilling prophecy.

In fact, some workplaces do not worry if the exchange of die takes eight hours. That, of course, is an extreme case, but no one thinks much about the die exchange that takes one hour. In some workplaces, equipment procurement is often premised on these uncontrolled die-exchange procedures.

In places like these, the load-smoothing system of production and the exchange of die become irreconcilable opposites.

One of the characteristics of the Toyota system is to make the size of a lot in the workplace as small as possible. If the time spent for exchanging die is greater, the lot is likely to remain larger. When the lot is larger, it is often assumed that through it the time lost through the exchange of die can be recovered. But this can lead to the waste arising from overproduction.

Our aim is to please our customers by producing only those cars that they order. If we complain about the frequency of die exchange, we are in effect saying to our customers: "Why don't you order the same style and same type of cars?" That is not the way to do business.

The only alternative left for us is to shorten the time spent for the exchange of die.

PREPARATION AND CLEANUP ARE THE KEYS

It is not that difficult to shorten the time needed for the exchange of die.

The point is to make an advance preparation of those molds, jigs and tools that can be assembled ahead of time, and to clean and place in their storage places those molds, jigs and tools that are removed only after the machine starts moving again. This is called *thoroughness in the outside exchange of die.*[1]

We must concentrate on, and try to improve, those operations that cannot be performed without stopping the machine. With this alone, the time needed can be significantly reduced. This is called *thoroughness in the inside exchange of die.*[2]

If tools are to be used, be sure that all those needed are kept by the side of the machine and in the order they are to be used. Do not overlook the proper arrangement of materials. Focusing their attention of the die exchange, workers can perform it quickly and expertly. But this can come to nothing if they do not have the necessary materials. Things like this happen frequently.

Preparations and arrangements can be made through improvement in the work process. In other words, these can be accomplished through the workers' own ingenuity. The procedure must be standardized and written down in a standards manual with which workers can continue training and retraining to do the exchange of die. Time reduction becomes possible.

This training is very similar to fire drills practiced by many companies. In a fire drill, it is not unreasonable to expect that all the water hoses are readied within two minutes. Everyone observes the correct procedure. The fire fighters also know how to divide up their work without any waste or delay.

In exchanging die for large equipment, Toyota retains the services of a special unit organized by specialists in die exchange. Seven or eight years ago, it took three hours to exchange die in an eight hundred-ton press. Today it takes only three minutes.

---

[1] See *A Revolution in Manufacturing: The SMED System,* by Shigeo Shingo (Productivity Press, 1985). Mr. Shingo, who developed the quick die change method for Toyota, explains inside exchange of die (IED) and external exchange of die (OED) in detail, and outlines steps for reducing and streamlining both IED and OED. See also *Modern Approaches to Manufacturing Improvement,* edited by Alan Robinson (Productivity Press, 1990).

[2] Ibid.

Chapters 5, 6, 7, 8, and 9 are selections from Today and Tomorrow, *Henry Ford (Cambridge: Productivity Press, Reprint edition 1988)*

5

It Can't Be Done

One of the surprising facts about industry is the tenacity with which people cling to methods which were used long before power and machinery entered the world. The only tradition we need bother about in industry is the tradition of good work. All else that is called tradition had better be classed as experiment.

In scrapping old ideas, one of the first that needs scrapping is the notion that because man power is cheap, developed power need not be used. Labor is not a commodity. One's own workers ought to be one's own best customers, and until that is fully realized, it is quite impossible to make even a beginning on the application of the wage motive. It is not to be assumed that men are worth only what they will work for and that the manufacturer should adapt his wages and prices to what the traffic will bear — that is, pay his men the least that they can be had for and charge his customers all that they will stand for. A business ought not to drift. It ought to march ahead under leadership.

It seems hard for some minds to grasp this. The easy course is to follow the crowd, to accept conditions as they are, and, if one makes a good haul, to take it and plume one's self on being smart. But that is not the way of service. It is not the way of sound business. It is not even the way to make money. Of course, a man may, following this old line, fall into a bit of luck and make a million or two — just as a gambler sometimes wins heavily. In real business, there is no gambling. Real business creates its own customers.

Our own attitude is that we are charged with discovering the best way of doing everything, and that we must regard every process employed in manufacturing as purely experimental. If we reach a stage in production which seems remarkable as compared with what has gone before, then that is just a stage of production and nothing more. It is not and cannot be anything more than that. We know from the changes that have already been brought about that far greater changes are to come, and that therefore we are not performing a single operation as well as it ought to be performed.

We do not make changes for the sake of making them, but we never fail to make a change once it is demonstrated that the new way is better than the old way. We hold it our duty to permit nothing to stand in the way of progress — in the way of giving better service with all that follows in wages and prices.

It is not easy to get away from tradition. That is why all our new operations are always directed by men who have had no previous knowledge of the subject and therefore have not had a chance to get on really familiar terms with the impossible. We call in technical experts to aid whenever their aid seems necessary, but no operation is ever directed by a technician, for always he knows far too many things that can't be done. Our invariable reply to "It can't be done" is, "Go do it."

Take the matter of making plate glass. The methods in use at our Glassmere factory, essentially do not differ from the methods used centuries ago. Glass making is very old; it has traditions, and those traditions center around the clay pot in which the mixture is melted into glass. That pot, as has been said, must be made by hand. The clay is tamped and kneaded by the bare feet of men and then the pot is built up by hand. Of course, machinery has come in to carry these pots to and from the furnace, there are conveyors to do the handling, and machine grinding and polishing has replaced the old hand work, but the operation itself has not been fundamentally changed. Machinery has been brought in to do, in so far as possible, what was formerly done by hand.

But the whole operation had never been thoroughly studied to discover what was really fundamental. The easy course is always to substitute machine effort for a hand effort, and the full value of power is not then realized. The hard course is to start at the beginning and evolve a method which, instead of substituting the machine for the hand, takes for granted that a method can be discovered by which the entirety may be done by machinery and the worker considered only as an attendant upon the machine. This is the machine concept of industry as opposed to the hand concept.

It seemed to us that we ought to be able to manufacture plate glass continuously in a big ribbon and with no hand work at all. The glass experts of the world said all this had been tried and that it could not be done. We gave the task of doing it to men who had never been in a glass plant. They started experimenting at Highland Park. They ran up against every trouble that had been predicted and a number that had not been, but eventually they achieved their result. The little plant at Highland Park is producing two and a half million square feet a year, and the big plant at the River Rouge, which we built as soon as we knew that we could make first-class plate glass, is producing twelve million square feet a year. This big plant occupies about one half the space of the Glassmere plant, although it has nearly double its production, and also it employs only about one third as many men as Glassmere. Although we have not been able to expand our plants sufficiently to care for our needs, we are already saving about three million dollars a year on the glass that we do make as compared with what we have to pay outside.

Here is the new process. The batch is melted in huge furnaces, each with a capacity of 408 tons of molten glass. The temperature maintained is a melting heat of 2,500 degrees Fahrenheit and a refining heat of 2,300 degrees. The furnaces are charged every fifteen minutes with sand, soda ash, and other chemicals. The glass flows out in a continuous stream on to a slowly revolving iron drum, and passes under a roller which gives the right thickness, and rolls it into a sheet. From the drum it enters the lehr, moving at the rate of fifty inches a minute. The lehr is 442 feet long and anneals the glass under gradually diminishing heat.

The construction of the lehr was one of the hardest problems and the one on which all others had fallen down. We could not have constructed it without our experience in conveyors and accurate machine making. It is no small accomplishment to support a moving sheet of glass 442 feet long while it cools from a temperature of fourteen hundred degrees Fahrenheit at the roller to a point where it is cold enough to handle. The movement of the conveyor has to be absolutely even and the rollers on which the glass moves so perfectly lined and adjusted that at no point in the 442-foot journey will the glass be subjected to the slightest distortion. The diminishing temperature problem is solved by thermostatically controlled gas flames at varying intervals.

At the end of the lehr the glass is cut into 113-inch lengths, each sheet being the exact size required for six complete windshields, and then is carried by conveyers to the polishing machines.

The sheets are mounted in quick-setting stucco to hold them firmly in position, and passed on conveyor tables under a series of grinding and polishing wheels. Sand mixed with water flows through a hole in the center of the cast-iron grinding disc and works its way out to the edge. Finer and finer sand is used as the glass moves on its way, each grinder taking a cut. Eight grades of sand and six grades of garnet are used in the grinding and smoothing.

The plate is then washed. The glass then goes to the polishing discs, which are felt-covered and which use a mixture of iron rouge and water. At the end of the line, the glass is turned over and proceeds back on another grinding and polishing line from which it leaves as completely finished and polished plate glass that has not been touched by human hand.

There is no handling of the sand, nor is there any handling of the various grades of polishing sand. The silica sand and other materials used in composing batches of glass are likewise untouched by hand. From a vacuum machine, a heavy rubber hose goes into the car of material. The material is drawn up through the hose and falls into a hopper. A conveyor of the elevator type carries it aloft and dumps it upon a belt conveyor equipped so as to permit the discharging of the material into the storage bin where it belongs.

The grinding sand has to be graded while being used. This is done in distribution by a process known technically as levigation.

As the sand arrives at the plant, it is received and stored in large tanks beside the railroad tracks. Then, as it is called into use, it is washed by a stream of water into a well. From here a pump forces it through pipe lines that carry it across the plant to the first supply tanks above the furnaces, and near to the grinding and polishing lines. From the first supply tanks the sand flows through inclined pipes to the first grinders in the line. As the rough grinding goes on, the used sand is edged off into gutters beneath the grinding machines, and a pump forces it from the gutters into the levigation system.

Floating now in a comparatively large volume of water, the sand begins to grade itself. The larger, heavier grains sink to the bottom of the second tank; the others float at depths that vary according to their size. The overflow from the second tank takes these smaller and lighter grains into the third tank in the supply line, where another settling takes place. The overflow from the third tank feeds in turn the fourth tank; and the same process is continued until the eighth and last tank holds the finest sand.

Sand supplied to the grinders by all tanks beyond the second is pumped from the gutters back to the second tank, from which it is again distributed in the same fashion as before. From the first to last, the overflow feed and gravity serve each successive tank with sand suited to the grinders it supplies. Garnet used in the last grinders is graded by this same method.

The process sounds simple enough, and it is. Every well-thought-out process is simple. And with the simplicity and the absence of hand labor has come a greater safety. Glass making used to be considered a dangerous occupation. It is no longer so with us. For two years past we have lost less than one hour per man due to accident. And that we shall cut down.

Spinning and weaving have come down to us through the ages and they have gathered about them traditions which have become almost sacred rules of conduct. The textile industry was one of the first to make use of power, but also it was one of the first to use the labor of children. Many textile manufacturers thoroughly believe that low-cost production is impossible without low-priced labor. The technical achievements of the industry have been remarkable, but whether it has been possible for any one to approach the industry with an absolutely open mind, free from tradition, is another matter.

We use more than a hundred thousand yards of cotton cloth and more than twenty-five thousand yards of woollen cloth during every day of production, and even a very tiny saving per yard would mean a good deal to us in the course of a year. That is why, several years ago, we started our textile experiments, not with any thought of making over the textile industry — for we are manufacturers of motors — but with the thought of finding some way to avoid the fluctuations of the cotton market and to get our own requirements at a lower price.

At first, we took for granted that we had to have cotton cloth — we had never used anything but cotton cloth as a foundation material for tops and for artificial leather. We put in a unit of cotton machinery and began to experiment, but, not being bound by tradition, we had not gone far with these experiments before we began to ask ourselves: "Is cotton the best material we can use here?"

And we discovered that we had been using cotton cloth, not because it was the best cloth, but because it was the easiest to get. A linen cloth would undoubtedly be stronger, because the strength of cloth depends upon the length of the fibre, and the flax fibre is one of the longest and strongest known. Cotton had to be grown thousands of miles from Detroit. We should have to pay transportation on the raw cotton, if we decided to go into cotton textiles, and we should also have to pay transportation on this cotton converted into its motor-car use — very often back again to where it had been grown. Flax can be grown in Michigan and Wisconsin, and we could have a supply at hand practically ready for use. But linen making had even more traditions than cotton, and no one had been able to do much in linen making in this country because of the vast amount of hand labor considered essential.

Cotton goods were a luxury, and cotton growing was unimportant until Eli Whitney invented his gin, for until then, as everyone knows, the seeds had to be picked out of cotton by hand, which was not only a long and tiresome but an exceedingly wasteful and expensive process. The flax fibre has always been recovered by hand in Ireland, in Belgium, and in Russia — in fact, everywhere that flax is used. The methods are not much different from those used in the Egypt of the Pharaohs. That is why linen is expensive, and that is why so little flax is grown in the United States: we, fortunately, have not a sufficient supply of low-paid hand labor to make any crop which requires manual handling profitable.

We began to experiment at Dearborn, and these experiments have demonstrated that flax can be mechanically handled. The work has passed the experimental stage. It has proved its commercial feasibility.

To begin at the beginning. We put about six hundred acres into flax. We ploughed and prepared the ground by machinery, we sowed by machinery, we harvested by machinery, we dried and threshed by machinery, and finally took out the fibre by machinery. That has never successfully been accomplished before.

Flax has always required a lot of cheap hand labor. We cannot use anything in our business which requires hand labor.

Flax grows very well in Michigan and also in Wisconsin, although in Wisconsin the attention has been given to growing a flax not for the fibre but for the seed, which is crushed into linseed oil. Flax growing for fibre has not gone far in this country, because almost the only market for flax is abroad, where cheap hand labor is available. Flax is a peasant crop, and, before the war, the big producer was Russia: it had an abundance of people accustomed to living on nothing a year. Our own country has not been enough interested in flax growing to find out with exactness where it will grow. It seems to require a moist climate, but once the flax industry is established here, undoubtedly we shall be able to develop varieties so that nearly every section of the country will have a species which it can profitably raise.

The valuable fibre of the plant is on the outside of the stalk surrounding the woody core, and it has always been considered out of the question to mow flax as one would mow wheat, for it is essential to keep the stalks parallel, else the subsequent hand operations will be hampered. Also, cutting flax was supposed to leave too much valuable stalk attached to the root in the ground. Therefore, the foreign practice is to pull by hand and afterward, while the crop is on the ground, to comb out the seeds. A great deal of the valuable seed is lost.

Thus, right at the beginning, under the old methods, we have two expensive and wasteful hand operations — the pulling and what is called the "rippling." We experimented with a rather intricate pulling machine, but found it was not worthwhile and that we could do better cutting very close to the ground. In our mechanical process, it is not necessary to keep the stalks parallel after they are cut, and it is cheaper to waste a few seeds than to use hand labor. Therefore, we harvested it by machinery, leaving the seeds on the stalks.

The next operation in the old style is what is called "retting" — that is, rotting. The usual method is to tie the stalks into sheaves and put them under water for some weeks with weights on top to keep them from drifting away. When the stalks have sufficiently rotted, the sheaves are taken out and dried in the sun. This is all hand work and extremely unpleasant, dirty work, because the rotting flax gives out an almost unbearable odor. It is a matter of great judgment to discover exactly the right kind of water for retting, and also to know when to stop the process. The next operation, under the old methods, is the most tedious, wasteful, and expensive of all. This is known as "scutching" — by which the fibre is separated from the woody core.

Under the method we have developed, all these expensive hand operations are done away with. After cutting, we leave the stalks on the ground for some weeks; then we gather them up and bale them, just as though they were hay. Instead of drying the retted flax in the sun, we pass it through an oven on a conveyor, and this conveyor delivers the conditioned flax to what we call a ginning machine, and which is the very heart of our process because it entirely replaces the old hand process of stripping the fibre. The gin has six sections running at various speeds with fluted rolls and combing rolls — there is no use going into the technical details. The upshot of it is that this machine mechanically takes out all of the seeds and stalks and leaves us a fibre which is, in part, what is called "line flax," and, in part, "tow."

There is a saving both in labor and in recovery. These gins do not care how the stalks feed into them, so it is no longer necessary to bother about keeping the stalks parallel. It is calculated that one machine working eight hours and tended by two men will scutch as much flax as ten men working by hand through a twelve-hour day.

This flax is now being spun into two grades of linen, one a coarse cloth and the other a fine cloth. This is done on standard equipment which we bought abroad, but our men have already managed to make some improvements on this machinery, and others will come as we get more fully into the work. For instance, the usual practice is to spin the flax on spools and then rewind on to bobbins for the filling yarn. We are spinning the flax directly to the filling bobbins. Eventually, we shall, by a continuous process, feed the flax in at one end of the line and have a dyed, all-linen backing cloth at the other. This will meet with the artificial leather, so that the whole process will be practically continuous.

We regard this work in flax as among the most important experiments which we are carrying on, for not only will it result in a better product than we have as yet been able to turn out, but also it will be another money crop for the farmer. We alone shall require the product of about fifty thousand acres annually and flax fits very nicely into the rotation of crops. Thus we shall have a cash crop for the farmer and perhaps a new industry for the country. And this is not counting the value of the flax by-products — the linseed oil, or the tow, which makes excellent stuffing for upholstery. Our chemists are experimenting with the "shives" or chaff, to the end of finding some satisfactory cellulose compounds. These might be used in a variety of ways — as liquids for the coating of the tops, or as solids for handles, and in connection with electrical equipment.

This flax growing, spinning, and weaving can and ought to be decentralized, so that it can be complementary to well-conducted farming — that is, grain farming as distinguished from dairying, stock raising, or truck farming. The place for the gins, the spindles, and the looms is out in the country where the flax is grown. It could be made a village industry manned by farmers, who can apportion their time between farm and factory.

We are also feeling our way into the manufacture of woollen cloth for our own requirements on our usual plan of making the process continuous. To start with, we took a young man out of a drafting room and for three months put him at work in a mill with instructions to learn all that he could about weaving excepting the traditions. We have as yet made only minor changes and improvements in the standard machinery, and the output of our experimental plant is negligible as compared with our needs, but we find that it will be possible to effect a saving of nearly 30 percent on our woollen cloth — which will mean a saving of many million dollars a year. Whenever one can line up machinery for the making of exactly one thing and study everything to the end of making only that thing, then the savings which come about are startling.

6

Learning by Necessity

We do nothing at all in what is sometimes ambitiously called research, excepting as it relates to our single objective. We believe that anything else would be outside our province and possibly done at the expense of our own particular function which, to repeat, is making motors and putting them on wheels. In the engineering laboratory at Dearborn we are now equipped to do almost anything that we care to do in the way of experiment, but our method is essentially the Edison method of trial and error.

As it is, our task is rather a large one, for we must look well ahead to the possible depletion of sources, to the saving of material, and to the finding of substitute materials and fuels. Quite often, we merely put the results of our experiments away for future use in case market conditions should change. For instance, if gasoline should go above a certain price, then it would be practical to bring in substitute fuels. But our principal duty, as we conceive it, is not to wander from our own path, but to learn to do one thing well. Learning to do that one thing well has taken us into many fields. We want to save material and we want to save labor and scarcely a week passes in which some change is not made. Some are of minor and others of major importance, but the method of procedure is always the same. Curiously enough, some of our largest savings come in the manufacture of parts where we thought we were doing rather well.

In one case we found that by using two cents more worth of material in a certain small part we were able to reduce the total cost of it by 40 percent. That is, the amount of material under the new method cost about two cents per part more than under the old, but the labor was so much faster that, under the new method, the cost which was formerly $.2852 was now only $.1663 — we carry our costs out to four decimals. The new method required ten additional machines, but the saving was nearly twelve cents per part — that is, the cost was almost cut in two which, on a 10,000 a day production, meant a saving of $1,200 a day.

From the beginning of manufacturing until several years ago we had used wood for the steering wheels. This seemed a great waste, for only the best quality of wood could be used and no wood-working operation can be carried through with absolute precision. At the same time, out on the farm at Dearborn, we had tons of straw yearly going to waste or being sold for next to nothing. Out of this straw we developed a substance which we call Fordite, which looks like hard rubber but is not. The steering wheel rim, and, in all, about forty-five parts of the car, mostly having to do with the electrical work, are now made out of this straw, and the production is so large that the farm will produce only enough for about nine months. Then we have to buy straw. This is the process:

The straw, rubber base, sulphur, silica, and other ingredients are mixed in batches of 150 pounds each, which then go to the rubber mills, where they are mixed in heated rollers for forty-five minutes. Then the mass is fed into tubing machines in small strips and comes out through a round die, much as sausage from a grinding machine. As it comes out it is cut, on the bias, in lengths of fifty-two inches and then is ready to be rolled into an outside covering of fine rubber-like substance. This is then put into a mould under hydraulic pressure of 2,000 pounds to the square inch and heated by steam for nearly an hour. When they come out of the heat, the wheels are soft, but they soon take on a flint-like hardness that remains.

Next, these steering wheels go to the finishing rooms, where they are smoothly trimmed and polished. The pressed steel "spider," or cross piece, is then placed in the wheel and securely fastened by a machine which in one operation bores a small hole and in the next screws in the screw. The steering wheel is then ready for shipment and final assembly on the car.

We save about half the cost of wood — and we conserve wood.

The touring car uses about fifteen yards of artificial leather for the top, curtains, and upholstery, and we need altogether five grades. Using natural leather would be quite out of the question. In the first place, it would be too expensive, while, in the second place, not enough animals are slaughtered to begin to provide for our requirements. Our people had a hard time developing an entirely satisfactory artificial leather — it took them five or six years. First, they had to get the proper coating compound for the cloth which is the base of the leather, and then to make the operation continuous. Making our own leather not only renders us independent — which was the original purpose of the undertaking — but also saves us more than twelve thousand dollars a day. Essentially, these are the operations as we now perform them:

The cloth is fed into ovens. The ovens consist of a series of towers. At the base of each is a tank containing the coating compound. This is poured on the cloth as it travels through, a knife spreading it evenly and scraping off the surplus. After receiving the coating, the cloth ascends the tower to a height of thirty feet, at a temperature of about two hundred degrees. By the time it has descended, it is thoroughly dry. The second oven gives it another coat, dries it in the tower, and brings it down to the tank in No. 3 oven, and so on, until the first seven coats have been given.

It is then weighed to determine the amount of coating per running yard and sent to the embossing press, where it receives the graining under a pressure of 700 tons. One more oven gives it the finishing or sealing coat, adds lustre, and keeps the material pliable.

The compound is a mixture of castor oil and drop black mixed with a preparation of nitrated cotton dissolved in ethyl acetate and thinned with benzol. This is highly volatile, which accounts for the easy drying. The fumes of the ethyl acetate, alcohol, and benzol are driven off in the ovens, but they are recovered by a special apparatus we developed. The fumes are drawn through charcoal made from coconut shells until the charcoal becomes saturated. Steam is then turned in, which drives the fumes into a condenser, from which they are separated into the original compounds. As much as 90 percent of the fumes has thus been recovered when the work of the condenser has been concentrated on one smokestack. The manufacturing is continuous. As soon as a roll of cloth is nearly used up, the end is unrolled by hand and sewn to a new bolt. Thus the coating continues without interruption — an important factor when one considers that even a brief delay would cause the compound to harden on the knives.

There are no lights within the building, all artificial illumination being furnished from the outside on account of the fire .hazard. Every machine is grounded, and as many precautions against fire taken as in an explosive factory, and we have had no accidents at all.

The treating of steel by heat is of the highest possible importance, for it makes possible the use of lighter parts by increasing their strength. But it is a delicate process: a part must not be too soft or it will wear out, or again, if it is too hard, it will break. The exact state of hardness depends upon the use to which the part is to be put. This is elementary. But the treating of large quantities of parts so that each will be of the right hardness is far from elementary.

The old way was to guess. We cannot afford to guess. We cannot afford to leave any process to human judgment. In our former heat treat processes, we thought that we were fairly advanced. And we were advanced for the time, because the work could be done by men after only a little training and the results were uniform, owing to the mechanical regulation. But the heat treatment departments involved hot, hard labor, and we do not like to have jobs of that sort in the shops. Hard labor is for machines, not for men. And also the straight parts, such as axles, did not cool evenly, and after treatment they had to be straightened, which added to the cost.

We set a young man the task of bettering all our heat treatment operations. He felt his way for a year or two and then began to get results. He not only cut down the number of men, but he devised a centrifugal hardening machine which cools the shafts evenly all around. Thus, they do not bend, and the straightening operation is no more. The electric furnace replacing the gas furnace has been one of the large steps forward. Where four gas-fired furnaces, with six men and a foreman, did 1,000 connecting rods an hour for the drawing operation alone, now two electric furnaces will both harden and draw 1,300 rods an hour, with only two men — one to feed and the other to take off.

For the heat treatment, the axle shaft department uses a large two-deck furnace. A walking-beam, working slowly, moves the shafts forward into the lower chamber of the furnace at intervals of one minute. It takes twenty-eight minutes for a shaft to move completely through the lower chamber of the furnace, and during those twenty-eight minutes it is in a constant heat of 1,480 degrees Fahrenheit, the temperature being regulated by instrument control.

As the shafts slowly come out at the far end of the furnace, they are seized by an employee with tongs and placed one by one in a spinning machine. They are quenched in caustic solution at the rate of four per minute; the spinning motion given them by the machine makes the decrease in temperature practically instantaneous over the shaft's entire surface. This operation goes to insure a uniform hardness and avoids pulling them out of shape by uneven cooling.

The quenched shafts are carried by a conveyor to the upper chamber of the furnace, and move back toward the entrance end through a constant heat of 680 degrees Fahrenheit. It takes forty-five minutes for this treatment. Thoroughly drawn, they are sent by overhead conveyor to the final machining.

These changes may not seem important, but cutting out the item of straightening after the heat treatment has saved us around thirty-six million dollars in four years!

We investigated the making of electric storage batteries and, after a period of trial — we always try out everything thoroughly before we go into it — we found that we could make batteries cheaper than we could buy them.

In the making of springs, a similar advance has come, both in accuracy and man saving. In shaping the leaves, the forms used keep them so exact that they are interchangeable with corresponding leaves on other springs. The leaves are formed and hardened in oil in one operation. Next, they are tempered in nitrate at 875 degrees Fahrenheit, after which they are graphitized and used.

In 1915, the department employed four men to make fifty springs a day; at present, 600 men make 18,000 springs a day.

We must have inspectors at every stage of the work; otherwise, faulty parts might get into the assembly. Our inspectors in only a few cases are required to use judgment — mostly they apply a gauge, but we are working toward mechanical inspection. For instance, electricity at 20,000 volts now tests the timing of the eight cams on the Model T Ford camshaft, not only more precisely than was possible by the former method, but seven times faster. Operated by one man, the new electrical gauge displaces seven of the old type gauges and their operators. The electrical test takes ten seconds.

In the new gauge, the camshaft is inserted in bearings, so that the cams operate push rods just as they do in the assembled motor. Instead of operating against valves, however, the push rods in the gauge close and open electrical contacts as the shaft is revolved. These electrical circuits are supplied with current only when the opening and closing points on the contour of each cam are in contact with the push rods, a distributor in the handwheel by which the shaft is revolved taking care of this.

If, at a critical position of the cam, the contour is too high or low within very close limits, an electrical contact is made completing a circuit which causes an electrical indicator to flash. There are two of these indicators, one for high and one for low cams. On the handwheel is an index, the position of which at the time of the flash indicates which cam is faulty. If the cams are all accurate within specifications, the electrical indicator does not flash at any point during the revolution. The electric gauge may be set to detect errors of two ten thousandths of an inch.

But this is the sort of thing which is going on every day — we take it as our duty to use the public's money to the advantage of the public by pressing always for a better and cheaper product.

7

Learning from Waste

If one used nothing then one would waste nothing. That seems plain enough. But look at it from another angle. If we use nothing at all, is not then the waste total? Is it conservation or waste to withdraw a public resource wholly from use? If a man skimps himself through all the best years of his life in order to provide for his old age, has he conserved his resources or has he wasted them? Has he been constructively or destructively thrifty?

How are we to reckon waste? Usually, we count waste in terms of materials. If a housewife buys twice as much food as her family eats and throws the rest away, she is considered wasteful. But on the other hand, is the housewife who gives her family only half enough to eat thrifty? Not at all. She is even more wasteful than the first housewife, for she is wasting human lives. She is withdrawing from her family the strength which they need to do their work in the world.

Materials are less important than human beings — although we have not yet come quite around to thinking in that fashion. Once upon a time, society hung a man for stealing a loaf of bread. Now society treats such an offence differently. It takes that man, puts him in a prison, withdraws the benefit of an amount of labor which might make thousands of loaves of bread, and then actually feeds him many times as much bread as he stole! We not only waste this man's productive power, but also we call on our other producers to give up a part of their production to support him. That is flagrant waste.

It is necessary and will be necessary to put men in jail until the news gets about that the profits of dishonesty do not compare with the profits of honesty, but there is no reason for thinking of a jail as a tomb for the living. Under first-class, non-political management, every jail in the country could be turned into an industrial unit, pay higher wages to the men than they could earn in outside industry, provide them with good food and reasonable hours of labor, and then turn over an excellent profit to the State. We already have prison labor, but most of it is ill-directed, degrading labor.

A criminal is a non-producer, but when he has been caught and sentenced, it is very wasteful to continue him as a non-producer. He can surely be turned into a producer and probably into a man. Yet, because we value human time so lightly and materials so highly, we do not hear much about the waste of man power in prisons, nor do we hear much of the terrible waste of withdrawing support from the families of the convicts and throwing them on the community.

Conserving our natural resources by withdrawing them from use is not a service to the community. That is holding to the old theory that a thing is more important than a man. Our natural resources are ample for all our present needs. We do not have to bother about them as resources. What we do have to bother about is the waste of human labor.

Take a vein of coal in a mine. As long as it remains in the mine, it is of no importance, but when a chunk of that coal has been mined and set down in Detroit, it becomes a thing of importance, because then it represents a certain amount of the labor of men used in its mining and transportation. If we waste that bit of coal — which is another way of saying if we do not put it to its full use — then we waste the time and energy of men. A man cannot be paid much for producing something which is to be wasted.

My theory of waste goes back of the thing itself into the labor of producing it. We want to get full value out of labor so that we may be able to pay it full value. It is use — not conservation — that interests us. We want to use material to its utmost in order that the time of men may not be lost. Materials costs nothing. It is of no account until it comes into the hands of management.

Saving material because it is material, and saving material because it represents labor might seem to amount to the same thing. But the approach makes a deal of difference. We will use material more carefully if we think of it as labor. For instance, we will not so lightly waste material simply because we can reclaim it — for salvage involves labor. The ideal is to have nothing to salvage.

We have a large salvage department, which apparently earns for us twenty or more million dollars a year. Something of it will be told later in this chapter. But as that department grew and became more important and more strikingly valuable, we began to ask ourselves:

"Why should we have so much to salvage? Are we not giving more attention to reclaiming than to not wasting?"

And with that thought in mind, we set out to examine all our processes. A little of what we do in the way of saving man power by extending machinery has already been told, and what we are doing with coal, wood, power, and transportation will be told in later chapters. This has to do only with what was waste. Our studies and investigations up to date have resulted in the saving of 80,000,000 pounds of steel a year that formerly went into scrap and had to be reworked with the expenditure of labor. This amounts to about three million dollars a year, or, to put it in a better way, to the unnecessary labor on our scale of wages of upward of two thousand men. And all of that saving was accomplished so simply that our present wonder is why we did not do it before.

Here are a few examples: We formerly cut our crank cases out of trimmed steel plate exactly the width and length of the case. That steel cost $.0335 per pound because it had in it a good deal of labor. Now we buy an untrimmed sheet 150 inches long at $.028 per pound, shear it to 109 inches — the sheared portion going to make another part — and on the remaining plate we can lay our five crank cases, which are cut in one operation. This saves four million pounds of steel scrap a year, and the whole saving amounts to nearly half a million dollars. The windshield bracket is somewhat irregularly shaped, and we formerly cut it from $18 \times 32\frac{1}{2}$ inch rectangular steel sheets. A sheet gave us six brackets and a quantity of scrap. Now, by taking stock $15\frac{1}{2} \times 32\frac{1}{2}$ inches cut at a seven-degree angle, we get six windshield brackets as before, but also in the same operation we get ten other blanks for small parts. This saves a million and a half pounds of steel a year. The oil-can holder is in the shape of a cross, and we formerly stamped it out of steel with great waste at a cost of $.0635 each. Now we cut the two parts of the cross separately with almost no scrap and weld them together, and they now cost $.0478 each. The bushing on the steering gear, which is made of bronze, was formerly .128 inches thick. We found that it could be half as thick and do its work quite as well — which saves us 130,000 pounds of bronze a year, or more than thirty thousand dollars. The head lamp bracket pad is a cross, measuring $7\frac{1}{2} \times 3\frac{1}{2}$ inches, and we used to cut fourteen of them out of a sheet $6\frac{1}{2} \times 35$ inches. We reduced the size of the bracket to $7\frac{1}{8} \times 3\frac{1}{8}$ inches and now get the same number as before out of a sheet $5\frac{7}{8} \times 35$ inches — which saves more than a hundred thousand pounds of steel a year. We formerly cut the fan-drive pulley out of new stock. Now we cut it out of the salvage from the hand door stock — which saves nearly three hundred thousand pounds of steel a year. By making very slight changes in twelve small brass items, we are saving nearly half a million pounds of brass a year. On nineteen items cut from bars or tubing we have, by changing the cutting tools and multiples and the length of the stock, saved more than a million pounds of steel a year. For instance, on one part we used a bar 143 inches long and got eighteen pieces per bar; we found that we could get the same number of pieces out of a bar $140\frac{9}{32}$ inches long — thus saving more than two inches per bar. On many small parts which were formerly cold rolled, we have changed to hot rolling. This, on sixteen little items, saves about three hundred thousand dollars a year.

This general policy has been extended in a great number of directions. We found that in many plates and bars, bought according to standard sizes or to specifications, we were not only paying for the shearing and the scrap at the steel mill, but we were actually losing serviceable metal both in getting fewer parts out of the steel and also increasing our own scrap. Thus, there was a waste all around. We have been working on this only a year and have hardly had a start on what can be done.

Scrap, we take it, is something to be avoided and not to be remelted until no other course remains. We had considered the worn steel rails from the railroad as scrap steel to be remelted. Now we pass them through a roll which separates the head, the web, and the foot — which gives us excellent steel bars which can be used for a number of purposes. This idea also is going to be carried further. On the other hand, such steel as we at present must consider as scrap amounts to a thousand tons or more a day. We had been selling this scrap to Pittsburgh and buying it back again as steel — paying transportation charges both ways. Now we have erected at the River Rouge a series of electric furnaces and a large rolling mill, so that we can convert the scrap ourselves and save this item of double transportation. If we cannot avoid all of this scrap — and some of it is hardly avoidable — we can at least save the waste of human labor in handling and transportation.

The salvage of materials about the shops has developed into a large industry, which is uncommonly important because it employs sub-standard men — men who could not work in production. We can use men otherwise unemployable to salvage the labor of other men.

Thousands of broken tools and damaged plant equipment come in for reclamation every twenty-four hours. The value of the belting sent to the salvage department amounts to more than a thousand dollars a day. This is all repaired and reworked, the smaller scraps going to make life belts for window washers or to the cobbler shop to be used for soles or patches. Broken tools of all kinds — pliers, wrenches, shears, braces, bits, hammers, drills, gauges, chucks, planes, saws, dies, jigs, and fixtures are repaired and returned to stock. These repairs are not patchwork. The tools are actually rebuilt according to the original blue print and come up to specifications in every particular.

The department has a record of every machine operation in the industry and just what kind and size of tools are required. It can instantly tell what can be done with a damaged tool. Generally it can be profitably reworked to smaller size, there being several machines which can use a drill even less than an inch in length. If a drill, a broach, or a reamer is worn out, it is cut down to a smaller size, always in accordance with the original blue print. Cold-heading dies are all reworked to the next size, and so on down through the entire list of tools. All tool steel is classified and sorted before reworking. Tool handles of all kinds are salvaged; a broken shovel handle may make several screw driver or chisel handles. Picks, rakes, spades, crowbars, mops, brooms, and similar implements are all salvaged as long as it is profitable. Two men spend most of their time in repairing mop pails.

Pipes, valves, joints, and other steam-fitting apparatus are conditioned. Old paint is reclaimed to the extent of 500 gallons a day and is used for rough work. The salvage of oil and cutting compounds from steel shavings amounts to 2,100 gallons a day.

Metal scrap, such as copper, brass, lead, aluminum, babbitt metal, solder, steel, and iron are remelted. Since all our cast iron is classified under heads according to analysis, it is a simple matter to sort iron scrap and return it to the proper cupola for remelting.

Molding sand is salvaged for its intrinsic value, and because of the saving in freight and handling. Scrap oil is salvaged, and what is unfit for either lubrication or rust-proofing is burned for fuel. A process by which the cyanide used in heat treating can be diluted has been developed and the cyanide bills cut in halves. The laboratories have developed a cement by which canvas facing may be stuck to pulleys, thereby reducing slippage of belts and the consequent waste of power. Old fire brick is broken up and reworked. Dross from the melting pots gives a yield. In the Photographic Department the silver salts are recovered from the developing solutions and the saving amounts to nearly ten thousand dollars a year.

The great amount of paper and rags gathered in a day throughout the plants bothered us, and so did the hardwood scrap from the body plant. Since we have swung over to all-steel bodies for most of the styles, the wood scrap has been much reduced. Having developed a salvage department, we at once start to make it unnecessary. The first thought with the hardwood scrap was to make it into paper, but we were told that only soft wood could be used in paper making. But we went ahead with our plans for a mill and proved that it could be successfully done. The paper plant now uses 20 tons of scrap paper a day and produces 14 tons of binder board and 8 tons of special waterproof board which is the result of a process developed in our laboratories. The board is of such great tensile strength that a ten-inch strip can bear the entire suspended weight of a Ford car.

We use standard machinery with some improvements and adaptations of our own in order to make the process continuous and to cut down labor. Only thirty-seven men are required to operate the mill, which contains more than seventy-five separate units of apparatus.

Part of the product is used in backing the upholstery and the remainder for containers in which to ship parts — which saves wood.

The blast furnaces produce five hundred tons of slag a day, 225 tons of which go into the making of cement, the rest being crushed for roads.

The conversion of blast furnace slag into cement is quite common, but we could not afford to have the dust of the usual cement plant, and so we worked on a new process known as the "wet," which is now being experimented with by other American manufacturers.

As the molten slag runs from the blast furnace, it is met by a stream of cold water which granulates it to the size of coarse salt. The wet mass, of which the wet slag comprises sometimes as much as 45 percent, though usually only 10 to 25 percent, is pumped through a 1,300-foot pipe to the cement plant, where it pours into constantly moving de-watering elevators which permit all the water to be drained off before it reaches the belt conveyors at the top. These carry the granulated slag to the storage bins from which it is drawn as needed. Inasmuch as this slag contains about one percent iron, the conveyors pass under powerful magnets which pick up the iron particles, a considerable amount being recovered in a day. This is sent back to the blast furnace for reclamation.

From the storage bins the slag is carried to the mill where, mixed with crushed limestone and 30 percent or more water, it is ground to powder. Before the mixture leaves the mill, it is so fine that 90 percent will pass through a 200-mesh screen. This mixture, of the consistency of cream, is called "slurry," and is forced by air pressure into huge storage vats. The analysis of this mixture is taken hourly and corrections in the proportioning are made accordingly.

The slurry then goes to rotary kilns 150 feet long where, under intense heat, the cement is fused to clinker form, after which, with the addition of a small amount of gypsum, it is ground to powder, in which form it is ready for use. Gypsum is added to regulate the setting of the finished cement.

The plant gives us about two thousand barrels a day. We sell a little of it to our men for their own use — just so that they can buy cement below the market price.

The point, to repeat, in all of this is the saving of human labor so that it may be made more effective and more valuable. It was to save the human labor that had gone into their making that we bought two hundred ships from the Government. They had been built by the Emergency Fleet Corporation for use during the war, and there was no commercial demand for them. We are now breaking them up at our plant at Kearney, New Jersey. We can use some of the engines in our smaller plants, for many of the engines are first class. We do not expect to make any money out of the salvage of these ships — we did not go into it to make money. We simply did not like to see such a mass of fine material — so much labor — go to waste when we might reclaim it. We bought with the wage, not the profit, motive in our minds.

Industry owes it to society to conserve material in every possible way. Not only for the element of cost in the manufactured article, although that is important, but mostly for the conservation of those materials whose production and transportation are laying an increasing burden on society.

As it is now, every manufacturing concern exists only to make its own products. It has not been linked up with the community.

But it is becoming apparent that manufacturing concerns of size can be much more useful to the community than they now are, for example, in the matter of supplying fuel and power. Under the present system, coal hauled to a factory is just burned under its boilers, and a small fraction of its content utilized. Deliver a thousand cars of coal to the shops of a great manufacturing district, and that is the end. In a time of coal shortage, the job of keeping the factories supplied with fuel and the job of keeping the homes supplied with fuel are distinct, requiring two great supplies of coal.

Some day — in order to save human labor — we shall link all of this together. All phases of life should be and can be complementary.

8

Reaching Back
to the Sources

We look upon industry largely as a matter of management, to us management and leadership are quite the same. We have no patience with the kind of management that shouts orders and interferes with instead of directing the men at their work. Real leadership is unobtrusive, and our aim is always to arrange the material and machinery and to simplify the operations so that practically no orders are necessary. Unless management begins on the drawing board, it will never get into the shop.

It is the work, not the man, that manages. That work is planned on the drawing board and the operations subdivided so that each man and each machine do only one thing. This is a general rule, but it is flexible and has to be applied with common sense. If a machine can be devised to perform several operations at once, then it would be waste to have several machines. A man may sometimes as easily perform two operations as one — in which case he performs two operations.

It is often imagined that our system of production is founded on moving platforms and conveyors. We use moving platforms and conveyors only when they aid in the work. For instance, in making headlights we do not use conveyors, because the nature of the parts is such that they can more easily be moved on in boxes than by a conveyor. On the other hand, in many departments we find conveyors extremely useful, and especially so in assemblies — that is, bringing the component parts of a unit together — for then the assembly can start at one end of the moving platform or belt conveyor and have its various parts added as it moves along.

The thing is to keep everything in motion and take the work to the man and not the man to the work. That is the real principle of our production, and conveyors are only one of many means to an end.

The key of our production is inspection. More than 3 percent of our entire force are inspectors. This simplifies management. Every part in every stage of its production is inspected.

If a machine breaks down, a repair squad will be on hand in a few minutes. The men do not leave their work to get tools — new tools are brought to them, but they do not often need new tools, and machines do not often break down, for there is continuous cleaning and repair work on every bit of machinery in the place. When new tools are needed, there is no delay. Tool rooms are provided for every department. Once we had large supply rooms, and men lined up at the windows to get their tools. That was waste. We found it often cost us twenty-five cents' worth of a man's time (not counting overhead) to get a thirty-cent tool. With that, we abolished the central tool room — a man cannot be paid high wages for standing around waiting for tools. Nor, which amounts to the same thing, can the public be served.

Stooping to the floor to pick up a tool or a part is not productive labor — therefore, all material is delivered waist high.

Our system of management is not a system at all; it consists of planning the methods of doing the work as well as the work. All that we ask of the men is that they do the work which is set before them. This work is never more than a man can do without undue fatigue in eight hours. He is well paid — and he works. When management becomes a "problem," the fault will be found to be with the planning of the work.

Of course, if men are under some outside influence or control by which the amount of work which they do in a day is limited — if they have to answer to an outside authority, then management is impossible, and consequently, high wages cannot be paid for the production of low-priced products. The whole wage motive fails.

It was in order to eliminate lost motion — which is just as fatal in a factory as in a bearing — that we began, some years ago, the plant which we call Fordson and which has now become the heart of our industries. Four years ago, it had a blast furnace, several shops, and about three thousand men. We had taken over the ground and put up some buildings to manufacture Eagle boats for the Government during the war — fast little boats to go after the submarines. Now the plant covers more than a thousand acres, has a mile of river frontage, and employs upward of seventy thousand men.

It is not in the line of our thought to build many large plants. We believe that smaller plants have a function, too, and we have made some interesting experiments along that line. But Fordson handles raw materials and in order to avoid unnecessary transport we have had to group around the raw materials the heavier assemblies, such as the motors, and also the entirety of the making of the tractor.

The reason for Fordson is transport. The Rouge is not much of a river — although we have managed to use its power almost from its source. But now the river is dredged so that Great Lakes boats and the smaller ocean liners can come into our docks, and we have dug a good-sized turning basin. This opens the plant to water transport, and the ore and lumber boats can come directly into the plant from our mines and forests in Upper Michigan. Then also it is the terminus of the Detroit, Toledo & Ironton Railroad, which we own. This road connects with our coalfields and also crosses nine main trunk lines. Therefore, not only can all our essential raw materials meet at this plant with no extra handling, but also finished automobile parts can leave with equal ease for any part of the country or the world.

The whole plant has been built with the single thought of simplifying the handling of material, and the backbone of its transportation is what we call the "High Line." The High Line is a concrete structure forty feet high and three quarters of a mile long, with five railroad tracks and two protected footpaths across its top. The outer track, nearest the storage bins, is of open-girder construction and permits bottom-dumping cars to discharge their loads directly into the bins.

Underneath the tracks are the active storage bins which supply the blast furnaces and other units. Every bit of space under the tracks is utilized for the full three-quarters of a mile. Here are machine shops for making locomotive parts and other equipment, stock rooms, tool rooms, conduits, conveyors, and blacksmith shop. There are eighty-five miles of railroad track in the plant supplementing the High Line. This permits the transportation of car loads and even train loads of material to any part of the plant.

Most of the coal, iron ore, limestone, and lumber arrive by boat, and enormous storage facilities have been provided to carry the plant through the period when navigation is closed on account of ice. The primary storage bins extend for half a mile in length, and their total capacity is more than two million tons.

Cargoes are removed from incoming ships at the rate of 1,050 tons an hour by two mechanical unloaders, which can lift twelve tons at a dip. The primary storage bins are spanned by traveling bridges 520 feet long which transfer material from one bin to another or to the High Line, where the secondary or active storage bins are located, convenient to the blast furnaces.

The moment a vessel docks, the unloaders get to work and the record is the discharge of 11,500 tons of ore in ten and a half hours. The average time is around eleven hours, but this is being cut down by dropping a tractor into the hold when it is almost empty and scraping the ore into piles to be more easily picked up by the big unloaders.

Now see what all this means from the standpoint of production. Trace the operations. Coal comes up from our mines in Kentucky and is stored in bins under the High Line or goes directly to the coking ovens, being pulverized on the way. We have one hundred and twenty "high temperature" ovens with a capacity of 2,500 tons a day. These are all by-product ovens and beside them is the by- product plant in which we recover such of the products as may be used within the organization, excepting the ammonium sulphate which we sell outside, and we also sell our surplus of benzol. The coal delivered at the plant costs us about five dollars a ton, but when converted into coke and by-products, it is worth about twelve dollars a ton. We have erected an experimental paint and varnish plant further to utilize by-products. Part of the gas produced in distillation is used to heat the ovens so as to make the process continuous, another part is piped to Highland Park while what remains is sold to the local gas company — which is an indication of how eventually the industries of community and the community itself may be linked together. The tar and oil we use in our own industries. At no point in the coking process is hand labor used.

Near by the coking ovens are the blast furnaces. They are charged with iron ore, coke, and limestone from the bins along the High Line. The blast furnace charge is made in the ratio of two tons of ore, one ton of coke, half a ton of limestone, and three and a half tons of air. The products taken out are in the ratio of a ton of high silicon iron, half a ton of slag, and five and a half tons of gas, equal to 200,000 cubic feet. None of these products is wasted.

The gas is cleaned and filtered to remove blast furnace dust and part of it used in the stoves to pre-heat the blast. The balance is piped to the power house, where it forms the principal fuel. The blast furnace dust is also saved. Formerly, this dust, which is nearly 50 percent pure iron, was regarded as waste, and was either dumped or sold as scrap, for it was too fine to be melted in the furnaces or cupolas. This dust is caught up in collectors, unloaded in cars by gravity, and carried directly to the sintering plant, where it is mixed with steel or iron borings and agglomerated into heavy lumps, which will melt easily. This process not only reclaims a great amount of iron, but also avoids the former labor of hauling it away. At the time the sintering plant was first put into operation, we had accumulated enough blast furnace dust to furnish material for more than six hundred thousand cylinder block castings. A comparatively small force of men is required to operate the blast furnaces, all the heavy work being done by machines. Electric drills cut the clay plugs when the furnaces are tapped, and a compressed air gun shoots in clay balls to close it again. As has already been explained, a large portion of the slag goes directly to the cement plant.

Formerly the foundry operations were at Highland Park, but now all our iron casting is in the Fordson foundry to avoid transportation and the reheating of the metal. This foundry now extends over thirty acres and is entirely operated on the conveyor system. The foundry is paved, the floors are kept spotlessly clean, and a system of suction pipes, ventilators, and dust collectors keeps the place cool and free from dust — in fact, there is nothing but the casting being made and the hot metal to suggest that the place is a foundry.

The foundry is not segregated into departments. Instead, every department is coordinated into a continuous system of manufacture by the use of conveyors.

Core making takes place on an endless chain which feeds the conveyors carrying the molds to the pouring stations at the cupolas. Molds are also made on moving conveyors, and reach completion only a few yards away from the hot metal ladles. The return trip allows the casting to cool before they reach the shake-out station, where they are removed from the flasks and the sand shaken out. After the fins and rough edges are chipped off, another conveyor carries the still hot castings to the tumbling barrels, where they are revolved until the surfaces are smoothed.

The motor block is the heaviest casting used in the car. It was formerly manufactured at Highland Park, but it was a waste to transport these castings to Highland Park and then ship the completed motors out by rail to the branches past the very gates of Fordson. Therefore, we transferred the motor assembly to Fordson, putting it in a building 800 feet long by 600 feet wide. There are four main assembly lines or conveyors, and now the process of making the motors is continuous.

We start with the blast furnace and end with a completed motor stacked in a freight car. The casting leaves the foundry on a moving platform or conveyor to one of the assembly lines, it is machined, the other parts are added as it moves along, and when it reaches the end of its line, it is a completed and tested motor — and all of this without a stop.

Out of the same foundry come the tractor castings. They pass into the tractor division, and the tractors leave the final assembly under their own power and pass into the freight cars for shipment.

The processes all differ in detail from those described in *My Life and Work*, but the principles are the same. By bringing everything together in the Fordson, we have been able to cut very largely into the time of making — so much so that it is said we deliver our tractors before they have had time to cool! Unlike the motor car, we ship the tractor complete from the factory. The tractor is so compact that it does not pay to ship it in parts for assembly at a branch.

For several years we have had large electric furnaces — one a fifty-ton furnace — for the salvage of steel scrap — as has been noted. And now we are adding more furnaces and a rolling mill, so that we shall be in a position not only to cast but to roll all our steel scrap and, if we find it advisable, to make our own steel. I have great faith in steel; Model T came into being because of vanadium steel — no other steel up to that time gave the necessary strength without bulk. We are working on many special kinds of steel, and I believe that the lightness and strength necessary for the all-metal airplane will eventually be found in steel. We must be prepared to make the special steels exactly suited to our uses.

The real age of steel — when we begin to realize something of its possibilities — is only approaching. Tonnage still predominates, and not only are we transporting too much metal about the country as metal, but also nearly every steel product that we use is far too heavy. Every time one uses two pounds of steel when one pound of special steel would do the work, one puts an unnecessary burden on the public which reflects in higher prices, less consumption, and lower wages. Steel has more possibilities than any other metal.

An interesting side development of putting the work on the machines instead of on the man is the increased necessity for skilled workmen to repair machinery and tools and now to construct new machinery. Many people thought that machine production would destroy craftsmanship. Exactly the reverse has come about; we now need more expert machinists than ever we needed — we can always use more tool makers. Making and repairing machinery is now a large industry with us, employing several thousand men.

As we increase our fund of mechanical knowledge, productive machinery will steadily require less attention from its operators, and the shift will be to the making of this machinery. We are not as yet equipped to make more than a small part of the machinery that we use, and have thus far confined ourselves almost wholly to special machinery on our own designs. We have made some large machinery in connection with our new power plant. The condenser casting for the turbo-generators weighed ninety-six tons. We made the generators partly because we wanted to put into them some of our own ideas and partly because we could not get delivery from outside manufacturers as quickly as we needed.

The savings brought about at Fordson have been enormous — we do not know how great they are, because we have no method of comparing the savings on our present large production with the former cost of production.

9

The Meaning of Time

Ordinarily, money put into raw materials or into finished stock is thought of as live money. It is money in the business, it is true, but having a stock of raw material or finished goods in excess of requirements is waste — which, like every other waste, turns up in high prices and low wages.

The time element in manufacturing stretches from the moment the raw material is separated from the earth to the moment when the finished product is delivered to the ultimate consumer. It involves all forms of transportation and has to be considered in every national scheme of service. It is a method of saving and serving which ranks with the application of power and the division of labor.

If we were operating today under the methods of 1921, we should have on hand raw materials to the value of about one hundred and twenty million dollars, and we should have unnecessarily in transit finished products to the value of about fifty million dollars. That is, we should have an investment in raw material and finished goods of not far from two hundred million dollars. Instead of that, we have an average investment of only about fifty million dollars, or, to put it another way, our inventory, raw and finished, is less than it was when our production was only half as great.

The extension of our business since 1921 has been very great, yet, in a way, all this great expansion has been paid for out of money which, under our old methods, would have lain idle in piles of iron, steel, coal, or in finished automobiles stored in warehouses. We do not own or use a single warehouse!

How we do this will be explained later in this chapter, but the point now is to direct thought to the time factor in service. Having on hand twice as much material as is needed — which is only another way of saying twice as much stored human labor as is needed — is precisely the same as hiring two men to do the job that one man ought to do. Hiring two men to do the job of one is a crime against society. Also, to carry a product 500 miles to the consumer, if that product can be found within 250 miles, is a crime. For a railroad to deliver in ten days when it might deliver in five is grand larceny.

This country was built by transportation. The big through trunk lines made us a nation — we had no political barriers to trade, and the railroads removed the natural barriers. Manufacturing naturally centered in the East because the known deposits of coal and iron were in the East, and so, also, were most of the consumers of the finished products, but now we have great cities from coast to coast — too great a population for our railroads to serve, following the old way of doing nearly all the manufacturing in the East.

A big factory unit sometimes pays. Our Fordson plant pays because it brings raw materials together economically. Our finished product, in the way we ship and assemble, goes out with a minimum transportation charge. But if Fordson did not deal in heavy, bulky raw materials it would not pay. It pays because it combines quick transportation both inward and outward. As a general rule, a large plant is not economical. A small plant making only one part is with cheap power more economical than a large plant with equally cheap power making all the parts — even in separate departments. At least, that has been our experience. The cost of power and transportation is controlling.

It is not possible to repeat too often that waste is not something which comes after the fact. Restoring an ill body to health is an achievement, but preventing illness is a much higher achievement. Picking up and reclaiming the scrap left over after production is a public service, but planning so that there will be no scrap is a higher public service.

Time waste differs from material waste in that there can be no salvage. The easiest of all wastes, and the hardest to correct, is this waste of time, because wasted time does not litter the floor like wasted material. In our industries, we think of time as human energy. If we buy more material than we need for production, then we are storing human energy — and probably depreciating its value. One may buy ahead on speculation in the hope of realizing an unearned profit. That is both poor service and poor business, because, over a term of years, the profits of speculation will not exceed the losses, and the net result to the speculator is zero, while the community itself has lost by having to make detours from the ordinary highways of trade. On the other hand, it is a waste to carry so small a stock of materials that an accident will tie up production. The balance has to be found, and that balance largely depends upon the ease of transportation.

There can be no ease in transportation unless the unnecessary shipment of goods is avoided. The country has railroad facilities enough to carry all the goods that need carrying, but it has not facilities enough to provide for unnecessary transportation. To have a surplus of facilities would only be waste. We should do better to look to the necessity of the transportation than to extend the railroads. For instance, when we wholly manufactured our motor cars at Highland Park and shipped them out complete, the day we went into the production of 1,000 cars a day brought on one of the worst freight jams ever known. That jam might have been broken by spending some millions of dollars in extending the railroads and building new box cars. But a much better way was to ship our cars in a different fashion. It would scarcely be possible to ship our present 8,000 cars a day production in the old fashion way, and, if we did, our cars would cost the buyers much more than they now do.

Modern business is on a different basis from the old business. In the days when opportunities were few, it is not surprising that making work for someone was regarded as a worthy act, but now, if the principle of the wage motive be followed, there is more work to do than there are men to do the work. Making a job for a man is merely asking him to assist in lowering wages and raising prices. It would seem that the more traffic given to the railroads the more prosperous they would be, and through buying new equipment they would share their prosperity with the steel makers, the locomotive builders, and car builders, and everyone in the long line of industries which the railroads support.

This is true if the transport be necessary, but not at all true if the transport be unnecessary. If we carry wheat 500 miles to the mill and then carry the flour back over that same 500 miles, then there is a waste, unless the economy of milling at the central point exceeds the extra cost of double transportation. If the carriage is waste, it will find its way into the price of bread, and people will eat less bread, and the farmer will get less for his wheat, and the traffic of the railroad will decrease, and it will be less prosperous and so will all those who depend on it.

Exactly the same principle goes through every kind of business that depends on transportation — and the number of businesses which are not dependent on transportation are so few that they do not have to be considered.

The speed of the transportation is itself a factor, and its importance depends on the value of the commodity carried. If a railroad does not insist that its freight cars go through on time, and allows them to pile up and be forgotten on sidings, then, regardless of the value of the commodity carried, that railroad will have a lot of dead money in surplus equipment.

Handling freight roughly is another source of great waste. It is absurd that an article for shipment has to be protected against other than the ordinary jarring of travel. The function of the carrier is to receive goods and transport them to their destination with the utmost care. This function seems to have been forgotten. Ordinarily, goods have to be packed, not merely to resist jar and ordinary handling, but to resist any attack that may be made on them. This is especially true of goods for overseas. The labor and material involved in packing are enormous, and most of it is sheer waste — waste of human labor and of valuable lumber.

All of these problems we have had to meet in our industries, and we have shaped our industries with transport always in mind. Instead of shipping complete cars, we have thirty-one assembly plants located at trade centers throughout the United States to receive standard parts from the manufacturing plants and assemble them into finished cars and trucks. This calls for chassis assembly, body building, and all the paint, trim, and upholstery work. Some of the branches manufacture cushions, springs, and closed bodies. They all operate under the same system, use the same standard tools, and build cars in the same way. Together they furnish employment for around twenty-six thousand men.

Recently, a new type of assembly plant building has been worked out, and all new branches are being built to these specifications. This calls for a one-story structure with the conveyor lines laid out in such a way that trucking and handling are practically eliminated. The new one-story design permits the greatest efficiency. Production may be greatly increased without additional labor. In the Chicago plant, the greatest distance any material has to be trucked is twenty feet, this being the distance from the incoming freight car to the first conveyor. After this it is mechanically handled during the entire process of assembling the units into a finished car.

The location of a new plant is largely determined by the cost of its power and the price at which it may make and ship goods to a given territory. The saving in freight rates of a fraction of a cent per part often decides the location. The St. Paul plant is able to supply all the country west of the Mississippi River at a lower freight rate than any plant east of it. St. Paul, therefore, makes all the parts that cannot be made elsewhere at a cost to offset the freight-rate advantage. Different parts of a motor car come under separate freight classifications, each with a different tariff. A single first-class part in a case of fifth-class parts may bring the whole shipment under the first-class rate. Packing and shipping are watched in the interest of economy. The amount of machining done on a part sometimes affects its freight classification. In such cases, the lower rate is taken advantage of by having only part of the machining done at the factory and the remainder at the branch to which it is shipped.

Only a few years ago, seven touring car bodies made a full load for a standard thirty-six-foot freight car. Now the bodies are shipped knocked-down to be assembled and finished in the branches, and we ship 130 touring car bodies in the same sized car — that is, we use one freight car where we should formerly have used eighteen.

Our finished inventory is all in transit. So is most of our raw material inventory. When production stands at 8,000 a day, this means that our various factories manufacture and ship enough to make 8,000 complete cars. We know just how many machines and employees it will take to reach a given figure at a given time, and how to take care of seasonal demands without the danger of becoming overstocked. A thirty-day supply of any one material is the maximum carried by a department, with the single exception of the blast furnaces, which carry enough iron ore in storage to last them through the winter. The average department inventory is less than ten days' supply.

The average shipping time between the factory and the branches is 6.16 days, which means that there is an average of a little more than six days' supply of parts in transit. This is called the "float." If production is at the rate of 8,000 cars a day, there are parts enough in transit to make more than forty-eight thousand complete cars. Thus, the traffic and production departments must work closely together to see that all the proper parts reach the branches at the same time — the shortage of a single kind of bolt would hold up the whole assembly at a branch. The exact status of the float may be determined at any hour of the day.

The problem of coordination is simplified by standard carloads — of which we have twenty-five. The standard carload for front axles, for example, contains exactly 400 sets. Limited quantities of smaller parts, such as spring hangers, are always included with the shipment of larger parts, but these, too, are standardized. This is worked out in a manner that will take advantage of the lowest freight classification.

This method does away with filling out shipping orders. Instead, they are printed and books are kept on one master part only. The only time it is necessary to specify quantities is when special shipments are made.

Whenever a shipment starts, the car number is wired to the branch. The factory traffic department traces all shipments and sees that they are kept moving until they are in the branch's territory, where the branch stock traffic man picks them up and follows them through to the unloading platform. We take no chances with the ordinary flow of traffic. Men are stationed at junctions and other points throughout the country to see that the cars are not delayed. The traffic department knows the exact transit time between different points, and if a car is overdue more than an hour, the fact is known at headquarters.

Our production cycle is about eighty-one hours from the mine to the finished machine in the freight car, or three days and nine hours instead of the fourteen days which we used to think was record breaking. Counting the storage of iron ore in winter and various other storage of parts or equipment made necessary from time to time for one reason or another, our average production cycle will not exceed five days.

Take the usual procedure. Let us say one of our ore boats docks at Fordson at 8 A.M. on Monday. It has taken forty-eight hours for the boat to come from Marquette to the docks. Ten minutes after the boat is docked, its cargo will be moving toward the High Line and become part of a charge for the blast furnace. By noon Tuesday, the ore had been reduced to iron, mixed with other iron in the foundry cupolas, and cast. Thereupon follow fifty-eight operations which are performed in fifty-five minutes. By three o'clock in the afternoon the motor has been finished and tested and started off in a freight car to a branch for assembly into a finished car. Say that it reaches the branch plant so that it may be put into the assembly line at eight o'clock Wednesday morning. By noon the car will be on the road in the possession of its owner. If the motor, instead of being sent to a branch, goes into the assembly line for the Detroit district, then the completed car will be delivered before five o'clock Tuesday afternoon instead of at noon on Wednesday.

All of this is made possible by the transportation within the plant, the development of the Detroit, Toledo & Ironton Railroad, the dredging of the River Rouge, and the development of water transportation with our own ships. A few years ago the River Rouge (which flows into the Detroit River and through the Detroit River connects with the Great Lakes) was only a shallow, winding stream from seventy-five to a hundred feet in width and not more than a nine-hundred-ton barge could come up to the factory docks. It was then necessary to transfer the cargoes of the Great Lakes steamers to barges at the mouth of the River Rouge and tow them up. Now we have a short-cut canal, reducing the distance form the lake to our turning basin from nearly five miles to three miles. The canal and river have a surface width of 300 feet and an average depth of twenty-two feet — which is sufficient for all of our purposes.

Since completion of the dredging, we have been building a Great Lakes fleet and now have four vessels, two of which, the Henry Ford II and the Benson Ford, are somewhat unusual in that they are driven by Diesel engines and are designed not only to carry the greatest possible amount of ore, but also to give the officers and crew what are practically first-class hotel accommodations. These boats are each 612 feet long and will carry 13,000 tons of coal or ore. As with everything in our industries, these boats are designed to operate with the smallest possible number of men and are kept spotlessly clean. The engine rooms, for instance, are finished in gray and white enamel, with nickel-plated trimmings. Both the officers' and the crew's quarters are finished in hardwood, with shower baths enough for everyone. The heat is electrical, and all the auxiliary machinery, such as pumps, windlasses, and winches, is electrically driven. These boats are used only the Great Lakes, but, as far as possible, we are locating our branches on navigable waterways. The Memphis and the St. Paul plants are on the banks of the Mississippi River; the Jacksonville plant is on the St. Johns River, with docks for ocean freighters; and the Chicago plant is on the Calumet River, which flows into Lake Michigan. Our Green Island plant is at Troy, near the confluence of the Hudson and the Mohawk rivers. This plant connects with the Kearny, New Jersey, plant by boats on the Hudson. It is less expensive to load boats than freight cars, and the transportation by water in this case is not only faster than by rail but also is cheaper.

A further development has been serving the Atlantic Coast plants at Norfolk, Virginia; Jacksonville, Florida; New Orleans, Louisiana; and Houston, Texas, directly by steamships going out through the Great Lakes and the canals. These vessels deliver on the coast about as quickly as do the railroads, and we have the added advantage of providing special racks and the like aboard the ships, so that our engines and larger parts do not have to be crated. This is applying the single purpose machine idea to the ocean steamship — just as we have applied it to the freight car. Carrying out the same thought, we are organizing an ocean fleet, a part of which has been in operation for more than a year, to our European branches, to our South American branches, and to our Pacific Coast branches. Loading "loose" on these steamers saves us about twenty thousand dollars in crating alone on each trip, in addition to a large saving in cargo space. On two shipments to the Pacific Coast, we saved more than seventy thousand dollars as against shipping by rail. We now have five units in the ocean service and will add as many more as necessary. On all of them we are using Diesel engines. For transatlantic shipments we mostly load at our plants at Kearny, New Jersey, and Norfolk, Virginia, and for the care of these vessels, as well as for the establishment of a new branch, we bought a shipbuilding plant at Chester, Pennsylvania.

On the ships on the high seas, as well as on the lakes, we have put into effect our wage and cleanliness policies and also our labor-saving devices. On our ships, we pay a minimum of $100 a month with board and room — and we board them well. The inclusion of board and lodging makes the rate higher than the shore rate — which is as it should be. We pay the captain and the engineers wages commensurate with the responsibilities they assume. On the whole, our wages will run considerably higher than the highest wages elsewhere paid. We make money on these wages, for really, the whole total of wages paid on a ship is not very important — the important thing is to see that you get the full use out of the big investment, which is the ship.

If a ship is held a couple of weeks in port unloading and loading, the loss will probably be greater than the total wages for a year. Low-priced, irresponsible men will not care what happens to a ship or how long it stays in port. Our men are on their toes to see that our ships are kept moving. They know they must do that to hold their jobs, for every one of our ships, no matter in what part of the world it may be, is held to schedule just as closely as a railroad train. We keep a constant check on every movement of every ship, and any delay has to be explained, and so it is a rare thing for one of our ships to be in a port more than twenty-four hours.

There are a thousand economies to be brought about in ocean transportation. We are so new at shipping that we are only beginning to appreciate the vast savings which are so easily possible. These savings lie in every direction. There are too many men ashore getting commissions and brokerage fees and what-nots; there is almost no attempt at the scientific buying of supplies; the loading and unloading are about the same as they were a hundred years ago, and the element of time to the shipper is almost totally disregarded. A job at sea is as important as a job on shore — which will have to be recognized by the pay.

Modern business — modern life — cannot afford slow transportation.

Chapters 10 and 11 are selections from *Toyota Production System: Beyond Large-Scale Production*, Taiichi Ohno (Cambridge: Productivity Press, 1988)

10

Starting from Need

THE OIL CRISIS OPENED OUR EYES

The oil crisis, in the fall of 1973, followed by a recession, affected government, business, and society the world over. By 1974, Japan's economy had collapsed to a state of zero growth and many companies were suffering.

But at the Toyota Motor Company, although profits suffered, greater earnings were sustained in 1975, 1976, and 1977 than at other companies. The widening gap between it and other companies made people wonder what was happening at Toyota.

Prior to the oil crisis, when I talked to people about Toyota's manufacturing technology and production system, I found little interest. When rapid growth stopped, however, it became very obvious that a business could not be profitable using the conventional American mass production system that had worked so well for so long.

Times had changed. Initially, following World War II, no one imagined that the number of cars produced would increase to today's level. For decades, America had cut costs by mass-producing fewer types of cars. It was an American work style — but not a Japanese one. Our problem was how to cut costs while producing small numbers of many types of cars.

Then, during the 15-year period beginning in 1959-1960, Japan experienced unusually rapid economic growth. As a result, mass production, American style, was still used effectively in many areas.

We kept reminding ourselves, however, that careless imitation of the American system could be dangerous. Making many models in small numbers cheaply — wasn't this something we could develop? And we kept thinking that a Japanese production system like this might even surpass the conventional mass production system. Thus, the principal objective of the Toyota production system was to produce many models in small quantities.

SLOW GROWTH IS SCARY

In the periods of high growth before the oil crisis, the usual business cycle consisted of two or three years of prosperity with, at most, six months of recession. At times, prosperity lasted longer than three years.

Slow growth, however, reverses this cycle. An annual economic growth rate of 6 to 10 percent lasts at most six months to one year, with the next two or three years realizing little or no growth or even negative growth.

Generally, Japanese industry has been accustomed to an era of "if you make it, you can sell it," and the automobile industry is no exception. I am afraid that, because of this, many business managers aim for quantity.

In the automobile industry, the Maxcy-Silberston curve[1] has been used frequently. According to this principle of mass production, although there are limits to the extent of cost reduction, the cost of an automobile decreases drastically in proportion to the increase in quantities produced. This was proved thoroughly in the era of high growth and the principle has become embedded in the minds of people in the automotive industry.

In today's slow-growth era, however, we must downplay the merits of mass production as soon as possible. Today, a production system aimed at increasing lot sizes (for example, operating a die

---

[1] For comparative statistics between Japanese and U.S. auto makers, see pages 215-217 in Michael A. Cusumano's *The Japanese Automobile Industry* (The Council on East Asian Studies, Harvard University, distributed by Harvard University Press, 1985).

press to punch out as many units as possible within a given time period) is not practical. Besides creating all kinds of waste, such a production system is no longer appropriate for our needs.

"CATCH UP WITH AMERICA"

Imitating America is not always bad. We have learned a lot from the U.S. automobile empire. America has generated wonderful production management techniques, business management techniques such as quality control (QC) and total quality control (TQC), and industrial engineering (IE) methods. Japan imported these ideas and put them into practice. The Japanese should never forget that these techniques were born in America and generated by American efforts.

August 15, 1945, was the day Japan lost the war; it also marked a new beginning for Toyota. Toyoda Kiichiro (1894-1952), then president of the Toyota Motor Company, said, "Catch up with America in three years. Otherwise, the automobile industry of Japan will not survive."[2] To accomplish this mission, we had to know America and learn American ways.

In 1937, I was working in the weaving plant of Toyoda Spinning and Weaving. Once I heard a man say that a German worker could produce three times as much as a Japanese worker. The ratio between German and American workers was 1-to-3. This made the ratio between Japanese and American work forces 1-to-9. I still remember my surprise at hearing that it took nine Japanese to do the job of one American.

Had Japanese productivity increased at all during the war? President Toyoda was saying that we should catch up in three years, but it would be very difficult to raise productivity by eight

---

[2] In 1937, Toyota Motor Company was founded by Toyoda Kiichirō, the son of Toyoda Sakichi, an automatic loom inventor fascinated by motor vehicles and founder of Toyoda Spinning and Weaving and Toyoda Automatic Loom. The family name "Toyoda," which means "abundant rice field," was changed to "Toyota," by the automobile division for marketing purposes. The word is an alternate reading of the two logographs with which the family name is written. [Ibid., 59.]

or nine times in such a time period. It meant that a job then being done by 100 workers had to be done by 10 workers.

Furthermore, the figure of one-eighth or one-ninth was an average value. If we compared the automobile industry, one of America's most advanced industries, the ratio would have been much different. But could an American really exert ten times more physical effort? Surely, Japanese people were wasting something. If we could eliminate the waste, productivity should rise by a factor of ten. This idea marked the start of the present Toyota production system.

JUST-IN-TIME

The basis of the Toyota production system is the absolute elimination of waste. The two pillars needed to support the system are:

- *just-in-time*
- *autonomation*, or automation with a human touch.

Just-in-time means that, in a flow process, the right parts needed in assembly reach the assembly line at the time they are needed and only in the amount needed. A company establishing this flow throughout can approach zero inventory.

From the standpoint of production management, this is an ideal state. However, with a product made of thousands of parts, like the automobile, the number of processes involved is enormous. Obviously, it is extremely difficult to apply just-in-time to the production plan of every process in an orderly way.

An upset in prediction, a mistake in the paperwork, defective products and rework, trouble with the equipment, absenteeism — the problems are countless. A problem early in the process always results in a defective product later in the process. This will stop the production line or change a plan whether you like it or not.

By disregarding such situations and only considering the production plan for each process, we would produce parts without regard to later processes. Waste would result — defective parts on one hand, huge inventories of parts not needed immediately on the other. This reduces both productivity and profitability.

Even worse, there would be no distinction between normal and abnormal states on each assembly line. When there is a delay in rectifying an abnormal state, too many workers would make too many parts, a situation not quickly corrected.

Therefore, to produce using just-in-time so that each process receives the exact item needed, when it is needed, and in the quantity needed, conventional management methods do not work well.

USING A COMMON SENSE IDEA

I am fond of thinking about a problem over and over. I kept thinking about how to supply the number of parts needed just-in-time. The flow of production is the transfer of materials. The conventional way was to supply materials from an earlier process to a later process. So, I tried thinking about the transfer of materials in the reverse direction.

In automobile production, material is machined into a part, the part is then assembled with others into a unit part, and this flows toward the final assembly line. The material progresses from the earlier processes toward the later ones, forming the body of the car.

Let's look at this production flow in reverse: a later process goes to an earlier process to pick up only the right part in the quantity needed at the exact time needed. In this case, wouldn't it be logical for the earlier process to make only the number of parts withdrawn? As far as communication between the many processes is concerned, wouldn't it be sufficient to clearly indicate what and how many are needed?

We will call this means of indication *kanban* (sign board) and circulate it between each of the processes to control the amount of production — that is, the amount needed. This was the beginning of the idea.

We experimented with this and finally decided on a system. The final assembly line is taken as the starting point. On this basis, the production plan, indicating the desired types of cars with their quantity and due date, goes to the final assembly line. Then the method of transferring the materials is reversed. To supply parts used in assembly, a later process goes to an earlier process to withdraw only the number of parts needed when they are needed. In this reverse way, the manufacturing process goes from finished product back to the earliest materials-forming department. Every link in the just-in-time chain is connected and synchronized. By this, the management work force is also reduced drastically. And kanban is the means used for conveying information about picking up or receiving the production order.

Kanban will be described later in detail. Here, I want the reader to understand the basic posture of the Toyota production system. The system is supported by the just-in-time system, already discussed, and autonomation, described in the next section. The kanban method is the means by which the Toyota production system moves smoothly.

GIVE THE MACHINE INTELLIGENCE

The other pillar of the Toyota production system is called autonomation — not to be confused with simple automation. It is also known as automation with a human touch.

Many machines operate by themselves once the switch is turned on. Today's machines have such high performance capabilities, however, that a small abnormality, such as a piece of scrap falling into the machine, can damage it in some way. The dies or taps break, for instance. When this happens, tens and soon hundreds of defective parts are produced and quickly pile up. With an automated machine of this type, mass production of defective products cannot be prevented. There is no built-in automatic checking system against such mishaps.

This is why Toyota emphasizes autonomation — machines that can prevent such problems "autonomously" — over simple automation. The idea originated with the invention of an auto-activated weaving machine by Toyoda Sakichi (1867-1930), founder of the Toyota Motor Company.

The loom stopped instantly if any one of the warp or weft threads broke. Because a device that could distinguish between normal and abnormal conditions was built into the machine, defective products were not produced.

At Toyota, a machine automated with a human touch is one that is attached to an automatic stopping device. In all Toyota plants, most machines, new or old, are equipped with such devices as well as various safety devices, fixed-position stopping, the full-work system, and *baka-yoke* foolproofing systems to prevent defective products. In this way, human intelligence, or a human touch, is given to the machines.

Autonomation changes the meaning of management as well. An operator is not needed while the machine is working normally. Only when the machine stops because of an abnormal situation does it get human attention. As a result, one worker can attend several machines, making it possible to reduce the number of operators and increase production efficiency.

Looking at this another way, abnormalities will never disappear if a worker always attends to a machine and stands in for it when an abnormality does occur. An old Japanese saying mentions hiding an offensively smelly object by covering it up. If materials or machines are repaired without the managing supervisor's being made aware of it, improvement will never be achieved and costs will never be reduced.

Stopping the machine when there is trouble forces awareness on everyone. When the problem is clearly understood, improvement is possible. Expanding this thought, we establish a rule that even in a manually operated production line, the workers themselves should push the stop button to halt production if any abnormality appears.

In a product like the automobile, safety must always be of primary importance. Therefore, on any machine on any production line in any plant, distinctions between normal and abnormal operations must be clear and countermeasures always taken to prevent recurrence. This is why I made autonomation the other pillar of the Toyota production system.

THE POWER OF INDIVIDUAL
SKILL AND TEAMWORK

Implementing autonomation is up to the managers and supervisors of each production area. The key is to give human intelligence to the machine and, at the same time, to adapt the simple movement of the human operator to the autonomous machines.

What is the relationship between just-in-time and automation with a human touch, the two pillars of the Toyota production system? Using the analogy of a baseball team, autonomation corresponds to the skill and talent of individual players while just-in-time is the teamwork involved in reaching an agreed-upon objective.

For example, a player in the outfield has nothing to do as long as the pitcher has no problems. But a problem — the opposing batter getting a hit, for example — activates the outfielder who catches the ball and throws it to the baseman "just in time" to put the runner out.

Managers and supervisors in a manufacturing plant are like the team manager and the batting, base, and field coaches. A strong baseball team has mastered the plays; the players can meet any situation with coordinated action. In manufacturing, the production team that has mastered the just-in-time system is exactly like a baseball team that plays well together.

Autonomation, on the other hand, performs a dual role. It eliminates overproduction, an important waste in manufacturing, and prevents the production of defective products. To accomplish this, standard work procedures, corresponding to each player's ability, must be adhered to at all times. When abnormalities arise — that is, when a player's ability cannot be brought out — special instruction must be given to bring the player back to normal. This is an important duty of the coach.

In the autonomated system, visual control, or "management by sight," can help bring production weaknesses (in each player, that is) to the surface. This allows us then to take measures to strengthen the players involved.

A championship team combines good teamwork with individual skill. Likewise, a production line where just-in-time and automation with a human touch work together is stronger than other lines. Its power is in the synergy of these two factors.

COST REDUCTION IS THE GOAL

Frequently we use the word "efficiency" when talking about production, management, and business. "Efficiency," in modern industry and business in general, means cost reduction.

At Toyota, as in all manufacturing industries, profit can be obtained only by reducing costs. When we apply the cost principle *selling price* = *profit* + *actual cost*, we make the consumer responsible for every cost. This principle has no place in today's competitive automobile industry.

Our products are scrutinized by cool-headed consumers in free, competitive markets where the manufacturing cost of a product is of no consequence. The question is whether or not the product is of value to the buyer. If a high price is set because of the manufacturer's cost, consumers will simply turn away.

Cost reduction must be the goal of consumer products manufacturers trying to survive in today's marketplace. During a period of high economic growth, any manufacturer can achieve lower costs with higher production. But in today's low-growth period, to achieve any form of cost reduction is difficult.

There is no magic method. Rather, a total management system is needed that develops human ability to its fullest capacity to best enhance creativity and fruitfulness, to utilize facilities and machines well, and to eliminate all waste.

The Toyota production system, with its two pillars advocating the absolute elimination of waste, was born in Japan out of necessity. Today, in an era of slow economic growth worldwide, this production system represents a concept in management that will work for any type of business.

THE ILLUSION OF JAPANESE INDUSTRY

After World War II, when Toyoda Kiichiro, father of Japanese car production, advocated catching up with America in three years, this became Toyota's goal. Because the goal was clear, activity at Toyota became focused and vigorous.

My job until 1943 was in textiles, not automobiles; this was an advantage. In fact, the idea of automation with a human touch was obtained from the auto-activated looms of Toyoda Sakichi's textile plant. When I moved to automobile production, although I was new, I could spot its merits and shortcomings in comparison to the textile plant.

During the postwar rehabilitation, Japan's automobile industry had a rough time. Domestic production for 1949 was 25,622 trucks and only 1,008 passenger cars. Insignificant as domestic production seemed, Toyota's production plant was filled with eager people trying to do something. President Toyoda's words "Catch up with America" generated this spirit.

In 1947, I was in charge of the No. 2 manufacturing machine shop at the present main office plant in Toyota City, then called the Koromo plant. To catch up with America, I thought of having one operator care for many machines and also different types of machines rather than one person per machine. Therefore, the first step was to establish a flow system in the machine shop.

In American as well as in most Japanese machine shops, a lathe operator, for example, operates only lathes. In many plant layouts, as many as 50 or 100 lathes are in one location. When machining is completed, the items are collected and taken to the subsequent drilling process. With that finished, the items then go to the milling process.

In the United States, there is a union for each job function with many unions in each company. Lathe operators are allowed to operate only lathes. A drilling job must be taken to a drilling operator. And because the operators are single-skilled, a welding job required at the lathe section cannot be done there but must be taken to a welding operator. As a consequence, there are a large number of people and machines. For American industries to achieve cost reduction under such conditions, mass production is the only answer.

When large quantities are produced, the labor cost per car and depreciation burden are reduced. This requires high-performance, high-speed machines that are both large and expensive.

This type of production is a planned mass production system in which each process makes many parts and forwards them to the next process. This method naturally generates an abundance of waste. From the time it acquired this American system until the 1973 oil crisis, Japan had the illusion that this system fit their needs.

ESTABLISHING A PRODUCTION FLOW

It is never easy to break the machine-shop tradition in which operators are fixed to jobs, for example, lathe operators to lathe work and welders to welding work. It worked in Japan only because we were willing to do it. The Toyota production system began when I challenged the old system.

With the outbreak of the Korean War in June 1950, Japanese industry recovered its vigor. Riding this wave of growth, the automobile industry also expanded. At Toyota, it was a busy and hectic year, beginning in April with a three-month labor dispute over manpower reduction, followed by president Toyoda Kiichiro's assuming responsibility for the strike and resigning. After this, the Korean War broke out.

Although there were special wartime demands, we were far from mass production. We were still producing small quantities of many models.

At this time, I was manager of the machine shop at the Koromo plant. As an experiment, I arranged the various machines in the sequence of machining processes. This was a radical change from the conventional system in which a large quantity of the same part was machined in one process and then forwarded to the next process.

In 1947, we arranged machines in parallel lines or in an L-shape and tried having one worker operate three or four machines along the processing route. We encountered strong resistance among the production workers, however, even though there was no increase in work or hours. Our craftsmen did not like the new arrangement requiring them to function as multi-skilled operators. They did not like changing from "one operator, one machine" to a system of "one operator, many machines in different processes."

Their resistance was understandable. Furthermore, our efforts revealed various problems. For example, a machine must be set up to stop when machining is finished; sometimes there were so many adjustments that an unskilled operator found the job difficult to handle.

As these problems became clearer, they showed me the direction to continue moving in. Although young and eager to push, I decided not to press for quick, drastic changes, but to be patient.

PRODUCTION LEVELING

In business, nothing is more pleasing than customer orders. With the labor dispute over and the special demands of the Korean War beginning, a lively tension filled the production plant. How would we handle the demand for trucks? People in the production plant were frantic.

There was a shortage of everything from crude materials to parts. We could not get things in the quantity or at the time needed. Our parts suppliers were also short on equipment and manpower.

Because Toyota made chassis, when many parts did not arrive on time or in the right amounts, assembly work was delayed. For this reason, we could not do assembly during the first half of the month. We were forced to gather the parts that were arriving intermittently and irregularly and do the assembly work at the end of the month. Like the old song "*dekansho*" that tells of sleeping half the year, this was *dekansho* production and the approach nearly did us in.

If a part is needed at the rate of 1,000 per month, we should make 40 parts a day for 25 days. Furthermore, we should spread production evenly throughout the workday. If the workday is 480 minutes, we should average one piece every 12 minutes. This idea later developed into production leveling.

Establishing (1) a production flow and (2) a way to maintain a constant supply of raw materials from outside for parts to be machined was the way the Toyota, or Japanese, production system should be operated. Our minds were filled with ideas.

Because there were shortages of everything, we must have thought it all right to increase manpower and machines to produce and store items. At the time, we were making no more than 1,000 to 2,000 cars a month, and keeping a one-month inventory in each process. Except for needing a large warehouse, this did not seem too big a burden. We did foresee a big problem, however, if and when production increased.

To avoid this potential problem, we looked for ways to level all production. We wanted to get away from having to produce everything around the end of the month, so we started by looking inside Toyota itself. Then, when outside suppliers were needed, we first listened to their needs and then asked them to cooperate in helping us achieve leveled production. Depending on the situation, we discussed the supplier's cooperation in terms of manpower, materials, and money.

IN THE BEGINNING, THERE WAS NEED

So far, I have described, in sequence, the fundamental principles of the Toyota production system and its basic structure. I would like to emphasize that it was realized because there were always clear purposes and needs.

I strongly believe that "necessity is the mother of invention." Even today, improvements at Toyota plants are made based on need. The key to progress in production improvement, I feel, is letting the plant people feel the need.

Even my own efforts to build the Toyota production system block by block were also based on the strong need to discover a new production method that would eliminate waste and help us catch up with America in three years.

For example, the idea of a later process going to an earlier process to pick up materials resulted from the following circumstance. In the conventional system, an earlier process forwarded products to a later process continuously regardless of the production requirements of that process. Mountains of parts, therefore, might pile up at the later process. At that point, workers spent their time looking for storage space and hunting for parts instead of making progress in the most important part of their jobs — production.

Somehow this waste had to be eliminated and it meant immediately stopping the automatic forwarding of parts from earlier processes. This strong need made us change our method.

Rearranging the machines on the floor to establish a production flow eliminated the waste of storing parts. It also helped us achieve the "one operator, many processes" system and increased production efficiency two and three times.

I already mentioned that in America this system could not be implemented easily. It was possible in Japan because we lacked function-oriented unions like those in Europe and the United States. Consequently, the transition from the single-skilled to the multi-skilled operator went relatively smoothly, although there was initial resistance from the craftsmen. This does not mean, however, that Japanese unions are weaker than their American and European counterparts. Much of the difference lies in history and culture.

Some say that trade unions in Japan represent a vertically divided society lacking mobility while function-oriented unions of Europe and America exemplify laterally divided societies with greater mobility. Is this actually so? I don't think so.

In the American system, a lathe operator is always a lathe operator and a welder is a welder to the end. In the Japanese system, an operator has a broad spectrum of skills. He can operate a lathe, handle a drilling machine, and also run a milling machine. He can even perform welding. Who is to say which system is better? Since many of the differences come from the history and culture of the two countries, we should look for the merits in both.

In the Japanese system, operators acquire a broad spectrum of production skills that I call manufacturing skills and participate in building up a total system in the production plant. In this way, the individual can find value in working.

Needs and opportunities are always there. We just have to drive ourselves to find the practical ones. What are the essential needs of business under slow growth conditions? In other words, how can we raise productivity when the production quantity is not increasing?

A REVOLUTION IN CONSCIOUSNESS IS INDISPENSABLE

There is no waste in business more terrible than overproduction. Why does it occur?

We naturally feel more secure with a considerable amount of inventory. Before, during, and after World War II, buying and hoarding were natural behaviors. Even in this more affluent time, people bought up tissue paper and detergent when the oil crisis came.

We could say this is the response of a farming society. Our ancestors grew rice for subsistence and stored it in preparation for times of natural disaster. From our experience during the oil crisis, we learned that our basic nature has not changed much.

Modern industry also seems stuck in this way of thinking. A person in business may feel uneasy about survival in this competitive society without keeping some inventories of raw materials, work-in-process, and products.

This type of hoarding, however, is no longer practical. Industrial society must develop the courage, or rather the common sense, to procure only what is needed when it is needed and in the amount needed.

This requires what I call a revolution in consciousness, a change of attitude and viewpoint by business people. In a period of slow growth, holding a large inventory causes the waste of over-production. It also leads to an inventory of defectives, which is a serious business loss. We must understand these situations in depth before we can achieve a revolution in consciousness.

11

Evolution of the Toyota Production System

REPEATING *WHY* FIVE TIMES

When confronted with a problem, have you ever stopped and asked *why* five times? It is difficult to do even though it sounds easy. For example, suppose a machine stopped functioning:

1. *Why* did the machine stop?
   There was an overload and the fuse blew.
2. *Why* was there an overload?
   The bearing was not sufficiently lubricated.
3. *Why* was it not lubricated sufficiently?
   The lubrication pump was not pumping sufficiently.
4. *Why* was it not pumping sufficiently?
   The shaft of the pump was worn and rattling.
5. *Why* was the shaft worn out?
   There was no strainer attached and metal scrap got in.

Repeating *why* five times, like this, can help uncover the root problem and correct it. If this procedure were not carried through, one might simply replace the fuse or the pump shaft. In that case, the problem would recur within a few months.

To tell the truth, the Toyota production system has been built on the practice and evolution of this scientific approach. By asking *why* five times and answering it each time, we can get to the real cause of the problem, which is often hidden behind more obvious symptoms.

"Why can one person at Toyota Motor Company operate only one machine, while at the Toyoda textile plant one young woman oversees 40 to 50 automatic looms?"

By starting with this question, we obtained the answer "The machines at Toyota are not set up to stop when machining is completed." From this, automation with a human touch developed.

To the question "Why can't we make this part using just-in-time?" came the answer "The earlier process makes them so quickly, we don't know how many are made per minute." From this, the idea of production leveling developed.

The first answer to the question "Why are we making too many parts?" was "Because there is no way to hold down or prevent overproduction." This led to the idea of visual control which then led to the idea of kanban.

It was stated in the previous chapter that the Toyota production system is based fundamentally on the absolute elimination of waste. Why is waste generated in the first place? With this question, we are actually asking the meaning of profit, which is the condition for a business's continued existence. At the same time, we are asking why people work.

In a production plant operation, data are highly regarded — but I consider facts to be even more important. When a problem arises, if our search for the cause is not thorough, the actions taken can be out of focus. This is why we repeatedly ask *why*. This is the scientific basis of the Toyota system.

COMPLETE ANALYSIS OF WASTE

When thinking about the absolute elimination of waste, keep the following two points in mind:

1. Improving the efficiency makes sense only when it is tied to cost reduction. To achieve this, we have to start producing only the things we need using minimum manpower.
2. Look at the efficiency of each operator and of each line. Then look at the operators as a group, and then at the efficiency of the entire plant (all the lines). Efficiency must be improved at each step and, at the same time, for the plant as a whole.

For example, throughout the 1950 labor dispute over manpower reduction and the ensuing business boom of the Korean War, Toyota struggled with the problem of how to increase production without increasing manpower. As one of the production plant managers, I put my ideas to work in the following ways.

Let's say, for instance, one production line has 10 workers and makes 100 products per day. This means the line capacity is 100 pieces per day and the productivity per person is 10 pieces per day. Observing the line and workers in further detail, however, we notice overproduction, workers waiting, and other unnecessary movements depending on the time of day.

Suppose we improved the situation and reduced manpower by two workers. The fact that 8 workers could produce 100 pieces daily suggests that we can make 125 pieces a day, increasing efficiency without reducing manpower. Actually, however, the capacity to make 125 pieces a day existed before but it was being wasted in the form of unnecessary work and overproduction.

This means that if we regard only work that is needed as real work and define the rest as waste, the following equation holds true whether considering individual workers or the entire line:

$$\text{Present capacity} = \text{work} + \text{waste}$$

True efficiency improvement comes when we produce zero waste and bring the percentage of work to 100 percent. Since, in the Toyota production system, we must make only the amount needed, manpower must be reduced to trim excess capacity and match the needed quantity.

The preliminary step toward application of the Toyota production system is to identify wastes completely:

- Waste of overproduction
- Waste of time on hand (waiting)
- Waste in transportation
- Waste of processing itself
- Waste of stock on hand (inventory)
- Waste of movement
- Waste of making defective products

Eliminating these wastes (see Glossary for categorical explanations) completely can improve the operating efficiency by a large margin. To do this, we must make only the quantity needed, thereby releasing extra manpower. The Toyota production system clearly reveals excess manpower. Because of this, some labor union people have been suspicious of it as a means of laying off workers. But that is not the idea.

Management's responsibility is to identify excess manpower and utilize it effectively. Hiring people when business is good and production is high just to lay them off or recruiting early retirees when recession hits are bad practices. Managers should use them with care. On the other hand, eliminating wasteful and meaningless jobs enhances the value of work for workers.

MY PLANT-FIRST PRINCIPLE

The production plant is manufacturing's major source of information. It provides the most direct, current, and stimulating information about management.

I have always firmly believed in the plant-first principle, perhaps because I started out on the plant floor. Even today, as part of top management, I have been unable to separate myself from the reality found in the production plant. The time that provides me with the most vital information about management is the time I spend in the plant, not in the vice president's office.

Some time in 1937-1938, my boss at Toyoda Spinning and Weaving told me to prepare standard work methods for textile work. It was a difficult project. From a book on standard work methods I bought from Maruzen, I managed to do the job.[1]

A proper work procedure, however, cannot be written from a desk. It must be tried and revised many times in the production plant. Furthermore, it must be a procedure that anybody can understand on sight.

When I first came to the Toyota Motor Company during the war, I asked my workers to prepare standard work methods. Skilled workers were being transferred from the production plant to the battlefield and more and more machines were gradually

---

[1] Maruzen is a chain of Japanese bookstores.

being operated by inexperienced men and women. This naturally increased the need for standard work methods. My experience during that period laid the foundation for my 35 years of work on the Toyota production system. It was also the origin of my plant-first principle.

WRITING THE STANDARD WORK SHEET YOURSELF

In each Toyota Motor Company plant, as well as in the production plants of cooperating firms adopting the Toyota production system, visual control is thoroughly established. Standard work sheets are posted prominently at each work station. When one looks up, the *andon* (the line stop indication board) comes into view, showing the location and nature of trouble situations at a glance. Furthermore, boxes containing parts brought to the side of the production line arrive with an attached kanban, the visual symbol of the Toyota production system.

Here, however, I want to discuss the standard work sheet as a means of visual control, which is how the Toyota production system is managed.

Standard work sheets and the information contained in them are important elements of the Toyota production system. For a production person to be able to write a standard work sheet that other workers can understand, he or she must be convinced of its importance.

We have eliminated waste by examining available resources, rearranging machines, improving machining processes, installing autonomous systems, improving tools, analyzing transportation methods, and optimizing the amount of materials at hand for machining. High production efficiency has also been maintained by preventing the recurrence of defective products, operational mistakes, and accidents, and by incorporating workers' ideas. All of this is possible because of the inconspicuous standard work sheet.

The standard work sheet effectively combines materials, workers, and machines to produce efficiently. At Toyota, this procedure is called a work combination. The result is the standard work procedure.

The standard work sheet has changed little since I was first asked to prepare one 40 years ago at the textile plant. However, it is based thoroughly on principles and plays an important role in Toyota's visual control system. It clearly lists the three elements of the standard work procedure as:

1. Cycle time
2. Work sequence
3. Standard inventory

Cycle time is the time allotted to make one piece or unit. This is determined by production quantity; that is, the quantity required and the operating time. Quantity required per day is the quantity required per month divided by that month's number of operating days. Cycle time is computed by dividing operating hours by the quantity required per day. Even when cycle time is determined this way, individual times may differ.

In Japan, it is said that "time is the shadow of motion." In most cases, delay is generated by differences in operator motion and sequence. The job of the field supervisor, section chief, or group foreman is to train workers. I have always said that it should take only three days to train new workers in proper work procedures. When instruction in the sequence and key motions is clear, workers quickly learn to avoid redoing a job or producing defective parts.

To do this, however, the trainer must actually take the hands of the workers and teach them. This generates trust in the supervisor. At the same time, workers must be taught to help each other. Because people are doing the work, rather than machines, there will be individual differences in work times caused by physical conditions. These differences will be absorbed by the first worker in the process, just as in the baton touch zone in track relay. Carrying out the standard work methods in the cycle time helps worker harmony grow.

The term "work sequence" means just what it says. It does not refer to the order of processes along which products flow. It refers rather to the sequence of operations, or the order of operations in which a worker processes items: transporting them, mounting them on machines, removing them from machines, and so on.

Standard inventory refers to the minimum intra-process work-in-process needed for operations to proceed. This includes items mounted on machines.

Even without changing machine layout, standard inventory between processes is generally unnecessary if work is carried out in the order of machining processes. All that is needed are the items mounted on the various machines. On the other hand, one item's worth (or two where two items are mounted on machines) of standard inventory will be required if work proceeds by machine function rather than by the process flow.

In the Toyota production system, the fact that parts have to arrive just-in-time means that standard inventories have to be met that much more rigorously.

TEAMWORK IS EVERYTHING

I touched on the subject of harmony in discussing cycle times. Now I would like to spend some time giving you my thoughts on teamwork.

Work and sports have many things in common. In Japan, competition is traditionally individual, as in *sumo* wrestling, *kendo* swordsmanship, and *judo*. In fact, in Japan we do not "compete" in these activities but rather we "seek the way and study it" devotedly. This approach has its analogy in the work arena, where the art of the individual craftsman is highly valued.

Competitive team sports came to Japan after Western culture was imported. And in modern industry, harmony among people in a group, as in teamwork, is in greater demand than the art of the individual craftsman.

For example, in a boat race with eight rowers per boat, a baseball team with nine players, a volleyball game with six people per side, or a soccer team with eleven members, the key to winning or losing is teamwork. Even with one or two star players, a team does not necessarily win.

Manufacturing is also done through teamwork. It might take 10 or 15 workers, for example, to take a job from raw materials to finished product. The idea is teamwork — not how many parts were machined or drilled by one worker, but how many products were completed by the line as a whole.

Years ago, I used to tell production workers one of my favorite stories about a boat rowed by eight men, four on the left side and four on the right side. If they do not row correctly, the boat will zigzag erratically.

One rower might feel he is stronger than the next and row twice as hard. But this extra effort upsets the boat's progress and moves it off course. The best way to propel the boat faster is for everyone to distribute force equally, rowing evenly and at the same depth.

Today a volleyball team has six players; previously there were nine. If a nine-member team tried to play a six-member team using the same plays, players might be injured bumping into one another. They would probably lose also because having more players is not necessarily an advantage.

Teamwork combined with other factors can allow a smaller team to win. The same is true in a work environment.

Sports gives us so many helpful hints. In baseball, for example, if someone drew boundaries around the infield defense zone and said only the second baseman could play there while the third baseman could only play in another designated area, the game would not be as much fun to watch.

Similarly, at work things do not necessarily run smoothly just because areas of responsibility have been assigned. Teamwork is essential.

THE SKILL OF PASSING THE BATON

About the time I began work on the Toyota production system, the Korean War was coming to an end. Newspapers were calling the so-called 38th parallel a national tragedy. The same is true in work. We cannot draw a "38th parallel" in each other's work area.

The work arena is like a track relay — there is always an area where the baton may be passed. If the baton is passed well, the total final time can be better than the individual times of the four runners. In a swimming relay, a swimmer cannot dive before the previous swimmer's hand touches the wall. In track, however, rules are different and a strong runner can make up for a weak runner. This is an interesting point.

In a manufacturing job done by four or five people, the parts should be handed over as if they were batons. If an operator in a later process is delayed, others should help set up his or her machine. When the work area returns to normal, that worker should get the baton and everyone else should return to their positions. I always tell workers they should be skillful in baton passing.

In work and in sports, it is desirable for team members to work with equal strength. In actuality, this is not always the case, particularly with new employees who are unfamiliar with the work. At Toyota, we call the baton-passing system the "Mutual Assistance Campaign." It provides the power to generate more powerful teamwork.

I feel the most important point in common between sports and work is the continuing need for practice and training. It is easy to understand theory with the mind; the problem is to remember it with the body. The goal is to know and do instinctively. Having the spirit to endure the training is the first step on the road to winning.

AN IDEA FROM THE U.S. SUPERMARKET

To repeat, the two pillars of the Toyota production system are just-in-time and automation with a human touch, or autonomation. The tool used to operate the system is kanban, an idea I got from American supermarkets.

Following World War II, American products flowed into Japan — chewing gum and Coca-Cola, even the jeep. The first U.S.-style supermarket appeared in the mid-1950s. And, as more and more Japanese people visited the United States, they saw the intimate relationship between the supermarket and the style of daily life in America. Consequently, this type of store became the rage in Japan due to Japanese curiosity and fondness for imitation.

In 1956, I toured U.S. production plants at General Motors, Ford, and other machinery companies. But my strongest impression was the extent of the supermarket's prevalence in America. The reason for this was that by the late 1940s, at Toyota's machine shop that I managed, we were already studying the U.S. supermarket and applying its methods to our work.

Combining automobiles and supermarkets may seem odd. But for a long time, since learning about the setup of supermarkets in America, we made a connection between supermarkets and the just-in-time system.

A supermarket is where a customer can get (1) what is needed, (2) at the time needed, (3) in the amount needed. Sometimes, of course, a customer may buy more than he or she needs. In principle, however, the supermarket is a place where we buy according to need. Supermarket operators, therefore, must make certain that customers can buy what they need at any time.

Compared to Japan's traditional, turn-of-the-century merchandising methods such as peddling medicines door to door, going around to customers to take orders, and hawking wares, America's supermarket system is more rational. From the seller's viewpoint, labor is not wasted carrying items that may not sell, while the buyer does not have to worry about whether to buy extra items.

From the supermarket we got the idea of viewing the earlier process in a production line as a kind of store. The later process (customer) goes to the earlier process (supermarket) to acquire the required parts (commodities) at the time and in the quantity needed. The earlier process immediately produces the quantity just taken (restocking the shelves). We hoped that this would help us approach our just-in-time goal and, in 1953, we actually applied the system in our machine shop at the main plant.

In the 1950s, American-style supermarkets appeared in Japan, bringing the object of our research even closer. And when in America in 1956, I finally fulfilled my desire to visit a supermarket firsthand.

Our biggest problem with this system was how to avoid throwing the earlier process into confusion when a later process picked up large quantities at a time. Eventually, after trial and error, we came up with production leveling, described later.

WHAT IS KANBAN?

The operating method of the Toyota production system is *kanban*. Its most frequently used form is a piece of paper contained in a rectangular vinyl envelope.

This piece of paper carries information that can be divided into three categories: (1) pickup information, (2) transfer informa-

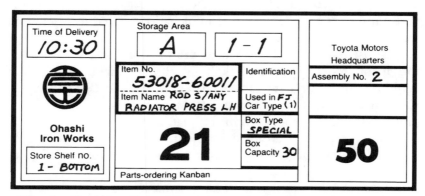

When the Ohashi Iron Works delivers parts to the headquarters factory of Toyota Motors, they use this parts-ordering kanban for subcontractors. The number 50 represents the number of Toyota's receiving gate. The rod is delivered to storage area A. The number 21 is an item back number for the parts.

Figure 11-1. A Sample of Kanban

tion, and (3) production information. The kanban carries the information vertically and laterally within Toyota itself and between Toyota and the cooperating firms.

As I said earlier, the idea came from the supermarket. Suppose we take kanban into the supermarket. How would it work?

Commodities purchased by customers are checked out through the cash register. Cards that carry information about the types and quantities of commodities bought are then forwarded to the purchasing department. Using this information, commodities taken are swiftly replaced by purchasing. These cards correspond to the withdrawal kanban in the Toyota production system. In the supermarket, the commodities displayed in the store correspond to the inventory at the production plant.

If a supermarket had its own production plant nearby, there would be production kanban in addition to the withdrawal kanban between the store and the production department. From the directions on this kanban, the production department would produce the number of commodities picked up.

Of course, supermarkets have not gone that far. In our production plant, however, we have been doing this from the beginning.

The supermarket system was adopted in the machine shop around 1953. To make it work, we used pieces of paper listing the part number of a piece and other information related to machining work. We called this "kanban."

Subsequently, this was called the "kanban system." We felt that if this system were used skillfully, all movements in the plant could be unified or systematized. After all, one piece of paper provided at a glance the following information: production quantity, time, method, sequence or transfer quantity, transfer time, destination, storage point, transfer equipment, container, and so on. At the time, I did not doubt that this means of conveying information would certainly work.

Generally in a business, *what*, *when*, and *how many* are generated by the work planning section in the form of a work start plan, transfer plan, production order, or delivery order passed through the plant. When this system is used, "when" is set arbitrarily and people think it will be all right whether parts arrive on time or early. Managing parts made too early, however, means carrying a lot of intermediate workers. The word "just" in "just-in-time" means exactly that. If parts arrive any time prior to their need — not at the precise time needed — waste cannot be eliminated.

In the Toyota production system, overproduction is completely prevented by kanban. As a result, there is no need for extra inventory and, consequently, there is no need for the warehouse and its manager. Generation of countless paper slips also becomes unnecessary.

INCORRECT USE CAUSES PROBLEMS

With a better tool, we can get wonderful results. But if we use it incorrectly, the tool can make things worse.

Kanban is one of those tools that if used improperly can cause a variety of problems. To employ kanban properly and skillfully, we tried to clearly understand its purpose and role and then establish rules for its use.

Kanban is a way to achieve just-in-time; its purpose is just-in-time. Kanban, in essence, becomes the autonomic nerve of the production line. Based on this, production workers start work by themselves, and make their own decisions concerning overtime.

The kanban system also makes clear what must be done by managers and supervisors. This unquestionably promotes improvement in both work and equipment.

The goal of eliminating waste is also highlighted by kanban. Its use immediately shows what is waste, allowing for creative study and improvement proposals. In the production plant, kanban is a powerful force to reduce manpower and inventory, eliminate defective products, and prevent the recurrence of breakdowns.

It is not an overstatement to say that kanban controls the flow of goods at Toyota. It controls the production of a company exceeding $4.8 billion a year.

In this way, Toyota's kanban system clearly reflects our wishes. It is practiced under strict rules and its effectiveness is shown by our company's achievements. The Toyota production system, however, advances by the minute and close supervision of the kanban rules is a never ending problem.

Functions of kanban	*Rules for use*
1. Provides pick-up or transport information.	1. Later process picks up the number of items indicated by the kanban at the earlier process.
2. Provides production information.	2. Earlier process produces items in the quantity and sequence indicated by the kanban.
3. Prevents overproduction and excessive transport.	3. No items are made or transported without a kanban.
4. Serves as a work order attached to goods.	4. Always attach a kanban to the goods.
5. Prevents defective products by identifying the process making the defectives.	5. Defective products are not sent on to the subsequent process. The result is 100% defect-free goods.
6. Reveals existing problems and maintains inventory control.	6. Reducing the number of kanban increases their sensitivity.

THE TALENT AND COURAGE TO RETHINK
WHAT WE CALL COMMON SENSE

The first rule of kanban is that the later process goes to the earlier process to pick up products. This rule was derived from need and from looking at things upside-down, or from the opposite standpoint.

To practice this first rule, a superficial understanding is not enough. Top management must change its way of thinking and make a commitment to reverse the conventional flow of production, transfer, and delivery. This will meet with lots of resistance and requires courage. The greater the commitment, however, the more successful will be the implementation of the Toyota production system.

In the 30 years since I moved from textiles to the world of automobiles, I have worked continuously to develop and promote the Toyota production system, even though I doubted my ability to succeed.

This may sound presumptuous, but the growth of the Toyota production system has tended to coincide with the growth of my own responsibilities at Toyota.

In 1949-1950, as manager of the machine shop in what is now the main plant, I made the first step toward the "just-in-time" idea. Then, to establish the flow of production, we rearranged the machines and adopted a multi-process system that assigns one operator to three or four machines. From then on, I utilized my growing authority to its fullest extent to expand these ideas.

During this period, all the ideas I boldly put into practice were intended to improve the old, conservative production system — and they might have looked high-handed. Toyota's top management watched the situation quietly, and I admire the attitude they took.

I have a good reason for emphasizing the role of top management in discussing the first rule of kanban. There are many obstacles to implementing the rule that the later process must take what it requires from the earlier process when it is needed. For this reason, management commitment and strong support are essential to the successful application of this first rule.

To the earlier process, however, this means eliminating the production schedule they have relied upon for so long. Production workers have a good deal of psychological resistance to the idea that simply producing as much as possible is no longer a priority.

Trying to make only the items withdrawn also means changing the setup more often unless the production line is dedicated to one item. Usually, people consider it an advantage for the earlier process to make a large quantity of one item. But while producing item A in quantity, the process may not meet the need for item B. Consequently, shortening setup time and reducing lot sizes becomes necessary.

Among the new problems, the most difficult surface when the later process picks up a large quantity of one item. When this happens, the earlier process immediately runs out of that item. If we try to counter this by holding some inventory, however, we will not know which item will be withdrawn next and will have to keep an inventory of each item: A, B, and so on. If all earlier processes start doing this, piles of inventory will form in every corner of the plant.

Therefore, to realize a system in which the later process picks up requires us to transform the production methods of both the earlier and the later processes.

Step by step, I solved the problems related to the system of withdrawal by the later process. There was no manual and we could find out what would happen only by trying. Tension increased daily as we tried and corrected and then tried and corrected again. Repeating this, I expanded the system of pickup by the later process within the company. Experiments were always carried out at a plant within the company that did not deal with parts ordered from outside. The idea was to exhaust the new system's problems within the company first.

In 1963, we started handling the delivery of the parts ordered from outside. It took nearly 20 years. Today we frequently hear a chassis maker asking the cooperating firm to bring parts just-in-time as if "just-in-time" was the most convenient system. However, if used for picking up parts ordered from outside without first changing the production method within the company, kanban immediately becomes a dangerous weapon.

Just-in-time is an ideal system in which the items needed arrive at the side of the production line at the time and in the quantity needed. But a chassis maker cannot simply ask the cooperating firm to employ this system, because adopting just-in-time means completely overhauling the existing production system. Therefore, once decided upon, it should be undertaken with a firm and determined mind.

ESTABLISHING THE FLOW IS THE BASIC CONDITION

After World War II, our main concern was how to produce high quality goods and we helped the cooperating firms in this area. After 1955, however, the question became how to make the exact quantity needed. Then, after the oil crisis, we started teaching outside firms how to produce goods using the kanban system.

Prior to that, the Toyota Group guided cooperating firms on work or production methods, in the Toyota system. Outsiders seem to think that the Toyota system and kanban are the same thing. But the Toyota production system is the production method and the kanban system is the way it is managed.

So, up until the oil crisis, we were teaching Toyota's production methods, focusing on how to make goods as much as possible in a continuous flow. With this groundwork already done, it was very easy to give guidance to Toyota's cooperating firms on kanban.

Unless one completely grasps this method of doing work so that things will flow, it is impossible to go right into the kanban system when the time comes. The Toyota Group was able to adopt and somehow digest it because the production plant already understood and practiced the idea of establishing a flow. When people have no concept of this, it is very difficult to introduce the kanban system.

When we first tried to use the kanban system on the final assembly line, going to a machine shop of an earlier process to withdraw the items needed at the time and in the quantity needed never worked. This was only natural and not the fault of the machine shop. We realized that the system would not work unless we set up a production flow that could handle the kanban system going back process by process.

Kanban is a tool for realizing just-in-time. For this tool to work fairly well, the production processes must be managed to flow as much as possible. This is really the basic condition. Other important conditions are leveling production as much as possible and always working in accordance with standard work methods.

At Toyota's main plant, the flow between the final assembly line and the machining line was established in 1950 and the synchronization started on a small scale. From there, we kept going in reverse toward the earlier processes. We gradually laid the groundwork for the company-wide adoption of kanban so that the work and transferring of parts could be done under the kanban system. This happened gradually by gaining the understanding of all people involved.

It was only in 1962 that we could manage the kanban system company wide. After achieving this, we called the cooperating firms and asked them to study it by watching how it really worked. These people knew nothing about kanban and making them understand it without a textbook was difficult.

We asked the cooperating firms from nearby to come, a few at a time, to study the system. For example, the outside die press people came to see our die press operation and the machine shop people came to see our machine shop. This way of teaching gave us the ability to demonstrate an efficient production method in an actual production plant. As a matter of fact, they would have had difficulty understanding the system without seeing it in action.

This teaching effort started with the cooperating firms nearby and spread to the Nagoya district. In the outlying Kanto district, however, progress was delayed in part due to the distance. However, a bigger reason was because part makers in the Kanto district were supplying their products not only to Toyota but to other companies as well. They felt they could not use the kanban system just with Toyota.[2]

We decided that this would take time for them to understand, and we set out patiently. In the beginning, the cooperating firms saw kanban as troublesome. Of course, no top management

---

[2] There are three distinct regional markets in Japan: Kantō, encompassing the Tokyo area; Kansai, in the Kyoto-Osaka region; and Nagoya, wherein lies Toyota City. Each region personifies different business qualities. [David J. Lu, *Inside Corporate Japan* (Cambridge, MA: Productivity Press, 1987), Ch. 1.]

came; no directors in charge of production or managers of production departments showed up in the beginning. Usually people in charge of the operation would come, but no one very important.

At first, I believe, many firms came without knowing what was involved. But we wanted them to understand kanban and if they didn't, Toyota employees would go and help. People from nearby firms understood the system early although they faced resistance in their companies. And today it is a pleasure to see all this effort bear fruit.

USE YOUR AUTHORITY TO ENCOURAGE THEM

In the beginning, everyone resisted kanban because it seemed to contradict conventional wisdom. Therefore, I had to experiment with kanban within my own sphere of authority. Of course, we tried to avoid interfering with the regular work going on.

In the 1940s, I was in charge of the machine shop and the assembly line. At the time, there was only one plant. By the end of the labor dispute in 1950, there were two production departments in the main plant, No. 1 and No. 2. I managed the latter. Kanban could not be tried in No. 1 because its forging and casting processes would affect the plant as a whole. Kanban could be applied only in No. 2's machining and assembly processes.

I soon became manager of the Motomachi plant when it was completed in 1959 and began experimenting with kanban there. Because the crude materials came from the main plant, however, kanban could be used only between the machine shop, press shop, and assembly line.

In 1962, I was named manager of the main plant. Only then was kanban implemented in forging and casting, making it a company-wide system at last.

It took 10 years to establish kanban at the Toyota Motor Company. Although it sounds like a long time, I think it was natural because we were breaking in totally new concepts. It was, nonetheless, a valuable experience.

To make kanban understood throughout the company, we had to involve everyone. If the manager of the production department understood it while the workers did not, kanban would not have worked. At the foreman level, people seemed quite lost because they were learning something totally different from conventional practice.

I could yell at a foreman under my jurisdiction, but not at a foreman from the neighboring department. Thus, getting people in every corner of the plant to understand naturally took a long time.

During this period, Toyota's top manager was a man of great vision who, without a word, left the operation entirely to me. When I was — rather forcefully — urging foremen in the production plant to understand kanban, my boss received a considerable number of complaints. They voiced the feeling that this fellow Ohno was doing something utterly ridiculous and should be stopped. This must have put the top manager in a difficult position at times, but even then he must have trusted me. I was not told to stop and for this I am grateful.

In 1962, kanban was adopted company-wide; it had earned its recognition. After that, we entered a high-growth period — the timing was excellent. I think the gradual spread of kanban made possible the strong production yield.

While in charge of the assembly line, I applied the just-in-time system there. The most important processes for assembly were the earlier processes of machining and body painting. The bodies came from the die press section. The machining process was difficult to connect by kanban to the crude material section but we were satisfied to accumulate experience as we worked to link up the machining process. This period was valuable because we could identify kanban's inadequacies.

MOUNTAINS SHOULD BE LOW AND VALLEYS SHOULD BE SHALLOW

To make the second rule of kanban work (having the earlier process produce only the amount withdrawn by the later process) manpower and equipment in each production process must be prepared in every respect to produce the quantities needed at the time needed.

In this case, if the later process withdraws unevenly in terms of time and quantity, the earlier process must have extra manpower and equipment to accommodate its requests. This becomes a heavy burden. The greater the fluctuation in quantity picked up, the more excess capacity is required by the earlier process.

To make matters worse, the Toyota production system is tied through synchronization not only to each production process within the Toyota Motor Company but also to the production processes of the cooperating firms outside Toyota using kanban. Because of this, fluctuations in production and orders at Toyota's final process have a negative impact on all earlier processes.

To avoid the occurrence of such negative cycles, the large chassis maker, specifically Toyota's final automobile assembly line (the "first process"), must lower the peaks and raise the valleys in production as much as possible so that the flow surface is smooth. This is called production leveling, or load smoothing, in the Toyota production system.

Ideally, leveling should result in zero fluctuation at the final assembly line, or the last process. This is very difficult, however, because more than 200,000 cars monthly come off the several assembly lines at Toyota in an almost infinite number of varieties.

The number of varieties reaches thousands just by considering the combinations of car size and style, body type, engine size, and transmission method. If we include colors and combinations of various options, we will rarely see completely identical cars.

Modern society's diverse wants and values are clearly seen in the variety of cars. In fact, it is certainly this diversity that has reduced the effectiveness of mass production in the automobile industry. In adapting to this diversity, the Toyota production system has been much more efficient than the Ford-style mass-production system developed in America.

Toyota's production system was originally conceived to produce small quantities of many types for the Japanese environment. Consequently, on this foundation it evolved into a production system that can meet the challenge of diversification.

While the traditional planned mass-production system does not respond easily to change, the Toyota production system is very elastic and can take the difficult conditions imposed by diverse market demands and digest them. The Toyota system has the flexibility to do this.

After the oil crisis, people started paying attention to the Toyota production system. I would like to make clear that the reasons lie in the system's unsurpassed flexibility in adapting to changing conditions. This capacity is the source of its strength even in a low-growth period when quantity does not increase.

CHALLENGE TO PRODUCTION LEVELING

Let me tell a story about a specific case of production leveling. In Toyota's Tsutsumi plant, production is leveled on two assembly lines making passenger cars: Corona, Carina, and Celica.

In one line, the Corona and Carina flow alternately. They do not run Coronas in the morning and Carinas in the afternoon. This is to maintain a level load. The lot size for single items is kept as small as possible. Great care is taken to avoid generating undesirable fluctuation in the earlier process.

Even the production of large numbers of Coronas is leveled. For example, suppose we make 10,000 Coronas working 20 days a month. Assume that this breaks down to 5,000 sedans, 2,500 hardtops, and 2,500 wagons. This means that 250 sedans, 125 hardtops, and 125 wagons are made daily. These are arranged on the production line as follows: one sedan, one hardtop, then a sedan, then a wagon, and so on. This way, the lot size and fluctuation in production can be minimized.

The finely tuned production carried out in the final automobile assembly line is Toyota's mass production process. That this type of production can be carried out demonstrates that the earlier processes, such as the die press section, have settled into the new system after breaking away from the traditional planned mass-production system.

In the beginning, the idea of leveling to reduce lot size and minimize the mass production of single items placed too heavy a demand on the die press section. It had been a long-accepted production fact that continuous punching with one die in the press brings the cost down. It was considered common sense to produce in the largest lots possible and punch continuously without stopping the press.

The Toyota production system, however, requires leveled production and the smallest lots possible even though it seems contrary to conventional wisdom. So, how did the die press section cope with this problem?

Making lots small means we cannot punch with one die for very long. To respond to the dizzying variety in product types, the die must be changed often. Consequently, setup procedures must be done quickly.

The same is true for other machine sections, all the way back to the earlier processes. Even the cooperating firms supplying parts are using buzz words like "reduce lot size" and "shorten setup time" — ideas completely contrary to past practice.

In the 1940s, Toyota's die changes took two to three hours. As production leveling spread through the company in the 1950s, setup times went to less than one hour and as little as 15 minutes. By the late 1960s, it was down to a mere 3 minutes.

In summary, the need for quick die changes was generated and steps were taken to eliminate the adjustments — something never discussed in previous work manuals. To do this, everybody chipped in with ideas while workers were trained to shorten changeover times. Within the Toyota Motor Company and its cooperating firms, people's desire to achieve the new system intensified beyond description. The system became the product of their effort.

PRODUCTION LEVELING AND MARKET DIVERSIFICATION

As I already mentioned, production leveling is much more advantageous than the planned mass-production system in responding to the diverse demands of the automobile market.

We can say this with confidence. Generally speaking, however, diversification of the market and production leveling will not necessarily be in harmony from the beginning. They have aspects that do not accommodate each other.

It is undeniable that leveling becomes more difficult as diversification develops. However, I want to emphasize again that, with effort, the Toyota production system can cope with it well enough. In keeping market diversification and production leveling in harmony, it is important to avoid the use of dedicated facilities and equipment that could have more general utility.

For example, taking the Corolla, the world's largest mass-produced car in 1978, a definite production plan can be set up on a monthly basis. The total cars needed can be divided by the number of work days (the number of days on which actual production can be carried out) to level the number of cars to be made per day.

On the production line, even finer leveling must be done. To let sedans or coupes flow continuously during a fixed time interval is contrary to leveling in that the same item is allowed to flow in a batch. Of course, if two production lines were used, one for sedans and one for coupes exclusively, leveling would be easier.

But this is not possible because of restrictions in space and equipment. What can be done? If one production line is set up so that sedans and coupes can both be assembled in any sequence, then leveling would be possible.

Viewed from this perspective, mass production using dedicated facilities, once the strongest weapon for reducing cost, is not necessarily the best choice. Of increasing importance are efforts to put together specialized, yet versatile production processes through the use of machines and jigs that can handle minimal quantities of materials. More effort is needed to find the minimum facilities and equipment required for general use. To do this, we must utilize all available knowledge to avoid undermining the benefits of mass production.

By studying every process like this, we can keep diversification and production leveling in harmony and still respond to customer orders in a timely manner. As market demands grow more diverse, we must put even more emphasis on this point.

KANBAN ACCELERATES IMPROVEMENTS

Under its first and second rules, kanban serves as a withdrawal order, an order for conveyance or delivery, and as a work order. Rule three of kanban prohibits picking up or producing goods without a kanban. Rule four requires a kanban to be attached to the goods. Rule five requires 100 percent defect-free products (that is, do not send anything defective to the subsequent process). Rule six urges us to reduce the number of kanban. When these rules are faithfully practiced, the role of kanban expands.

A kanban always moves with the needed goods and so becomes a work order for each process. In this way, a kanban can prevent overproduction, the largest loss in production.

To ensure that we have 100 percent defect-free products, we must set up a system that automatically informs us if any process generates defective products; that is, a system in which the process generating defective products feels the pinch. This is indeed where the kanban system is unrivaled.

Processes producing in a just-in-time system do not need extra inventory. So, if the prior process generates defective parts, the next process must stop the line. Furthermore, everyone sees when this happens and the defective part is returned to the earlier process. It is an embarrassing situation meant to help prevent the recurrence of such defects.

If the meaning of "defective" goes beyond defective parts to include defective work, then the meaning of "100 percent defect-free products" becomes clearer. In other words, insufficient standardization and rationalization creates waste *(muda)*, inconsistency *(mura)*, and unreasonableness *(muri)* in work procedures and work hours that eventually lead to the production of defective products.

Unless such defective work is reduced, it is difficult to assure an adequate supply for the later process to withdraw or to achieve the objective of producing as cheaply as possible. Efforts to thoroughly stabilize and rationalize the processes are the key to successful implementation of automation. Only with this foundation can production leveling be effective.

It takes a great effort to practice the six rules of kanban discussed above. In reality, practicing these rules means nothing less than adopting the Toyota production system as the management system of the whole company.

Introducing kanban without actually practicing these rules will bring neither the control expected of kanban nor the cost reduction. Thus, a half-hearted introduction of kanban brings a hundred harms and not a single gain. Anyone who recognizes the effectiveness of kanban as a production management tool for reducing cost must be determined to observe the rules and overcome all obstacles.

It is said that improvement is eternal and infinite. It should be the duty of those working with kanban to keep improving it with creativity and resourcefulness without allowing it to become fixed at any stage.

CARRYING CARTS AS KANBAN

I have described the kanban as the piece of paper contained in a rectangular vinyl envelope. An important role of kanban is to provide the information that connects the earlier and later processes at every level.

A kanban always accompanies the goods and thus is the essential communications tool for just-in-time production. In the following case, the kanban functions even more effectively when combined with carrying carts.

In Toyota's main plant, a carrying cart of limited load capacity is used to pick up the assembled engines and transmissions in the final assembly line. A kanban is attached to the engine, for example, carried on this carrying cart.

But the carrying cart itself simultaneously performs the role of a kanban. Thus, when the standard number of engines at the side of the final assembly line (three to five units) is reached, the worker in the section that attaches the engine to the vehicle takes the vacant carrying cart to the engine assembly point (the earlier process), picks up a cart loaded with the necessary engines, and leaves the vacant carrying cart.

In principle, a kanban should be attached. In this case, however, even if the kanban itself is not attached to the carrying cart, the earlier and later processes can talk to each other, decide on the number of carrying carts to be used, and agree on the pickup rules so that the same effectiveness can be achieved by using simple number plates.

For example, when there is no vacant cart in the unit assembly line, there is no place to put completed units. Overproduction is automatically checked even if someone wants to make more. The final assembly line also cannot hold any extra inventory other than that on the carrying carts.

As the basic idea of kanban spreads throughout manufacturing, many tools like the carrying cart kanban can be devised. Nonetheless, we should not forget to always use the principles of kanban.

Let me raise another example. In an automobile production plant, chain conveyers are used as a way to rationalize, or improve, transportation. Parts can be suspended from the conveyor while being painted or carried to the assembly line on it. Of course, it goes without saying that no part can be hung on the conveyor without a kanban on the hanger.

When many types of parts are carried by this chain conveyer, indicators designating the parts needed are attached to the hangers at regular intervals to eliminate any mistake in the type of part, quantity, or time it is required. Thus, by installing a means of conveying only the parts indicated, smooth delivery and withdrawal of needed parts can be achieved. Production leveling is maintained by circulating the part-indicators with the conveyer.

THE ELASTIC NATURE OF KANBAN

I would like to give another example that demonstrates the true meaning of kanban.

The propeller shaft is an important auto part that causes problems sporadically in assembly. To prevent uneven rotation, workers attach small pieces of iron as balance weights during the finishing stage.

There are five types of balance weights. A piece suitable for a particular degree of imbalance in the propeller shaft is selected from the five types and attached. If there is no imbalance, no balance weight is needed.

In some cases, many pieces have to be attached. The number of different balance weights used is irregular. Unlike ordinary parts, the amount needed is not known when the production plan is written. Thus, with these parts, unless production is well managed, an urgent need may arise, while in other cases, unnecessary inventory piles up.

We might say this is not a serious problem because it is only a small piece of iron. In reality, however, it is a big problem because extra indirect workers may be kept idle. This is yet another challenge to Toyota's kanban system.

Kanban must work effectively to maintain just-in-time in the plant. And for kanban to be effective, stabilization and production leveling are indispensable conditions. Some people think, however, that kanban can be used only to manage parts processed in daily stable quantities — but this is a mistake. Others think kanban cannot be used without a steady withdrawal of parts. This is also wrong thinking.

Kanban was introduced to manage the balance weight problem, one of the most difficult processes in automobile production. Since the amount was not stable, the first step toward effectively managing the production, transfer, and use of the balance weight was to know at all times how many of the five weights were held in each process. With these amounts in mind, we had to find a way to trigger production or transfer so that an urgent need or excess inventory could not arise.

What was the result? By attaching a kanban to the actual balance weights, types and quantities available could be identified accurately. With the kanban circulating between the processes, production and transfer of the parts could be initiated in the necessary sequence at all times. As a result, inventories of the five weights were kept constant and, eventually, reduced drastically.

The kanban system is not inflexible or stiff. As Toyota's experience with the balance weights demonstrates, kanban is an effective tool even for management of special parts where the amount used is unstable and where kanban may seem inapplicable at first.

Chapter 12 is a selection from *Just in Time for Today and Tomorrow*, Taiichi Ohno with Setsuo Mito (Cambridge: Productivity Press, 1988)

12

Management's Power to Grasp and Act on the *Now!* Needs of the Marketplace

THEME: NOT THE PAST OR FUTURE BUT THE *NOW!*

The Ford system was one of the moving forces behind the modernization of U.S. industry and the arrival of the American Century. Mass production was a powerful means to reduce costs and popularize the automobile, a product of modern civilization with its seemingly unlimited possibilities.

The system that Henry Ford developed has been called technically "assembly based on a flow system," but perhaps it is most appropriately described as a "planned mass-production system." That word "planned" has such a profound meaning that indeed we may call it a villain. Let me explain. In the case of the Ford system, "planned" means to strive to maximize the quantity produced within a given time period. This reduces costs and thereby lowers the price to the consumer, which in turn popularizes the automobile making it easier to sell. This is the plan in theory.

In terms of popularizing the automobile, however, Alfred P. Sloan of General Motors outrivaled Henry Ford's Model T. He saw the marketplace's coming diversification and successfully upgraded the popular car through a strategy of product differentiation. This created a new era in competition. But in manufacturing terms, he was unable to surpass Ford's planned mass-production system.

Mass production accelerates the shift from human labor to production by machines. Its goal is to reduce costs and make production as simple as possible.

Systems design in the twentieth century — such as the one established and popularized by Henry Ford — was based on an overall view of assembly of finished goods in a continuous production flow, rather than a partial view of individual parts, machines, or factories. This was just one of the complete systems of "mass production, mass sales" that brought modern manufacturing into a new age.

After its defeat in World War II, Japan began the process of rebuilding its economy and reentering international society. In the process, it developed manufacturing and management systems suited to Japanese markets. Of course, there were many visible signs of a mini-American-style consumer market rising from its postwar ruins. This was in part responsible for the country's rapid economic growth up until the 1973 oil crisis.

Masses of consumers stormed the market with ever-increasing demands for material satisfaction. It goes without saying that companies supplying those needs rushed to imitate the planned mass production of the Ford system. But regardless of how booming market demands may have been, it was not necessarily wise to copy exactly American-style mass production.

Even putting aside the issue of the different size and character of the Japanese market, we would have expected Japanese companies at least to strive to improve that system before adopting it. They should have modified it to suit their own market and industry conditions.

However, these companies did not do this during their time of expansion. They rushed headlong into the "big guns and warships" mentality; that is, to have the most mass-production equipment. In any case, with the possibility of selling anything they could make, Japanese companies "pushed" production onto the marketplace.

There are limits to material growth, however. At some point, it must stop or even reverse, which is precisely what happened after the first oil crisis. The starting point for the Toyota production system was recognizing that the Ford system was not necessarily the best for managing the highs and lows of material growth.

Here are the basic precepts underlying the Toyota production system:

1. Material growth is limited. It will grow, eventually decline, and approach zero.
2. Economic activity produces waves of all sizes. Waste necessarily will be created in the production activities of companies producing to meet these waves.
3. Putting aside for now the original intent of its creator, the Ford system's planned mass production in fact does produce production waste during prosperity — although it remains hidden. During recession, overproduction becomes apparent.
4. American management and its planned mass production is too often ivory-tower theory and backward looking.
5. No matter how great the market demand, each customer is different and has unique preferences. American planned mass production creates complacent suppliers who are unable to respond to needs of the marketplace and individual customers.
6. A *push* system cannot meet market needs. A *pull* system is needed so customers pull from the factory exactly what they need when they need it. A *planned* system is no more than an ivory-tower theory ignoring market trends and relying too much on market research and other past information.

The theme of the Toyota production system is not the past, not the future, but the current (*Now!*) needs of the marketplace and customer. Although extremely difficult to grasp, the *Now!* needs must drive the organization. The process of developing the Toyota production system is the history of pursuing that goal.

The approaching Information Age brings with it the management possibility of grasping the *Now!* information coming from the marketplace.

The Convenience Store Grasps the *Now!*

I think the convenience store is an inevitable product of the Information Age. By answering the needs of the times, it has taken root as a social and a business system. The convenience store conceals a great deal of human imagination at work.

Being 1,000 square feet at most, it appears at first to be nothing more than a mini-supermarket. But, as implied, it is above all "convenient" for the customer. We don't make it a point to go every evening, but if we feel like getting a copy of a recent magazine we can find one easily at the convenience store. Next to the magazines is hot coffee, which we drink if we feel like it. We easily can start up a conversation with the shopkeeper and discuss what is selling well and so forth.

We may be surprised to discover that this little shop contains anywhere from 3,000 to 3,500 items. This number would include many relatively new products, of which 6,000 to 7,000 make their appearance during the course of a year. The substitution of these "players" is so rapid that it is said that over a two-year period the entire stock is new.

A position on the starting lineup of a professional baseball team may be hard to hold, but competition is much more severe for a position on the convenience store shelf. The product life cycle is very short. While not clear whether or not consumers' tastes change at such a dizzying pace, it is clear that the competition among retailers to meet those tastes is severe. We can imagine that the pressure must be intense.

With this intense competition the mind goes to work with different management strategies and puts out all sorts of new products. The results are many kinds of products: some good, some grotesque, some fraudulent. But in the end, those not up to snuff are weeded out by the consumers.

In market competition, sellers strive to grasp that quality of "salability" necessary for success in the marketplace. Negotiation between the customer and the seller (the chooser and the chosen) is a synergistic process that gives birth to salability and often produces a popular product.

What I would like to put forth as a hypothesis here is that what was pursued as salability until now is nothing more than past information and is, in fact, useless. Using that information leads to the production of mountains of unsalable goods. We will come back to the issue of how to grasp and use salability. But for now let us realize that it is not simple to implement a management system in which products are continually changed. A high degree of management skill and management technology is necessary.

Point-of-sale (POS) information management systems are being introduced enthusiastically in the distribution and financial industries. In convenience stores also terminals are being installed to enable the headquarters to gain precise minute-by-minute information on sales trends. Looking at this situation, we think that in some way the *Now!* of the market is being grasped. It now would seem possible to use this information in developing new products. Yet, this method failed to hold true long ago.

In fact, at the end of this exciting salability and information waits a pile of unsalable inventory. This was discovered by the auto industry when it encountered the negative growth brought on by the 1973 oil crisis. The auto companies presumed that they could sell whatever they made and that demand was unlimited. They competed to see who could install the most efficient equipment and produce the greatest quantity of goods in any given time period. The receiver of this unlimited output was the dealer who became the source of information on salability.

Yet salability became "unsalability" in the face of the first oil crisis, and a new way to find true salability could not be found. Salability in fact was not *Now!* information — it merely traced past trends.

Convenience stores have thought up a clever way to avoid this danger and grapple successfully with the *Now!*. What we might call the originality of the convenience stores is that they do not get carried away with information about salability. Rather, they focus on that which does not sell, thereby grasping thoroughly the nature of unsalability. They then mercilessly remove those products from the shelves.

By rapidly removing such products, they make space available for products developed with information on salability. In this way, salability is not completely useless. The *Now!* is realized by creating empty shelves based on understanding unsalability, a cycle that allows the shopkeeper to create continuously an energetic *Now!* atmosphere in the store.

It is dangerous to chase salability too closely because it is based on past information. A forecast of the future is also based on past information. The most important information to understand is the present. But is it really possible to grasp the *Now!*? If we think we have grasped it, is it alright to put that understanding in the shape of a new product and launch it in the marketplace? Undeniably, the convenience store is the model for dealing with and living in the *Now!*

Toyota's two pillars, just-in-time and autonomation, differ from convenience stores in their time of arrival and in their approach. Yet they are similar in seeking to lead management into a new way of grappling with the *Now!*

What is *Now!* is both a philosophical and a very real question for people today. Looking ahead to the twenty-first century and a rapidly advancing Information Age, it is extremely important to find a way to grapple with and live in the *Now!*

DIALOGUE A: AN INFORMATION SYSTEM THAT PROVIDES EXACTLY WHAT IS NEEDED WHEN IT IS NEEDED

Mito: You have said that if Henry Ford were alive today he would produce a production system just like Toyota's. It must be then that his successors distorted his original intentions.

Ohno: Planned mass production, symbolized by the phrase "mass production, mass sales," brought unlimited material prosperity and gave rise to the American Century. Therefore, the entrepreneurs who used this system and those who studied it in business schools are totally entranced by its power.

During Japan's period of rapid growth from the late 1950s to the early 1970s, and in the United States since the end of the Great Depression, there has never been a sense of material scarcity. In fact, it has been an era of continuous prosperity. There have been peaks and valleys, but the general long-term trend has been towards increasing prosperity.

People end up taking such prosperity for granted. The entrepreneurs who should be sensitive to the fragility of prosperity and the university-trained professional managers came to believe that America's prosperity would continue forever.

Believing that "bigger is better," they increased the size of plants and facilities to giant proportions. Believing that "more is better," they strove to push production speed to the outer limits.

Coupling mass production with America's specialty — mass sales — they became lost in a dream. They ignored the negative side of this policy — that "mass production, mass sales" is accompanied by many forms of waste.

Mito: The "planned" in "planned mass production" carried with it an ironic meaning. America also had been a place where anything produced could be sold. Production was based on the American idea of scientific control. They felt that their success was due to the power of American-style marketing, which analyzed diverse data gathered with sophisticated market research.

But we now realize that the magical American management and marketing were in fact ivory-tower theories producing outmoded management methods based on past information. As long as prosperity continued, the waste within the organizations remained hidden.

Ohno: A glance might enable us to see some waste scattered here and there. During the years of continuous prosperity, however, more than enough surplus profits offset that waste, making management indifferent to small amounts. In an absolute sense, however, those amounts were not small. Since the system was inherently flawed, they could not grasp to what a serious extent the waste really was.

Organizations like these were weakened by bureaucratic control. Carried away with prosperity, however, the managers could not see this reality at all. This was true of Japan as well in its period of rapid growth.

The eyes of Japanese managers were blinded by prosperity and unable to see the hidden danger. That which forced all managers, indeed everyone in the world, to pay attention to hidden waste was the first oil crisis in the fall of 1973. In that regard, the oil crisis was a revolutionary event globally. That year, the "bigger is better" way of thinking came to an end.

It was also the year Japan entered a new dimension. For the first time since its defeat in World War II, Japan had reached a mature and gradual economic growth.

Waste Wreaks Havoc to the Extent That Growth Slows Down

Mito: Entering a new dimension means that the rules and previously established order no longer apply. The "mass production,

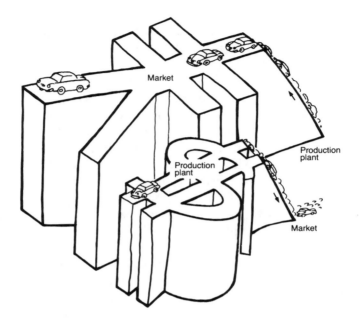

Figure 12-1. In the Toyota production system, the market *pulls* the needed goods. In the Ford system, the company forcefully *pushes* products on the market.

mass sales" system went bankrupt. The shock of the first oil crisis was enough to make the manufacturing industry reconsider its "big guns and warships" management philosophy and start to deal with its useless inventory-producing machines. It took pains to deal with the suddenly exposed waste and started looking in the direction of the Toyota production system. Oil prices had increased four or five times and more innovative thinking was demanded.

Ohno: There is a limit to the growth of all material things. Growth slows down, sometimes reversing itself. If mentally unprepared for this, we will be unable to deal with the situation when it occurs.

The Toyota production system strives to eliminate all waste because waste wreaks havoc when growth slows down or stops. In a period when anything made can be sold, useless inventory does not attract attention — but once growth drops, it shows.

As the name implies, useless inventory cannot be sold even at fire-sale prices. Useless work in process and finished goods lie idle in the warehouse while interest must be paid on the working capital. Any profits made are quickly consumed by the warehousing costs.

"Rationalization" means to get rid of fat. As they say, "an ounce of prevention is worth a pound of cure," but somehow people don't take this to heart. Only when they become overweight do they worry about keeping trim. And then, it's not easy.

Mito: The auto industry has its well-known Maxcy-Silberston curve. As the production system expands to meet rising demands, the cost curve moves in the opposite direction as average costs decrease. The Ford system was able to enjoy the fruits of this curve as long as the demand kept rising. Yet, as long as there are mountains, there must also be valleys — the demand for automobiles cannot rise forever.

When the demand starts to move back down the curve, the costs will increase as dramatically as they had decreased when moving up the curve. We can, in fact, draw a reverse Maxcy-Silberston curve.

There is a need for some sort of shock absorber to deal with decreases in demand. Since the Toyota production system is a mechanism for feeling even the smallest fluctuations in demand, it plays the role of just such a shock absorber.

Ohno: If the road is just a little rough, we can run along as usual without bumping too much. For a manager, however, there is nothing better than having a mechanism or shock absorber for dealing with changes in the external environment beyond his or her control. This is a fundamental aim of the Toyota production system.

On the surface, the economy appears to be running along smoothly. If we look at a graph of any given period of prosperity, it might be possible to imagine the future based on past trends. It is not enough, however, for managers of a private enterprise to rely on general trends. They must be aware of changes in market conditions. They must *feel* the sales fluctuations of their companies' products as they occur.

The Toyota production system allows managers to feel the competition in the marketplace and the pains of market changes.

By feeling such changes, it is possible to formulate a response. To feel such pain is to witness the continuously fleeting moments of time and grasp the information from the absolute *Now!* Being able to grasp and effectively utilize such information is a key to management survival in the Information Age.

The relationship between action and time is elusive. Any action or information quickly becomes part of the past. To rely on such past information is to fail to grasp the essence of the *Now!* market and will lead to the production of a large mountain of unsold goods.

The Toyota production system responds just-in-time to the needs of the *Now!* market by providing exactly what is needed when it is needed. Putting aside for a moment the production plant, let's return to the example of the convenience store. It anticipates the Information Age. Positioned at the very nerve center of the marketplace, through its extensive POS system, the convenience store incorporates consumer needs as they arise.

Composed of strategic software and hardware, a POS system serves as a management information weapon in a fiercely competitive market. If managers have a penetrating mind and a sense of the times, they can grasp precisely the *Now!* and put the information to use to their hearts' content.

The Convenience Store Has Penetrated the Consumer Mind

Mito: Itoh Masatoshi of Itoh Yokado is just such a manager. Two years after the first oil crisis, he visited you and left no doubt that he was quite inspired by the discussion.

Ten years later in November 1985, he introduced POS systems into every department of each store in the Itoh chain. As a first step into the Information Age, 8,000 POS registers were installed. With this system, Itoh Yokado is said to control all of its 600,000 items. This makes it possible to know instantaneously how much of which product is selling.

Within the Itoh Yokado Group, 7-Eleven Japan first introduced the POS system. Management decided on the system as an effective weapon to aid decision making by providing *Now!* information. It took the lead in Japan's distribution industry by installing POS systems companywide beginning in September

1982. The ultimate decision, of course, was made by Mr. Itoh. It was Suzuki Toshifumi, President of 7-Eleven Japan, however, who took everything the American 7-Eleven had to offer and improved upon it to create a superior Japanese model.

7-Eleven Japan was established in November 1973, immediately after the oil crisis. Mr. Suzuki had visited the United States in the late 1960s and was apparently impressed with the appearance and atmosphere of the successful 7-Eleven chain of the Southland Corporation.

At first he was surprised to find that 7-Eleven stores operated 16 or 24 hours a day. Moreover, he was amazed to find that in the small space of 1,000 square feet individual stores managed over 3,000 items. He felt the convenience store was just as the name implied — convenient. From that point on, he began collecting and assimilating all the information needed to construct such a system in Japan — distribution, store construction, the flow and arrangement of goods, and sales.

Ohno: Every product or industry has a natural life. This knowledge may have directed Mr. Suzuki's thinking. That is to say, looking at the United States, perhaps he saw a trend from centralization to dispersion. The supermarket had become a mature industry — and new growth was in fast-food chains and convenience stores located closer to the consumers' homes.

DIALOGUE B: LOOKING AT AMERICA FIRES THE IMAGINATION

Mito: Mr. Suzuki's process of conceptualization has much in common with your observations of U.S. supermarkets. He had contact with American convenience stores early on and was able to give full vent to his imagination. You, on the other hand, despite having fallen in love with the concept, were unable to visit a supermarket right away. Your imagination worked in unusual and interesting ways. By the time you actually saw a supermarket, you realized that what you previously had imagined to be a Toyota production system was actually a pseudo-Toyota Ohno system. From that realization the entire Toyota production system began to take shape.

It is a valuable case study to compare how your respective imaginations reacted to stimuli from the environment and developed your systems.

Ohno: As income rises, material needs are satisfied and leisure time and time at home increases. The trend, therefore, turns away from a system based on large mass-sales supermarkets to one based on convenience stores located closer to the customers' homes. Suzuki Toshifumi's foresight is demonstrated in his instant perception of this trend and his bringing of such enterprises to the Japanese market.

Mito: Your contribution was from the production plant floor where you created a production flow in order to eliminate waste. You did this by analyzing the relationships between workers, between machines, and between workers and machines. Ultimately, you found it impossible to eliminate all waste by dabbling in just one area of the plant.

You realized you would have to figure out how to respond quickly and accurately to the car dealers who were the actual source of information. This is where the diverse consumers come to purchase the particular car they want. As a manufacturer, you grappled with the theme of providing the market with exactly what it needed when it needed it. Changing the main point of reference from the production plant to the marketplace was quite an innovation.

Ohno: Indeed it was revolutionary. Reflecting on industrial history in Japan since the Meiji Restoration [1867-1912], we find the underlying current has been material scarcity. Therefore, the categorical imperative on the national, company, and individual level has been to produce things as rapidly as possible. The ingrained way of thinking among entrepreneurs — manufacturers in particular — was to produce rapidly and to produce a lot. Whatever was made could be sold.

Japan's manufacturing advanced rapidly in the postwar era. The 1960s marked its first experience with material prosperity. One would expect managers to lose their bearings in this new environment. No one had dared expect such a long period of peace and prosperity. On the industrial front, existing thinking was not enough to respond to the changed environment. The main change was that one could not grasp the basic manufacturing issues and address them directly without focusing on the marketplace.

Mr. Suzuki's changes in the distribution and retailing business were revolutionary. Because, however, he was not in manufacturing, he naturally encountered resistance.

The Foresight and Imagination of Suzuki Toshifumi

Mito: When speaking with Mr. Suzuki, I found it most interesting that while in the process of visiting American convenience stores he had never heard of the Toyota production system. At that time, companies in secondary industries only knew that Toyota seemed to be doing something unusual. To those in tertiary industries, the system was unknown.

You spoke of Mr. Suzuki's actions as revolutionary. In that respect, you two have something in common. You saw Toyota grow into a mammoth organization insensitive to the feelings of individual consumers. Mr. Suzuki realized the same thing about supermarkets.

Itoh Yokado also grew rapidly, becoming more bureaucratic. Essential information failed to be delivered at the needed times. Both of you realized the importance of looking at business from a market viewpoint and broke away from the current thinking. These similarities occurred even though the two of you worked in different environments.

Ohno: It does seem that as supermarkets evolved from groups of individual stores into nationwide chains that the "bigger is better" syndrome crept into current thinking. Retailing's key function, purchasing, became centralized. From that point on, it became difficult to escape the vicious spiral of "mass production, mass purchasing, mass sales." This is the same "big guns and warships" pattern we saw in the automobile industry under the Ford system.

Suzuki Toshifumi recognized that "big guns and warships" could not grasp individual consumer needs and created too much waste in the supermarket system. He foresaw the entry of smaller stores into the neighborhoods where consumers actually lived.

I dislike "big guns and warships" for the same reason. In the production plant, we must respond personally to individual orders.

Human Tenacity in Pursuit of a Complete System

Mito: Itoh Masatoshi saw the necessity of changing the retailing business. Following the first oil crisis, he went in search of a new system and saw the Toyota production system as a possible answer. Meanwhile Mr. Suzuki, his trusted subordinate, was traveling both inside and outside Japan developing new ideas. As a result, he reached an agreement with the Southland Corporation and 7-Eleven of the United States.

In certain respects, Mr. Itoh and Mr. Suzuki's relationship is comparable to that of yourself with Toyoda Eiji. At first the Toyota production system was not widely accepted in the company and for many years was repulsed as an "Ohno system." Of course, Mr. Suzuki did not encounter such resistance in implementing his plans with 7-Eleven. The similarity is that you both were trusted by your superiors and encouraged to develop your ideas into a company system. Isn't it true?

Ohno: It is true with all projects that without the trust of your superiors you cannot succeed. Toyoda Eiji and Saito Naoichi were my two superiors at this time. No matter how much criticism the system received, never once did they say "Stop!" Best of all, they quietly supported me along the way.

This relationship of trust with my superiors was unflinching. I never heard a word of criticism from outside the department: they took it all for me and never passed it on. Itoh Masatoshi and Suzuki Toshifumi likewise had a mutual trust that allowed Mr. Suzuki to carry out his plans.

Mito: A relationship based on trust gives birth to a perseverance that blossoms when it encounters a crisis.

For example, Mr. Suzuki was absorbed in the convenience store project when the first oil crisis hit. He viewed it as an opportunity to rejuvenate the company. Considering his tenacity, we realize that this was not only natural but almost inevitable. His meticulous planning and preparation created new opportunities for him to take decisive action.

Ohno: Human foresight and insight come from understanding social changes. Mr. Suzuki ably demonstrated this understanding through his work. His success was no accident.

Mito: You and Mr. Suzuki are similar in that regard. Individuals with foresight seize upon the signs of change and act upon them immediately. This ability is clear when change occurs. Although it may appear that success is due to chance, for certain individuals change is chance, meaning that any change can be an opportunity for success.

Mr. Suzuki knew prior to the oil crisis that consumers' values were changing and tastes were becoming more diverse. What had been thought of as "the public" was splintering in different directions. The ensuing economic crisis made this obvious.

In a mature economy, the compact, decentralized convenience chains should be more suitable than large, centralized supermarkets. Therefore it was extremely opportune that 7-Eleven emerged on the scene when it did. Founded as York Seven, the chain was renamed 7-Eleven in January 1978.

Ohno: Putting it that way fires my imagination. On the one hand, Mr. Itoh took a scalpel to the huge organization and made structural changes. Meanwhile Mr. Suzuki started with what we might call the blank canvas of the Japanese archipelago and made it his goal to paint a 7-Eleven in every corner of the picture.

Information Is the Password to the Future

Mito: Suzuki Toshifumi made quite an achievement in establishing convenience stores throughout Japan. In the franchise-chain system, the headquarters — in this case, 7-Eleven Japan — provides various kinds of know-how and assistance to the individual affiliated stores. In exchange for this know-how and support, sales profits are divided between headquarters and the stores — 45 percent for headquarters, 55 percent for the affiliate. This is a rational system. It gives the headquarters the resources with which to develop the software necessary to enter the Information Age.

This system of franchising convenience stores has brought both the distribution and information revolutions not only to industry but to all of society. What you are doing in Toyota plants, making individual products for individual consumers — first got its start in the various 7-Eleven stores. In the small space of 1,000 square feet, over 3,000 different items are constantly turned over.

In this system, just as in the Toyota production system, small lots and "leveled" thinking are indispensable. In developing this system, it is necessary to break away from using traditional wholesalers who only cover their own territories. We must not be confined by the old system, but must encourage the development of a new breed of wholesalers — vendors who will deliver directly to the retail outlet.

In order to construct a convenience store system, we must be able to do several things. We must have a fixed set of items deliverable on schedule in the appropriate quantities to the various stores in the chain. Because Mr. Suzuki saw the necessity of breaking away from the traditional way of doing things, he met with great resistance at first, just as you did.

Nevertheless, this resistance was overcome because of the overriding economic and social advantages offered by the convenience stores. The possibilities created by the ability to master the flow of information are limitless.

Ohno: There is, of course, the benefit of extended hours of operation, which provides convenience to the consumer. Then there is the constant turnover of different products which makes goods available that the consumer wants and removes those no longer desired. This has been one of the main forces behind the growth of convenience stores.

The turnover of goods is in fact driven by the turnover of information. A principle tool enabling 7-Eleven to capture this information was the POS system.

Can You Grasp the *Now!?*

Mito: 7-Eleven took advantage of the convergence of computers and communications early on. Recognizing the value of this development, managers use POS to achieve the maximum utility from available store space. It has become a management tool that fully utilizes all information.

In the POS system, each time something is entered on the store's cash register, the item, number, time, and price is transmitted to the home computer. The home computer analyzes this information, enabling management to develop product, purchasing, and delivery strategies for maximum total effect. In the Information Age, this is the goal towards which all companies strive.

Suzuki Toshifumi's insight was in realizing our need to solve an apparent contradiction. Most information traditionally received by management was already part of the past. *Now!* information is scarce indeed.

Ohno: That's a good point. I have often criticized the Ford system for this reason. The marketing elite from headquarters often uses old information to develop the ivory-tower plans they unilaterally impose on the plant floor. This leads to the production of mountains of useless inventory.

"What is *Now!?*" sounds like a philosophical question — but it really isn't. We ultimately are asking how the production plant is going to respond quickly to individual orders for products originating in the marketplace.

Take, for example, the customer who enters a bakery and orders ten cookies. That order for ten is the *Now!* information. Many different cookies are kept in stock. Twenty or 30 of each kind are made based on previous sales trends with the possibility that some will not sell. There is also the chance that the bakery will not have in stock what the customer wants, making it better to bake ten cookies when you get the order. *Produce only what is needed when it is needed in the amount needed.* This is the heart of just-in-time. However, it is easier in theory than in practice.

At this point, you begin wondering how best to grasp the *Now!* The Ford system, no matter how you look at it, is based on the past. When I was pondering this point, it occurred to me that the secret was somehow hidden in the design of the American supermarket.

Ultimately, the development of the Toyota production system was the pursuit of the *Now!* information before it became part of the past. It may indeed be possible now to give consumers exactly what they want when they want it.

Competition among companies in a free marketplace will become more severe as sellers bend over backwards to please the customer. But it makes no sense to sell at a loss. The only solution is to cut costs to maintain profits at a lower price.

Today, information systems will be the point of competition among companies. Whoever can best grasp and utilize *Now!* information will win.

Unsalability Is More Important Than Salability

Mito: I find it interesting that Mr. Suzuki says a 7-Eleven will not be a store of best sellers. One would think a storekeeper would want to keep popular items in stock and give them additional shelf space. Retailing has always pursued this type of salability.

However, this is also the path to mountains of unsold inventory and reliance on past information. Mr. Suzuki rejected this method. It would not be the same 7-Eleven if he did otherwise. He saw the opportunity to rely on unsalability rather than salability.

In other words, salability information is valuable when developing new products and improving old ones. However, to produce new products one after another based on past trends is no longer rooted in the present. To that end, emphasis must be on unsalability. We must constantly remove products that are not selling to create space on the shelves. You can rotate this now available space between the new and improved products based on salability. By constantly removing those products demonstrating unsalability, we create a *Now!* situation. Putting new products on empty shelves is an act that goes beyond the present to the future. Thus we see how 7-Eleven's have no connection at all with past information.

Ohno: When selling thousands of items to many, diverse consumers, it is not easy to see the whole picture. It is easier to focus on unsalability by removing non-selling products and rotating newly developed products on the shelves. This way we can be in touch with the *Now!* information continuously and provide exactly what is needed, when needed, in the quantities needed.

Don't Drown in Computer Hardware

Mito: The 7-Eleven system makes the most of human intelligence. It is a powerful concept that removes non-selling products in order to grasp current information and give life to the shelf space.

These days, POS systems are popular in all companies and industries because of the spread of personal computers and the accelerated connection between computers and telecommunications. 7-Eleven has taken advantage of all the latest information-processing machines, office automation equipment, and various computer terminals. Although the system is a product of all this hardware, the key is really the unique software 7-Eleven uses to run the system. Anyone can buy hardware but without software, it will be useless.

Some people say, irrationally, that the Toyota production system is outdated because it uses little scraps of paper (kanban) instead of sophisticated computers that enable you to transmit information instantly from a keyboard.

Ohno: I don't oppose introducing personal computers or other terminals into the factory. But to forget the original purpose of kanban and ridicule the scraps of paper invites a terrible result.

Using the keyboard of a personal computer to say "Give me this much of that at this time" simply plays the same role of kanban. The issue is knowing what the advantage is. There is no merit in excessively fast transmission of information. The essence of the Toyota production system is just-in-time. To transmit information too fast invites overproduction and its wastes.

These little scraps of paper, on the other hand, check overproduction. Furthermore, they prevent producing defective goods, concealing problems, and help control inventory. Of course, the personal computer is amazing as a product of modern civilization. But its true value in the production plant will be demonstrated only when combined with extensive telecommunications networks.

Mito: As you suggest, as it enters the Information Age, Japan suffers from an imbalance between hardware and software. This lag in software development is especially clear in comparison to America. For example, the United States is ahead in Information Networking Systems (INS), Value-Added Networks (VAN), Local Area Networks (LAN), and Cable Television (CATV), among others. As information is able to transcend national borders via space satellites, these systems have great significance.

However, in facing the Information Age, we must realize that even a scrap of paper is superior to a computer if the computer is not used intelligently. The scrap of paper is, in fact, information and mental software.

Merely installing a personal computer in every home and establishing a telecommunications network will not be enough.

Creating a flow of information will not even be enough. Money and goods must flow through this network as well. We must be able to place an order on the keyboard and arrange for the transfer of funds and home delivery of the product. The Toyota production system is an advanced information system. When given strategic software, it will blossom and achieve success as a management system of the Information Age.

MITO'S COMMENTARY

Studying Henry Ford's Awareness of Time and Waste, We Realize That Were He Alive Today He Would Do the Same as Taiichi Ohno.

Taiichi Ohno believes that were Henry Ford alive today, they would both be creating the same kind of system. He argues that Mr. Ford had a keen awareness of time and waste.

The following is a passage from Henry Ford's book, *Today and Tomorrow*, first published in 1926:

> *The time element in manufacturing stretches from the moment the raw material is separated from the earth to the moment when the finished product is delivered to the ultimate consumer. It involves all forms of transportation and has to be considered in every national scheme of service. It is a method of saving and serving which ranks with the application of power and the division of labor.*[1]

If we were operating today under the methods of 1921, we should have on hand raw materials to the value of about one hundred and twenty million dollars, and we should have unnecessarily in transit finished products to the value of about fifty million dollars. Instead of that, we have an average investment of only about

---

[1] Henry Ford with Samuel Crowther, *Today and Tomorrow*, Garden City, NY: Doubleday, Page & Company, 1926, 108-109. (Long out of print, this book is currently available in a 1988 anniversary reprint edition from Productivity Press.)

fifty million dollars, or, to put it another way, our inventory, raw and finished, is less than it was when our production was only half as great.

> *The extension of our business since 1921 has been very great, yet, in a way, all this great expansion has been paid for out of money which, under our old methods, would have lain idle in piles of iron, steel, coal, or in finished automobiles stored in warehouses. We do not own or use a single warehouse!*

It's amazing that even in the 1920s this kind of thinking was going on in the implementation of the Ford system. "For the masses" was the principle of this thoroughly rational system. Its goal was the total elimination of waste. The following words of Ford come straight from the heart of an entrepreneur:

> *Hiring two men to do the job of one is a crime against society. Also, to carry a product 500 miles to the consumer, if that product can be found within 250 miles, is a crime. For a railroad to deliver in ten days when it might deliver in five is grand larceny.*[2]

We find the essence of his thinking about wasting time in the following excerpt:

> *It is not possible to repeat too often that waste is not something which comes after the fact. Restoring an ill body to health is an achievement, but preventing illness is a much higher achievement. Picking up and reclaiming the scrap left over after production is a public service, but planning so that there will be no scrap is a higher public service.*
>
> *Time waste differs from material waste in that there can be no salvage. The easiest of all wastes, and the hardest to correct, is this waste of time, because wasted time does not litter the floor like wasted material. In our industries, we think of time as human energy. If we buy more material than we need for production, then we are storing human energy —*

---

2 Ibid., 109.

and probably depreciating its value. One may buy ahead on speculation in the hope of realizing an unearned profit. That is both poor service and poor business, because, over a term of years, the profits of speculation will not exceed the losses, and the net result to the speculator is zero, while the community itself has lost by having to make detours from the ordinary highways of trade.[3]

We see the "superrationalism" underlying Henry Ford's entrepreneurial spirit. Mr. Ford once scolded his financial officer for not considering the cost of products that couldn't be sold. His argument is convincing.

Had Henry Ford and Alfred P. Sloan Met in Competition, Perhaps the Outcome Would Have Been an American-Style Toyota System.

From 1924 to 1926 the American automobile market underwent a revolutionary change. Since the introduction of the Model T in 1908, luxury cars had been designed for a limited set of consumers. At a stroke, however, luxury cars were no longer a limited commodity but available to the public as well.

The market changed. Mr. Ford's concept of the automobile as a cheap mode of transportation evolved into Alfred P. Sloan's (1875-1966) idea that cars for the general public would improve continuously. The following comments are from Mr. Sloan's book, *My Years with General Motors:*

> *In the 1920s the American economy began a new period of expansion. Along with this came new phenomena and the market changed from what it had been in the past. It was a turning point for the automobile industry.*
>
> *These changes can be broken into four categories. One, the introduction of installment plan sales. Two, the trade-in of used cars. Three, the advent of the sedan. Four, the appearance of annual models. (If we include changes in the environment for the automobile we must add the improvement of the public*

---

[3] Ibid., 110.

*roads.) These changes now have deep roots in the automobile
industry. It is impossible to avoid consideration of them.*

*Before 1920 and for a short time thereafter, the pur-
chaser of an automobile was a first-time buyer and usually
paid in cash. He bought either a roadster or a touring car,
and the model did not differ from the year before and did not
seem as though it would change in the future. These conditions
continued for a while and, even if there was a change, it was
nothing climactic. Each of the changes occurred separately
and at its own pace, until one day we realized that there had
been a revolution in the marketplace.*[4]

Alfred Sloan was suggesting that the Model T was out of date
because customers desired newer and more luxurious automobiles.
This new era did not pass unnoticed. Mr. Sloan immediately organized GM strategy around a full-line policy. In today's language,
he foresaw the diversification of the marketplace. Entrepreneurial
businesspeople must see this diversification and develop a strategy
of segmentation.

However, we can find no evidence that he developed a new
GM production system corresponding to his new strategy of the
full- line policy. Nevertheless, his insight was brilliant. He foresaw
that which was to come in the near future: the birth and exploding
growth of the consumer society.

In his book *The Americans: The Democratic Experience*,
Daniel J. Boorstin gives a full account of American consumer
society. He describes how Sloan the manufacturer, by introducing a new automobile model yearly, turned interest toward the
consumer.

*This was the annual model. The spirit and purpose of
the annual model were, of course, quite opposite to those of
Ford and his Model T. "The great problem of the future,"
Sloan wrote to Lawrence P. Fisher, maker of Fisher Bodies, on
September 9, 1927, "is to have our cars different from each
other and different from year to year." The annual model,*

---

[4] Alfred P. Sloan, *My Forty Years with General Motors*, Garden City, NY:
Doubleday, 1964.

then, was part of a purposeful, planned program. And it was based on creating expectations of marvelous, if usually vague, novelties-always-to-come.

Sloan and his able collaborators at General Motors set up a styling department (which by 1963 would employ more than fourteen hundred workers). They showed a concern for color, they "invented" new colors, and gave aphrodisiac names to old colors. Now for the first time their automobile designers included women. "It is not too much to say," Sloan explained, "that the 'laws' of the Paris dressmakers have come to be a factor in the automobile industry — and woe to the company which ignores them."[5]

Mr. Sloan's entrepreneurial spirit was in no way inferior to his rival's. By capitalizing on the diversification of the market, with his wide variation strategy he was able to overpower Henry Ford and achieve great success. Yet with such an extreme emphasis on the marketplace, he failed to devote sufficient time to rationalizing his production system. Because of this lack of competition, the Ford system, its hidden defects aside, became more deeply rooted in the American auto industry.

In stronger words, Alfred Sloan incurred high costs both in losses and waste to produce a very ostentatious Cadillac just to upstage the Model T. To cover himself, he charged a very high price.

In the 1960s and 1970s, as external labor-union problems compounded the many internal problems of the production plant, the American automobile industry fell apart. While a decisive and thorough management revolution is going on, the 1980s find the unions beginning to adjust their attitudes.

Did Henry Ford's sense of time and awareness of waste really get to the heart of the matter? And just how insightful were Mr. Sloan's ideas of diversification and segmentation? It seems that the Toyota production system is the best of both worlds.

---

[5] Daniel J. Boorstin, *The Americans: The Democratic Experience*, New York: Vintage Books, 1974, 552.

Sooner or Later, All Growth Levels Off.
While an Economist May Concur with this Statement,
Managers of Private Enterprises Must Continue to
Seek Ways to Create New Growth Opportunities

All real growth is structural. The interrelationship of the elements of such growth changes and becomes more complex over time.

Insofar as all organizations are living things, they are growing. For growth to continue, regeneration is indispensable. Fresh air is needed. New strengths will come forward and replace the old. The forces of positive and negative growth will collide and ultimately result in harmony. An organization's form and essence can regenerate itself completely within five or ten years.

The Toyota production system gives the impression of being a "hard" system promoting a concrete, fixed way of doing things in its pursuit of mechanizing, automating, and rationalizing the production plant. As a management system, however, Toyota has left that dimension behind. Taiichi Ohno accepts the challenge of helping organizations regenerate themselves because he recognizes that growth is limited. This is why the Toyota system, as a system, should be "soft" — not hard.

The Dispersal of Production Leveling Marked the End
of the Maxcy-Silberston Curve. Toyota's Production System
Was Best Suited to Soften the Shock of Its Reversal.

Maxcy-Silberston curve is the concept of economies of scale that resulted from the research of the English economists Aubrey Silverston of Cambridge University and George Maxcy of Hull University. Their book *The Motor Industry*, published in 1959, presents the results of years of detailed analysis of the special characteristics of the British automobile industry.

The researchers asked what the impact was on the cost per unit when production quantities leapt from 100,000 to 200,000 units, and then to 300,000 and 400,000. The response from the automobile manufacturers was conservative. They said volumes initially doubled while total cost per unit declined 8 percent. When volume doubled the second time, however, total cost declined 5 percent. When questioned about manufacturing cost rather than total cost per unit, the decreases were even greater. They discovered that a manufacturer with a present production level of 100,000 units contemplating an increase to 400,000 units could expect a reduction of 25 percent of the controllable costs, or about 15 percent of the total cost of the automobile.

This research was done in England over a quarter of a century ago. Yet the concepts have been used and popularized in the belief that the percentage of profits increases with volume. The Maxcy-Silberston curve, in fact, became an index for all subsequent automobile manufacturers. So too did the idea that profits would decrease as volume decreased, as was the case in several recessions.

This fear was experienced following the 1973 oil crisis when Japan experienced its 1974 zero growth. The automobile industry could not escape the effects of the crisis. Restrictive laws on gasoline were passed, and the consumer movement to conserve gasoline made matters worse. Only through emphasis on total quality control (TQC) and the resultant increase of exports to America was the Japanese economy able to recover. It is safe to say that the oil crisis made a deep impact on the mind of every manager in Japan.

A concrete example of this was the rapid diffusion of the Toyota production system immediately after the oil crisis. Manufacturing firms involved in the automobile industry experienced a tremendous shock when they suddenly found themselves on a reverse Maxcy-Silberston curve.

In fact, from this point on, the Toyota production system began spreading to other industries as well. Until then most companies had indulged themselves because they could sell anything they made. They were disinclined to listen to the diverse needs of their customers. They soon realized, however, the impossibility of increasing profits because the production gains dictated by the Maxcy-Silberston curve were not materializing.

In this respect, this curve and all the other logical extensions of the Ford "bigger is better," "planned mass production" system became myths.

Free Information!

If you liked this book, you may be interested in our other publications on continuous improvement in productivity, quality, and total employee involvement. Just drop this card in the mail and we'll put you on our mailing list.

Name _____

Title _____

Company _____

Street Address _____

City _____ State _____ Zip _____

Phone ( ) _____ Fax ( ) _____

Country (if outside the U.S.) _____ E-mail _____

Title of book this card was in _____

Key Code 2CARD

The old-fashioned neighborhood grocery is today the con-venience store with 7-Eleven Japan's Suzuki Toshifumi at the forefront. We cannot discuss the distribution industry the way we can operations such as steel, automobiles, and paper pulp. Lying somewhere between capital and human logic, distribu-tion is a marginal industry some think should do no further industrialization.

The above words are from Tsutsumi Seiji, (1927-), leader of the Seibu Seven Group.

To expand a little, the distribution industry is viewed from many non-economic perspectives, including political, social, and cultural. The industry itself believes it constantly must strive to modernize to keep up with the desires of its many consumers — "modernize" meaning capital logic or capital intensive. Necessarily, as the industry has modernized, it has accelerated the urbanization trend throughout the Japanese archipelago, changing the residen-tial environment of many communities.

In other words, the supermarket, empowered with capital logic, has developed through the maximum use of land and labor, revolutionizing the distribution industry. But its excessive enthusi-asm in fulfilling consumer's material needs has also disrupted the traditional landscape of many small retailers in the typical commu-nity. Mr. Tsutsumi currently is examining his company's impact on these developments.

How should the distribution industry modernize without destroying the traditional balance between history, culture, and business? The best qualified to be called a success in this struggle is the convenience store (CVS). The leader in this field is 7-Eleven Japan, spearheaded by Mr. Suzuki.

7-Eleven Japan was born in the midst of the first oil crisis. Mr. Suzuki already had perceived that the development of mass retail outlets would peak with the maturity of the consumer mar-ket. He saw retailing's need to get much closer to the consumer's home. He began investigating the American model.

In 1971 he visited Southland corporate headquarters in Dallas, Texas, to begin negotiations. When deciding whether or not there was in fact a need for convenience stores in Japan, he was struck most by the fact that conveniences for daily living were not keeping pace with advances in material prosperity.

For example, even though the trends toward a 24-hour city and the late-night family in which family members work, study, or play late at night were continuing, there were no signs of late-night stores in the neighborhoods. People's only choice was to make instant noodles at home. But it was not just the needs of the late-night consumer that were unsatisfied. He saw the time had come in Japan when consumers would appreciate the convenience offered by 7-Eleven in the morning, daytime, and evening. This just happened to coincide with the 1973 oil crisis.

---

1. Visiting Prospective Owners

A recruiting field counselor (RFC) visits an area where a new affiliate store is desired. Candidates are interviewed to see if they can fulfill the conditions required for operating a 7-Eleven.

2. Market Research

Market conditions of the prospective location are observed from different angles and the data analyzed.

3. Information about the 7-Eleven System

The philosophy and details for operation and management of a 7-Eleven store are explained until the prospective owner understands and consents.

4. Explaining the Franchise Contract

The contract is explained carefully.

5. Signing the Franchise Contract

Following explanation and consideration, the contract is signed.

6. Store Planning and Design

The design department undertakes the layout of a functional store that is easy to work in and, of course, easy to buy in. The customer path, proper temperature and lighting, and efficiency in everything from equipment to maintenance is considered.

7. Signing the contrusction Contract

An architect and construction company are brought in and a contract signed.

8. Preparation for Opening

Construction is carried out. Display stands stipulated in the design are ordered and installed. Various manuals are delivered. Opening preparations begin to accelerate.

9. Owner Education and Training

The new owner receives ten days of training required to run the store, including the opeation of the computer system.

10. Delivery and Display of Products prior to Opening

Products and vendors are selected with the advice of the RFC. Efficient delivery and product display is arranged prior to opening.

11. "Turn-key"

When preparations are complete for the store to open the following day, the cash register key is handed over ceremoniously to the new owner. The RFC steps back, passing the baton to the operation field counselor (OFC).

12. Opening

The opening is announced in the local newspaper and through distribution of flyers.

13. Operation of the 7-Eleven System

The point-of-sale (POS) system transmits information on the activity of products and customers. Another system arranges for the purchase and delivery of products. This unique combination of hardware and software supports the store owner.

14. Management Consulting Visits by the OFC

The OFC, familiar with both the 7-Eleven system and the marketplace, visits the new owner at least twice a week and serves as a pipeline for information and analysis from the network of stores linked through headquarters.

Table 12-1. 7-Eleven Japan's 14 Steps from Contract to Store Opening

The System That Absorbs the "Pains" of Market Changes

7-Eleven is a franchise chain system (FC) to which Mr. Suzuki and his staff devoted themselves to becoming masters. Their biggest challenge was developing a backup system to educate and strengthen the various stores, some of which are owned by headquarters and others by affiliated owners. Mr. Suzuki and his team met that challenge successfully.

To provide for the extended hours of year-round operation, work schedules of the owners, employees, and part-timers had to be arranged meticulously and various issues dealt with individually. For instance:

- How to manage the arrangement and delivery of 3,000 items.
- How to negotiate purchase prices that are less than a supermarket pays.
- How to share profits between headquarters and affiliate stores.
- How to appeal to neighborhood residents.
- What should be the advertising strategy.

"Management's strength is in its systematization. Because it is essential to gain acceptance from and an in-depth understanding of the consumer, the convenience store must fundamentally be a place run by and for people."

This was Mr. Suzuki's management vision. He wanted to create a convenience store that would feel pain with market changes. This management strategy is equivalent to the Toyota production system: provide what is needed when it is needed and in the quantities needed. Mr. Ohno developed his system on the plant floor; Mr. Suzuki stood in the marketplace. Yet the ideas of both are merging with an impact stimulating to the entire world of industry.

7-Eleven, the Information Store

7-Eleven Japan began installing POS systems in September 1982. The storekeeper inputs the item and quantity bought, the other products with which it was bought, and what kind of customer made the purchase. This data is assembled and analyzed at headquarters.

The winter 1985 edition of the *Itoh Yokado Quarterly* reported that "in this manner, we are able to computerize the management of over 5,000 items. Analyzing sales trends can help us better understand salability and unsalability to come up with product strategies . . ."

The introduction of POS systems in Japan marked a new era and the development of new dimensions in POS technology. POS innovations as of 1985 are as follows:

1. Data entry people with the ability to process ten times more information five times faster.
2. Equipment for graphic display of information in the stores.
3. Presentations of real-time graphics made possible by the combination of data entry people and graphic display equipment.
4. The increased technical ability to transmit information, giving stores an almost instantaneous understanding of market trends.
5. Capabilities to accommodate those products not easily computer coded (soft drinks, for example). These products can be entered now with special keys and codes allowing management to collect yet another kind of data.

These simple, flexible management software systems respond to changing market conditions and complement the advanced hardware already installed. With the "informationization" of the stores, Mr. Suzuki sought to achieve his goal of humanizing 7-Eleven. He, better than anyone, has understood exactly what the market *Now!* is and has used this information to his advantage.

7-Eleven has been able to modernize retailing without destroying the traditional balance between history, culture, and commerce. In January 1986, there were 2,604 7-Eleven stores in Japan. There were also 1,178 Lawson stores of the Daiei Chain and 708 Familymart stores of the Seibu Seven Group.

Mutual Trust Is Best Connected with an Invisible Thread. The Relationships between Toyoda Eiji and Taiichi Ohno and that between Itoh Masatoshi and Suzuki Toshifumi Approach this Ideal.

Max Picard, in his book *The World of Silence*,[6] says that silence is neither negative nor inexplicable. Rather, silence is a positive phenomenon existing independently in the world order. These are the very philosophical words of a philosopher, and they are mentioned

---

6 Max Picard, *Die Welt des Schweigens,* Erlenbach-Zurich: E. Reutsch, 1959. Published in German in 1948 and translated into English in 1952.

here because they explain a lot about the activities of Taiichi Ohno within Toyota.

In the spring of 1932, in the midst of the Great Depression, Taiichi Ohno graduated from the mechanical engineering department of Nagoya High School and joined Toyoda Spinning and Weaving. He started off in textiles but was transferred to Toyota Motors in 1943. After the war, he remained in the automobile company. He was impressed by Toyoda Kiichirō's just-in-time idea and inspired by the inventive genius of the founder Toyoda Sakichi. His own contribution was in the field of autonomation. Still in his thirties and full of energy, Mr. Ohno set out to develop an Ohno system to challenge the Ford system.

His career and influence advanced rapidly. In 1947, at age 33, he was put in charge of the main factory in the general assembly division at headquarters. In 1948 he became responsible for the No. 2 machining facility at the Koromo plant. In 1949 he was made machine shop manager. In 1953 he was second in charge of manufacturing and promoted to a company director. Throughout this period, he was given more and more freedom to experiment with just-in-time methods.

His efforts aroused opposition. He tried a "supermarket system" in 1953. To create a production flow, he rearranged equipment on the floor and connected the assembly plant to the body plant. He strove to implement visual control. These measures were revolutionary compared to existing operations.

They refuted the existing conventions in manufacturing and wounded the pride of many. Anger was directed not so much at Mr. Ohno himself but at his superiors. He would not agree, as the Ford system dictated, that the bigger the lot size, the better, and that they should try to limit the number of die changes. Indeed, it would be unusual had there been no opposition from those in manufacturing.

Throughout his 35 years at Toyota, Mr. Ohno's superiors were Toyoda Eiji, currently chairman, and Saitō Naichi. They absorbed all the discontent and grumbling directed at Mr. Ohno from the factory and never mentioned it to him. They only wanted him to continue finding ways to reduce manufacturing costs. These men were bound together by an invisible thread of mutual trust, which brings to mind earlier words.

Reflecting on the past, Taiichi Ohno says:

I knew all too well how they worried about me and what I was doing. Yet they never said "Do this!" or "Do that!" For my part, I never had to say "I'd like to do this" or "Please let me do that." I just did everything I thought had to be done. Had I asked permission, my resolve would have weakened because of the pressure to prove what I was doing. Had either side said anything, the relationship would have collapsed.

Max Picard says something similar when he notes that in the realm of silence, rather than us gazing at silence, silence watches us. In the same way, Itoh Masatoshi's relationship with Suzuki Toshifumi is supported by this silent thread.

The Toyota Information System Underlies the Toyota Production System. As We Enter the Information Age, It Will Demonstrate Not Only Refinement But Tremendous Development as Well.

The just-in-time system of providing exactly what is needed in the quantity and at the time needed is an essential element of the Toyota production system. This applies not only to hardware such as automobiles and parts but to the software of information as well.

In fact, Toyota's information system is integral to its production system. Mr. Ohno gives an overview of this arrangement.

First, the Toyota Motor Company has an annual plan. This means the rough number of cars — for instance, two million — to be produced and sold during the current year.

Next, there is the monthly production schedule. For example, the type and quantities of cars to be made in March are announced internally early on, and in February, a more detailed schedule is "set." Both schedules are sent to the outside cooperating firms as they are developed. Based on these plans, the daily production schedule is established in detail and includes production leveling.

In the Toyota production system, the method of setting up this daily schedule is important. During the last half of the previous month, each production line is informed of the daily production quantity for each product type. At Toyota, this is called the daily level. On the other hand, the daily sequence schedule is sent only to one place — the final assembly line. This is a special characteristic of Toyota's information system. In other companies, scheduling information is sent to every production process.

This is how the Toyota information system works in production: when the production line workers use parts at the side of the line for assembly, they remove the kanban. The preceding process makes as many parts as were used, eliminating the need for a special production schedule. In other words, the kanban acts as a production order for the earlier processes.[7]

The main — as well as unique — feature of the Toyota information system is that it determines what is the Now! information. By trying not to send excess information, it prevents waste arising from overproduction. At the same time, it avoids the confusion that results in other firms when production plans are changed.

As we proceed into the Information Age, Toyota will take advantage of the convergence between computers and telecommunications to produce an even more refined Toyota information system. Furthermore, the progression toward an information network will accelerate with Toyota at the center and include all the factories, dealers, affiliated companies, and parts suppliers. We plan to develop a global Toyota information system to match the times.

---

[7] Taiichi Ohno, *Toyota Production System: Beyond Large Scale Production*, Cambridge, Massachusetts: Productivity Press, 1988, pp 48-49.

Chapters 13 and 14 are selections from *The Idea Book: Improvement Through TEI (Total Employee Involvement)*, Japan Management Association, editors (Cambridge: Productivity Press, 1988)

13
The Joy of Creation and Invention

THE UNIQUE HUMAN BEING

If people did not think, we would not be much different from dogs, cats, rats, and other animals. In fact, lacking the sharp fangs of dogs, the agility of cats, or the environmental adaptability of rats, we are generally weaker and more vulnerable than animals. The wonder of humanness lies in the ability to think.

Through thinking, humans have learned to control nature and make life more convenient and rewarding. Most of us learned in school who invented the conveniences that surround us — the light bulb, telephone, printing press, automobile, steam engine, and so on. But what about the inventors of the tools you are using now — for example, the pen or pencil in your hand? Can you name the inventor of a piece of office equipment, or a shop machine, or a hand tool and its components? How about the inventors of desks, chairs, blackboards, coffee cups, plates, shoes, or clothing? Nobody knows them.

At work and at home we are surrounded by products whose inventors we don't know. Each product, nevertheless, is the embodiment of human creativity and improvements on prior ideas. Every invention reflects human history — the story of ordinary people applying their creative drive to the pursuit of convenience, ease, and a higher quality of life. Civilization rests on such past achievements and the unique adaptability that has enabled humans to survive and thrive on the earth.

WHY WE MAKE SUGGESTIONS

Instead of asking, "Why do we make suggestions?" we might ask, "What makes us express our creativity? Why are we always looking for ways to improve things?" The answer is obvious. It is human nature to use our creativity to make things better and easier.

Of course, it is important for any organization that its members adhere to established standards and do their work properly. However, if we followed the rules blindly without making any creative contribution, we would be no different from machines and robots.

Many ideas occur to us while we work: "This action seems awkward," or "This is wasteful!" or "Our customers would like the product better if we did it this way." These ideas give us important clues to make our work more successful.

The job you are doing now is not perfect. It may involve many inefficiencies. The equipment and machinery, the jigs and fixtures, the office automation systems, and the work standards were probably designed by talented individuals. None of them, however, have direct knowledge of the inconveniences you, the user, experience.

Correcting such deficiencies and inconveniences is up to you. Only you can provide the answer, because the inconveniences you notice are intrinsically your experience.

Improvement is the process through which you develop your own solutions. The *suggestion system* is the process through which your solutions are adopted by management.

Look around you. What you see is the job you must do. You know a lot about the job and its peculiarities. Does the equipment or tool you use have a peculiarity only you know about? Is there an inconvenience that only you know? Is there a method you've always felt should be used?

You can probably answer yes to one of these questions. No matter how trivial it may seem, any change that improves a process or eliminates an inconvenience is welcomed. A greater benefit is achieved when many small problems are solved one by one.

If a worker only follows orders, he or she is little more than a robot or a part of a machine.

However, a human being senses and thinks while working.

Figure 13-1.

Idea

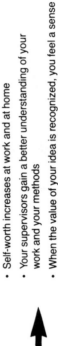

- There is no need to make things more complicated than they already are. It's important to realize that you are using the machine, not the other way around. This will make "thinking" enjoyable so that you can forget the passage of time and overcome minor obstacles.
- You will learn to look at a piece of paper or a bolt with quality, cost, and safety in mind.

Suggestion

- Writing your suggestions improves analytic skill, reasoning ability, and writing skill. This leads to confidence.

Applying the idea at the workplace

- It is very satisfying to see your suggestion steadily improving a workplace. Other workers will welcome ideas that make their jobs easier.

Results

- Easier work
- Safer working conditions
- Reduced work errors
- Improved productivity and reduced cost
- Improved service and more satisfied customers

Personal recognition

- Self-worth increases at work and at home
- Your supervisors gain a better understanding of your work and your methods
- When the value of your idea is recognized, you feel a sense of accomplishment that motivates you to do more.

Receiving a reward

- One of the biggest thrills in a suggestion system is to receive a reward. As one worker put it, "I can remember how happy I was to receive $250 for proposing 35 suggestions in one month. I like going out, but my pocket money doesn't go very far when bar hopping. The award made a big difference in my personal budget."

Self-motivation

- You have something to look forward to and you can be hopeful about the future.

- You gain an increased understanding of the work.

- One good improvement may be the trigger you need to qualify for a higher level job. The personal benefits of making suggestions increase as you make more suggestions on your own initiative. Creative suggestion-making is an important self-educational tool.

Improved interpersonal relationships in the workplace

- Everyone appreciates suggestions that improve the working environment and alleviate some of its pressures and problems. It is satisfying to be able to help fellow workers, and to benefit in turn from their suggestions. This promotes good interpersonal relationships in the workplace.

The company and the individual workers improve together

Figure 13-2.

WHAT A SUGGESTION SYSTEM CAN DO

A suggestion system has a simple basic structure. Each day, as workers find solutions to problems encountered on the job, they write up and present their improvements as suggestions. The suggestions are then evaluated and rewarded on the basis of certain criteria. Details differ between companies, but the underlying character of the suggestion system remains the same.

Suggestions make jobs easier, safer, and more efficient, reduce errors and cost, improve service, and make customers happier. However, it is important to realize that the benefits of a suggestion system are not limited to improved efficiency and reduced cost. There are substantial personal benefits for the workers.

A suggestion system actively supported by workers revitalizes the workplace. Communication and commitment improve because solving problems and suggesting improvements require a heightened sense of cooperation throughout the company.

Workers increase their understanding about the job as they closely observe the problems around them, and they become more enthusiastic about working as they see their suggestions being adopted on the job. In a very real way, a successful suggestion is a barometer of the morale in the workplace.

How can a suggestion system produce this wide variety of benefits? *The IDEA Book* is book provides some of the answers. But the only way to experience the benefits of a suggestion system is to implement one of your own.

BENEFITS OF THE SUGGESTION SYSTEM: PERSONAL EXPERIENCES

Here are some comments from several workers about what they have gotten from participating in suggestion activities:

> *I spent my first days in the company trying to learn my job and become a capable and contributing worker. After I had learned the job pretty well, I recommended doing a task in a certain way. My recommendation was accepted and put to immediate use. My superior brought me a suggestion form*

and urged me to write up my improvement as a suggestion. That was the first time I had seen a suggestion form.

I did not know how to write a suggestion, but I did the best I could. Some time later, I received an envelope with a money reward in it. I can still remember how happy it made me feel.

***

Figure 13-3.

My first suggestion was not adopted. However, I remember receiving a small reward and a certificate for my effort and thinking, "Making suggestions isn't all that hard." Since then I have turned in suggestions regularly.

As I got used to making suggestions, more of them were adopted. This made me more confident and made the job more enjoyable. Regardless of the size of the improvement, knowing that I did something makes me feel very happy.

***

I wasn't shooting for high quality when I first started making suggestions. I wasn't even thinking of getting a reward. If you make enough suggestions, though, there's bound to be a few good ones, and I won $45 as a reward. Afterwards, one of my supervisors and several of the engineers came to me with questions.

That particular supervisor did not usually talk to me. When he came to me to talk, I knew I must have done something pretty important. I realized that my idea had been accepted, and this motivated me to make more suggestions. Now I try my best, and sometimes I make a very good suggestion.

***

I made my first suggestion after I had been working at my company for about three years. During one morning meeting, my plant manager passed out some suggestion forms and said: "X received a reward for making a good, creative suggestion. You should try too — you could earn a reward."

About a month after I made a suggestion, the plant manager came to me and said: "The engineers told me that you made a good suggestion." I was relieved, because I wasn't sure how good the idea was. Since then, I have continued looking for problems to improve at my workplace and writing suggestions.

I started by writing suggestions to made my work easier. I've won rewards of $15 or $25. Winning a reward makes me feel appreciated and motivates me to write more suggestions. Today, I feel that I am participating in managing my company through the suggestion system.

***

I became seriously committed to the suggestion system about ten years ago when my supervisor told me: "I don't care whether it's sports or work. Why don't you become the best in the division at something?" I had just received a $2 reward for a suggestion and I promised myself I would become the best suggester in the division. Since then I have made suggestions like crazy.

I feel so happy when a suggestion of mine is adopted and someone tells me that it has made his job easier or less physically demanding. Several years after I started making suggestions, I decided I was going to win the gold award. I did my best and won the gold award, which made me number

Figure 13-4.

one in the division. I still remember how happy I was. I also remember how good it felt when my supervisor told me my suggestion was saving the company $450 per month. Memories like these keep me motivated to continue making suggestions.

14

How to Make Improvements

To those who have never made one, a *suggestion* may sound like something very difficult. Many people think they can't do something as difficult as making a suggestion. They may be confusing *suggestions* with *inventions* or thinking of blue-ribbon suggestions they have seen written up in the company newspaper. This is looking at the highest level of creativity, but it is better to set your goals a little lower. Learning to make suggestions is not complicated, and there is no way to reach the top without first mastering some sound fundamentals.

START WITH SMALL IMPROVEMENTS

Start by looking for examples of waste, inconsistency, or inadequacy that are sure to be around you. The important thing is to identify problems close to you and solve these routine problems one by one.

Even people whose suggestions have won company or national-level awards started out by simply eliminating the waste, inefficiency, or inconsistency they saw around them. Steady effort in these areas lays the groundwork necessary for coming up with major improvement suggestions.

Unfortunately, we tend to accept a certain amount of waste as inevitable and ignore what we perceive as trivial problems. If left unchecked and allowed to grow, however, a trivial problem may become major enough to rock the foundation of the company. Given enough time, a leaky faucet can waste enough water drop by drop to fill a lake.

In a company, people, goods, and money are concentrated, and small problems increase geometrically in size. One screw, one piece of paper, five minutes wasted here and there can all add up to significant waste when they are repeated often enough.

PILING SMALL IMPROVEMENTS ON TOP OF EACH OTHER

Figure 14-1.

Efficiency is achieved when objective and method are balanced. If the method is insufficient for the task, it is inadequate. Waste occurs if the method is excessive for the object. When the method is sometimes wasteful and sometimes inadequate, it is called inconsistent. For example, a one-ton truck should be used for carrying a load of one ton. If you try to use a half-ton truck to carry one ton, the method is inadequate. If you use a two-ton truck, it is wasteful.

The job we do every day can be considered a means for accomplishing a certain end. If we evaluate the job in light of the objective and then eliminate waste, inadequacy, and inconsistency, the job will become easier, quicker, safer, cheaper, and more accurate. In other words, efficiency is improved. Look around you. There is waste, inadequacy, and inconsistency everywhere that you can start to reduce.

IMPROVEMENT STEPS

The road to improvement laid by our predecessors, from problem identification, to improvement, and then follow-up, is not a smooth or easy path. Obstacles along the way may be very difficult and may require a lot of trial and error to solve.

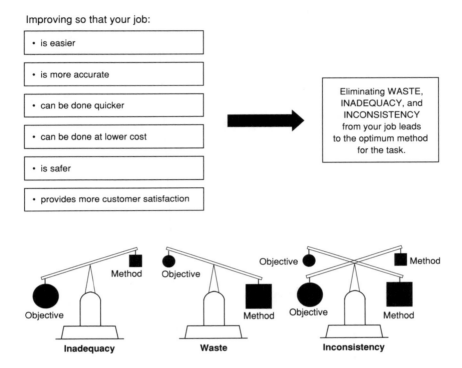

Improving so that your job:

- is easier
- is more accurate
- can be done quicker
- can be done at lower cost
- is safer
- provides more customer satisfaction

Eliminating WASTE, INADEQUACY, and INCONSISTENCY from your job leads to the optimum method for the task.

Objective Method **Inadequacy**

Objective Method **Waste**

Objective Method **Inconsistency**

Figure 14-2.

The improvement process can be broken down into two stages: *problem identification* and *problem solving*. The problem identification stage has four steps: identification, research, idea formulation, and organization. The problem solving stage has two steps: improvement implementation and improvement follow-up. These steps apply not only to the suggestion system but to all improvement activities.

Some companies or divisions accept only proposals for improvement, while others accept only suggestions that have actually been implemented. Generally speaking, improvement proposals were the only type of suggestions accepted until the mid-1960s, but starting in the mid-1970s, implemented suggestions began to account for the majority.

Improvement Steps

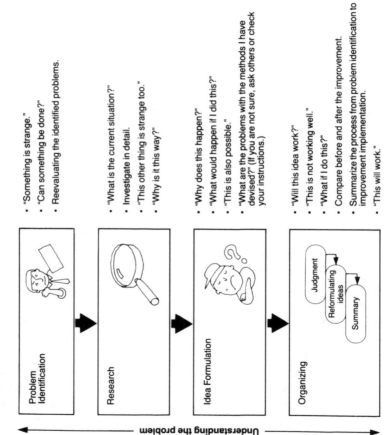

Problem Identification

- "Something is strange."
- "Can something be done?"
- Reevaluating the identified problems.

Research

- "What is the current situation?"
- Investigate in detail.
- "This other thing is strange too."
- "Why is it this way?"

Idea Formulation

- "Why does this happen?"
- "What would happen if I did this?"
- "This is also possible."
- "What are the problems with the methods I have devised?" (If you are not sure, ask others or check your instructions.)

Organizing

- Judgment
- Reformulating ideas
- Summary

- "Will this idea work?"
- "This is not working well."
- "What if I do this?"
- Compare before and after the improvement.
- Summarize the process from problem identification to improvement implementation.
- "This will work."

Understanding the problem

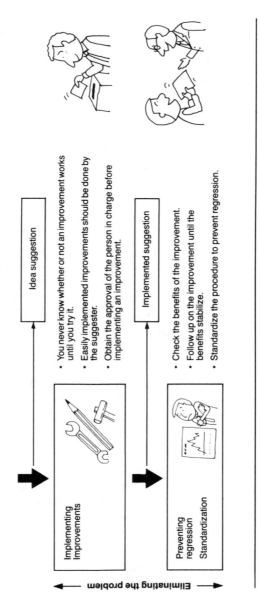

Eliminating the problem →

Implementing Improvements

→ **Idea suggestion**

- You never know whether or not an improvement works until you try it.
- Easily implemented improvements should be done by the suggester.
- Obtain the approval of the person in charge before implementing an improvement.

Preventing regression
Standardization

→ **Implemented suggestion**

- Check the benefits of the improvement.
- Follow up on the improvement until the benefits stabilize.
- Standardize the procedure to prevent regression.

The ABCs of creative suggestion-making:

a. **Think:** Use your mind continuously and improve your thinking power.
b. **Record:** Develop the ability to write and organize your thoughts.
c. **Devise:** Develop and implement the improvements yourself.
d. **Calculate:** Look ahead and become aware of raw cost.
e. **Action:** Be flexible in your action.

Figure 14-3.

STEP 1: PROBLEM IDENTIFICATION

"Hmmm, the equipment sounds different today."

"Hmmm, the work piece doesn't fit well today."

"There are so many errors in this calculation. I wonder what happened."

All problems are deeply rooted in the character of the workplace. The quality of an improvement depends on how deeply you dig to find the root cause. If you immediately jump to a conclusion about the cause, your solution will most likely produce only temporary relief of the symptoms of the problem.

The process of problem identification must be carried out thoroughly so that the real problem is found. Different ideas must be tried until the best solution is obtained.

One definition of a problem is *a deviation from the norm* — the difference between what is expected and what is actually occurring. Reducing or eliminating the difference between the two is solving the problem.

An implication of this definition is that a problem does not become apparent unless you know what the ideal, expected state is, no matter how long you observe a given phenomenon. In other words, it is impossible to detect a problem unless you know why you are doing the job and what that job's ideal state is.

All improvements start with the perception of a problem as a slight deviation from the ideal or standard, detected by a sharply honed instinct for catching problems. Most of us encounter numerous slight deviations from established standards during the course of our work each day. In many cases, however, we either ignore these deviations or fix them with makeshift solutions; we don't see them as areas for improvement for the long term.

Most jobs are already fairly well managed. If we do not develop our perception to notice these deviations, we may imagine that there are no problems to be solved. This attitude becomes stronger as familiarity with the job increases, and eventually we can lose all ability to detect deviations from the norm.

You should learn to analyze the workplace carefully in terms of its ideal, most efficient and convenient state. If you look at your workplace with this ideal in mind, you will probably notice mountains of problems. In that sense, the workplace is a source of creativity and inventiveness — a starting place for your ideas. Without a good approach to problem identification, however, the creative opportunities of the workplace will go unused.

Look at the workplace with a problem-finding attitude. The workplace will provide ample opportunities for creative problem-solving.

Figure 14-4.

Identifying Problems for Improvement

1. Become aware of problems:
    - "Hmm, this is strange."
    - "A defect has occurred."
    - "This process is inconvenient and time-consuming."

2. Have you overlooked these?
    - You think of a particular problem every morning before starting the day's work.
    - When you're start up the job, it never goes smoothly.
    - You can't get hold of what you need when you need it.
    - There's a drastic difference between busy and slow days.
    - Things are not returned to their proper place.
    - You feel frustrated because procedures are not followed.
    - A measure that works in other work areas doesn't work in yours.
    - Prior improvement ideas are not being implemented.
    - There's too much waiting and too much waste.
    - The same procedure produces varied results.

Five Main Tasks to Think About in the Workplace:

1. How to improve and maintain quality and reduce defects
2. How to reduce cost
3. How to improve productivity and meet delivery deadlines
4. How to increase safety
5. How to improve interpersonal relationships

Are There Problems With the "Four Ms" of the Workplace?

1. Me
2. Machine
3. Material
4. Method

Are There Waste, Inadequacy, and Inconsistency in the Workplace?

1. Is the method inadequate?
2. Is waste occurring?
3. Is there inconsistency in results?

Improvement Hints for the Week

1. Monday: Look for costs that can be reduced
2. Tuesday: Look for items requiring improvement
3. Wednesday: Look throughout the workplace
4. Thursday: Look for hazardous conditions
5. Friday: Look for organization and orderliness

STEP 2: RESEARCH

M misses a step while walking down a staircase and sprains his ankle. You might say that there's nothing more to the injury than carelessness, and you may be right. Many people walk down the same steps, and only M was injured. M says he had just had an argument with Q and was not paying attention to the steps.

However, on investigation, you learn that the steps had just been washed and were still wet. It also turns out that M was not wearing the required rubber-soled shoes and that the staircase, despite its steep angle, was not equipped with a handrail — two factors that could have contributed to M's accident.

Almost anyone would agree that it would be a very superficial analysis to attribute M's injury to his argument with Q. Nevertheless, we tend to assume that the first contributory factor we identify is the sole cause of the problem.

Asking "Why?" Five Times

Careful analysis of an occurrence will usually show there is more than one cause. You will also find a cause of a cause, and a cause of a cause of a cause. The causal chain ultimately extends to infinity.

It is therefore imperative to consider whether the first "cause" you detect for a particular phenomenon is really the true cause. This requires considering all the relevant facts, including the flow of work, the work procedure, the worker's movements, the jigs and fixtures, and the machines and equipment used. For each factor, you must ask the question "Why?" and search for the true cause. What you intuitively feel is the cause is usually not the whole story; the true cause is usually hidden. If you go back at least five "generations" of cause, you will be likely to find the true cause.

Figure 14-5.

QC Tools for Understanding the Current Situation

To solve a problem we must understand it. This means gathering all the relevant facts. The data you collect must be organized to be easily understood. This is especially true when tackling major, deep-rooted problems such as those brought up in group discussion. In such cases, QC charts and graphs, described in detail in the subsequent pages, should be used to make the problem more understandable and to make sure that all group members understand the problem in the same way. Using these QC tools will also lead to a thorough analysis of the workplace, enabling countless new problems to be identified in the course of solving the original problem.

Pareto Chart

Pareto analysis sorts raw data into several categories and presents the data on a bar chart arranged in decreasing order. A line graph indicates the cumulative value of the data, ending at 100 percent. Pareto charts are widely used for identifying a problem and understanding the distribution of defects thought to contribute to the problem. They provide information on the number of defects present overall and the percentage each specific defect contributes to the problem as a whole.

To create a Pareto chart:

1. Collect data over a specific period for a specific number of categories.
2. Sort data into categories.
3. Draw the graph.
   - Draw a horizontal axis (X) and two vertical axes (Y). Set out the categories along the X-axis in decreasing order of magnitude, starting with the largest category at the left. Mark the left Y-axis for the number of occurrences in each category. Mark the right Y-axis for percentage.
   - Enter the data as a bar chart.
   - Connect the cumulative values with a line.
4. Analyze and understand the causes and propose countermeasures.

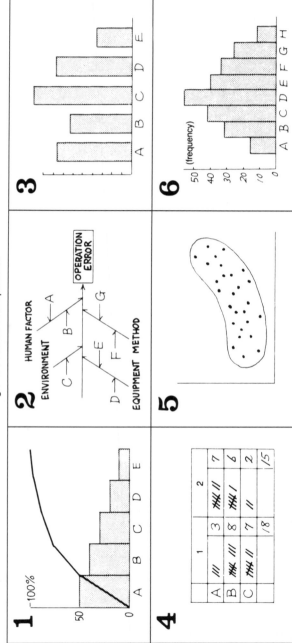

1. **Pareto chart** shows the distribution of factors contributing to a problem or situation.

2. **Cause-and-effect diagram** provides a systematic and ordered understanding of the causes of the problem.

3. **Bar graph** makes numbers more meaningful.

4. **Check sheet** helps make a graph based on available data.

5. **Scatter diagram** helps check the correlation among prepared data.

6. **Histogram** helps check the frequency distribution.

Figure 14-6. QC Tools

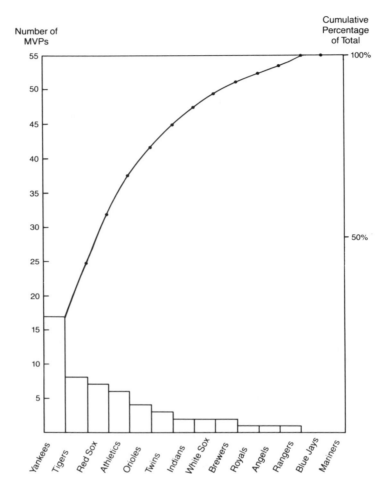

Team	Yankees	Tigers	Red Sox	Athletics	Orioles	Twins	Indians	White Sox	Brewers	Royals	Angels	Rangers	Blue Jays	Mariners
Number of Awards	17	8	7	6	4	3	2	2	2	1	1	1	0	0
Percent of total	31	15	13	11	7	6	4	4	4	2	2	2	0	0

Source: *The Complete Handbook of Baseball* (15th ed., Zander Hollander, ed., 1985) Signet Books

Figure 14-7. Pareto Chart: American League MVP Awards by Team (based on data since 1931)

The example shows how we could use Pareto analysis to chart the distribution of Most Valuable Players among American League teams over the last 54 years. This shows us which teams have benefited from the largest number of MVPs.

Cause-and-Effect Diagram

The cause-and-effect diagram is used to systematically analyze and organize the causes of a problem. Its purpose is to list the factors that contribute to a result and to organize them from broad to specific factors. It can be used to investigate the causes of defects and suggest solutions or to analyze and correct problems with efficiency or raw cost.

Cause-and-effect diagrams are sometimes referred to as fishbone diagrams because of their shape. The problem or effect to be analyzed is written at the right, where the fish's head would be. The factors that contribute to the effect are written as branches of the main trunk. Major causes are represented as branches directly attached to the main trunk. Smaller branches fanning out from them represent specific influences within each major cause.

To create a cause-and-effect diagram:

1. Identify the result or effect to be addressed and write it on the right of the diagram.
2. Determine the factors that contribute to this effect.
3. Sort the factors into major, minor, and intermediate causes. There is no fast rule about how to sort the factors. As you examine them you will organize them according to the relationships you discover between them.
4. Compare the finished diagram against the actual condition.

The example shows how to use a cause-and-effect diagram to pinpoint the major and minor causes of a common and frustrating problem — not receiving telephone messages.

Bar Graph

Bar graphs are used to analyze the cost of process defects, the number of defects per line, and so forth. Other types of graphs include line graphs, used to show changes in data over time, and

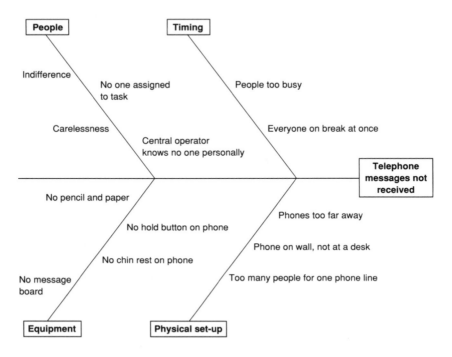

Figure 14-8. Cause-and-Effect Diagram: Missed Telephone Messages

pie charts, used to show, for example, the percentage of occurrences of an effect attributable to a specific cause.

Numerical data are more understandable when organized into a bar graph. A good graph must:

- Provide the overall picture at a single glance.
- Be simple and clear — the meaning of the graph should be obvious.
- Communicate at once — the meaning of the graph should be understandable without explanation.
- Allow the correct interpretation — the scales used, the line thickness, and other such elements must facilitate an accurate judgment about the facts described; and
- Provide a clue for a countermeasure — the graph should suggest the solution to correct the undesirable condition.

Here is a simple example using a bar graph to compare the output of five identical machines on the shop floor. Identifying the least productive machine is the first step toward isolating and correcting the factors causing its poor performance.

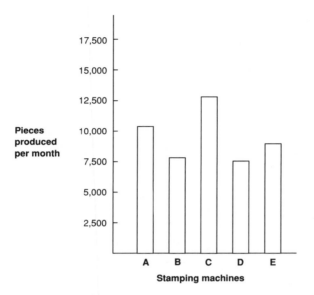

Figure 14-9. Bar Graph: Monthly Stamping Production by Machine

Check Sheet

A check sheet is a good way to begin to analyze the causes of a problem. A check sheet is a table for tallying how frequently different events or phenomena occur. It can be used to analyze data about the occurrence of defects or various problems with machines and tools.

A graph is more understandable than a list of numbers. Since it takes time to create a graph, however, it is more efficient to record the data in check sheet form as it is produced. Later the data can be used to make a graph.

Some hints for creating a good check sheet:

• The data should be accurate and easily noted.
• The data must be easily translated into a graph or chart after it is produced.

- The data recorded should be easily presentable as a report.
- The check sheet should convey information not readily expressible with numbers or words.
- The data must be understandable at a glance.

The example shows how to use a check sheet to chart some of the causes of employee absenteeism.

Reason	Division A	Division B	Division C	Annual Total
Illness	𝍌 𝍌 𝍌 𝍌 𝍌 𝍌 𝍌 𝍌 𝍌 ///	𝍌 𝍌 𝍌 𝍌 𝍌 //	𝍌 𝍌 𝍌 𝍌 𝍌 𝍌 𝍌 𝍌 𝍌 𝍌 𝍌 𝍌	135
Child Illness	𝍌 𝍌 𝍌 𝍌 𝍌 𝍌	𝍌 𝍌 𝍌 //	𝍌 𝍌 𝍌 𝍌 𝍌 //	74
Personal day	𝍌 𝍌	𝍌 ////	𝍌 𝍌 𝍌 //	36
Family death	////	//	////	10
Professional leave	𝍌 //	𝍌 𝍌	////	21
Total	99	65	112	276

Figure 14-10. Check Sheet: Absenteeism

Scatter Diagram

When you analyze problems in the workplace, you will identify many potential causes, and as you create a cause-and-effect diagram you will discover that some of the causes are related to each other. A scatter diagram is a way of charting paired data to highlight the causal relationships between them.

To create a scatter diagram:

1. Collect pairs of data for two causes or characteristics (A and B) you wish to study. It is good to have as large a sample as possible — at least 20 data pairs.
2. Plot the value for characteristic A along the horizontal axis and that for B along the vertical axis. Make sure the values on these axes include the maximum and minimum values of A and B in your sample.
3. Plot the particular combinations of A and B as points on the graph.
4. Analyze the correlation.
   - Is there a correlation?
   - Is it a positive correlation (an increase in A means an increase in B) or an inverse correlation (an increase in A causes a decrease in B)?
   - Is there a point that does not fit in the pattern of the correlation? Look for some abnormality that may have caused the deviant point.
   - What is the approximate shape of a line connecting the points?

The figure gives an example of a scatter diagram to check the relationship between employee salaries and years of experience. Monthly salary is plotted along the X-axis and years along the Y-axis. Each point on the diagram represents a particular individual's combination of these two factors.

The distribution of the points in the figure indicates that for this sample group, salary does tend to increase with job experience. Similarly, you could use such a chart to investigate the correlation between the dimensions of sample parts and of finished products made with the part.

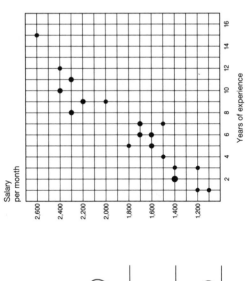

Positive
correlation

No
correlation

Inverse
correlation

Employee	Years Experience	Salary Per Month
1	2	1400
2	4	1500
3	3	1400
4	9	2000
5	12	2400
6	1	1200
7	7	1700
8	5	1800
9	10	2400
10	11	2300
11	8	2300
12	7	1500
13	15	2600
14	9	2200
15	5	1600
16	3	1200
17	6	1700
18	2	1400
19	1	1150
20	6	1600

Data

Figure 14-11. Scatter Diagram: Salary and Years of Experience

Histogram

A histogram is a special type of bar graph showing the frequency distribution of a large number of data. Histograms are frequently used for checking the distribution of a particular dimension of a component part.

A histogram is a convenient way to display at a glance the distribution of various characteristics of a group of data. To create a histogram:

1. Collect data.
2. Sort the collected data into equal-sized classes; for 30 to 50 pieces of data, five to seven classes are usually adequate.
3. Make a tally of the frequency of data in each class.
4. Use the frequency table to draw a bar graph, with the classes along the horizontal axis and the frequency scale along the vertical axis.
5. Check the distribution from the histogram.

The figure is an example of a histogram plotting the distribution of delivery delays of various lengths past the promised date, using number of days behind schedule as the measured class.

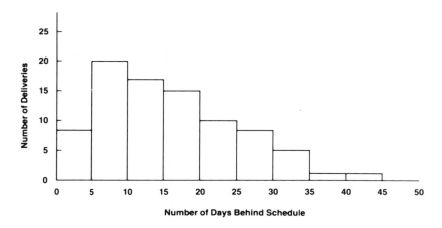

Figure 14-12. Histogram: Distribution of Delivery Delays

STEP 3: IDEA FORMULATION

Unlike mathematical problems, which usually have only one answer, problems dealing with workplace improvement have many possible solutions. The goal is to select the best answer from these possibilities. For this reason, solving an improvement problem is simultaneously easier and harder than solving a math problem.

People frequently ask whether to emphasize quantity or quality in making suggestions. When overall improvement is the goal, it is important initially to formulate as many ideas as possible. The sheer quantity of ideas inevitably leads to quality.

It is important to seek solutions and ideas for a given problem from as many angles as possible. If the problem is to be solved by a group, a brainstorming session should be held to generate as many ideas as possible. If you are working on the problem alone, you should hold a "solo" brainstorming session.

People prefer to maintain the status quo. They like to stay put, retain their viewpoint, and criticize. Such an attitude, however, does not contribute to good ideas, regardless of how well a problem is identified or studied. When you brainstorm, then, don't put a damper on your own or others' ideas by saying, "This is too time-consuming," or, "This is too costly." The rule at this stage is to remain open-minded and imaginative, considering any option, no matter how far-fetched. Feasibility should be considered at a later stage.

If a treasure is to be found from a suggestion activity, it must be unearthed during the idea formulation stage, so let your mind run free and come up with lots of ideas.

Basics of Idea Formulation and Applications

Checklist for Idea Formulation:

- Elimination: What will happen if something is eliminated?
- Reversal: What will happen if something is reversed?
- Normal and abnormal: Is something an abnormality or does it occur all the time?
- Constant and variable: What will happen if only the changing item is treated as an exception?

Type	5W2H	Description	Countermeasure
Subject Matter	What?	What is being done? Can this task be eliminated?	Eliminate unnecessary tasks
Purpose	Why?	Why is this task necessary? Clarify the purpose.	
Location	Where?	Where is it being done? Does it have to be done there?	Change the sequence or combination
Sequence	When?	When is the best time to do it? Does it have to be done then?	
People	Who?	Who is doing it? Should someone else do it? Why am I doing it?	
Method	How?	How is it being done? Is this the best method? Is there some other way?	Simplify the task
Cost	How much?	How much does it cost now? What will the cost be after improvement?	Select an improvement method

A number of simple guidelines have been developed to help people or groups generate new ideas. In general, these guidelines urge you to question everything, from every conceivable angle. The figure outlines the 5W2H Method, which stands for the five "w's" — what, why, where, when, and who — and the two "h's" — how and how much.

Osborn's Checklist

Described in A. F. Osborn's book, *Applied Imagination* (New York: Scribner's, 1963), this list suggests additional ways to examine and question a machine, part, or process for improvement ideas:

1. **Use it another way.**
   • Is there another way to use it while keeping the current setup?
   • Can anything else be produced?

2. **Borrow an idea from something similar.**
   • Ideas are formed by combining. See if ideas used elsewhere can be adapted to your improvement project.

3. **Change or replace it.**
   • Change the shape, color, sound, smell, movement, location, orientation, power source, and so on.
   • Rotate it.
   • Remove something that's there; add what's not there.

4. **Expand it.**
   • Add something; spend more time; increase the repetition; make it stronger, longer, or thicker; add some other value; double it; duplicate it; increase it; exaggerate it.

5. **Reduce it.**
   • Remove something; make it smaller or stronger; divide it; simplify it; reduce it; lighten it; express it in a more subdued way.

6. **Use alternatives.**
   • Use someone or something else. Use other elements, ingredients, materials, methods, locations, approaches, or tone of voice.

7. **Replace it.**
   • Use different elements or ingredients, dies, layout, sequence, or arrangement. Reverse the cause and effect. Change the pace, speed, or schedule.

8. **Reverse it.**
   • Turn it upside down; invert it; reverse the positions, front and back, positive and negative. Change the roles, orientation, or setup.

9. **Combine it.**
   • Mix it; make an alloy; assemble it.

Figure 14-13. How to Formulate Ideas

- Enlargement and reduction: What will happen if something is enlarged or reduced?
- Linking and separating: What will happen if some things are joined or taken apart?
- Concentration and dispersion: What will happen if some things are concentrated or dispersed?
- Addition and removal: What will happen if something is added or removed?
- Changing the sequence: What will happen if a different assembly procedure is used?
- Replacement and substitution: Can something be used for another purpose? Can it be replaced with something else?
- Parallel and serial: Can two or more things be done at the same time? Can they be done sequentially?
- Differences and similarities: Is there a method to easily separate different things? Is there a method to group similar things?

Elimination: What Will Happen if Something is Eliminated?

The ultimate improvement of a task is to discontinue doing it entirely. If the initial objectives can be achieved even after eliminating a task, then performing the task is wasteful. The formulation of statistics is an example of this. Clerical personnel spend hours preparing statistics from data sent from production floors. Most of the time, however, statistics are created without knowing who will be using them or for what purpose, and they sometimes remain unused. This sort of wasteful practice will not occur if the purpose of each task is well understood. It may not be possible to eliminate a task entirely, but you may find a simpler method to achieve the same purpose.

Reversal: What Will Happen if Something is Reversed?

A job required two workers to lift an object onto a scale and weigh it. The item was too heavy for one person to lift. Someone then suggested sinking the scale to floor level to eliminate the lifting, so a hole was dug to the right depth and the scale was placed in it. Now, just one worker can roll the item onto the scale.

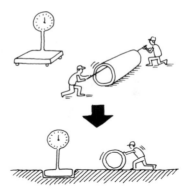

Figure 14-14. Reversal

Normal and Abnormal: Is Something an Abnormality or Does It Occur all the Time?

An exception or deviation is an event that occurs rarely. If you want to know how frequently a normal event occurs, it may be quicker to count the number of exceptional events. For example, count the number of people who are absent to know how many people are working. Checking the exception may allow a goal to be reached quicker.

Constant and Variable: What Will Happen if Only the Changing Item is Treated as an Exception?

Suppose the job is to stamp a serial number starting from 6291. This means that for nine stampings only the last digit changes. Instead of changing the stamp each time, you could do this task by first stamping nine items with "629," the unchanging portion, and then stamping the last digit onto the items. Tasks involving a changing portion and a constant portion can frequently be simplified after considering the two separately.

Enlargement and Reduction: What Will Happen if Something is Enlarged or Reduced?

A job may be difficult because it is either very small or very large. If a job is very small, consider using a magnifying lens or a

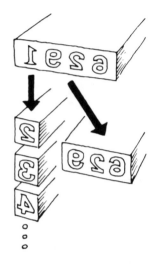

Figure 14-15. Constant and Variable

pair of forceps. If something is too large to handle easily, find a way to make it manageable, such as folding it. Consider ways that power tools and other devices can be used to handle the job more easily.

Figure 14-16. Enlargement and Reduction

Linking and Separating: What Will Happen if Some Things Are Joined or Taken Apart?

When people screw small parts together, the usual procedure is to grab the screw, start it in the hole by hand, and then tighten it with a screwdriver. You could greatly simplify the job by attaching a tool to the screwdriver that would grab the screw and link it to the screwdriver while you start it in the hole.

Concentration and Dispersion: What Will Happen if Something Is Concentrated or Dispersed?

Multiple drills and multiple spot-welders make jobs convenient by performing many different tasks at once. On the other hand, dividing a job into different functions may also simplify a job. As an example, imagine the task of gathering a deck of cards that are spread out, some face down and some face up. Rather than picking up all the cards first and then one-by-one flipping over the ones going the wrong way, it would be easier to first pick up the cards facing in the same direction, then gather the remaining cards and stack them together in the same direction.

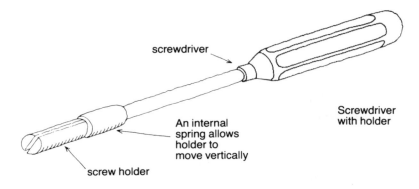

screwdriver

An internal spring allows holder to move vertically

Screwdriver with holder

screw holder

Figure 14-17. Concentration and Dispersion

Addition and Removal: What Will Happen if Something Is Added or Removed?

When you tighten a wood screw, the screwdriver may jump out of the slot if the screw is too tight or too shallow. Someone thought of adding a cross-slot for a better grip, and thus the Phillips head screw was invented.

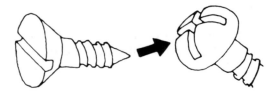

Figure 14-18. Addition and Removal

Changing the Sequence: What Will Happen if a Different Assembly Procedure Is Used?

You could put on a necktie in the following steps:

1. Button the shirt,
2. Raise the collar,
3. Position the necktie,
4. Knot the necktie, and
5. Lower the collar.

A better procedure that holds the tie in the right position would be:

1. Raise the collar,
2. Position the necktie,
3. Lower the collar,
4. Knot the necktie, and
5. Button the shirt.

Changing the sequence makes the job easier and keeps the collar from getting as wrinkled.

Replacement and Substitution: Use the Time Spent Waiting

Among job motions, unavoidable delay (waiting), empty movement (movement with nothing in hand), and holding (holding an object without moving) are usually easily improved. The figure shows how productivity was significantly improved, eliminating an empty movement by changing the position where pressed products were stored.

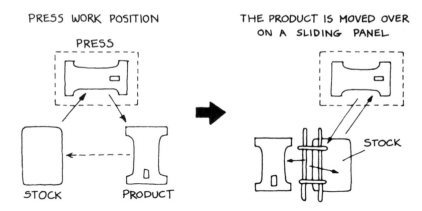

Figure 14-19. Replacement and Substitution

Parallel and Serial: Can Two or More Things Be Done at the Same Time? Can They Be Done Sequentially?

Instead of washing seven boxes one at a time, you could use a system like the one shown in the figure. The seven boxes are placed in a rack in offset positions so that when soapy water is poured into the top box, it will overflow into the remaining six boxes in succession. This is a good example of eliminating unnecessary processes by a three-dimensional use of space.

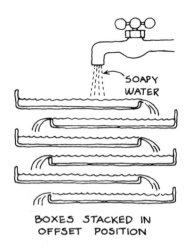

Figure 14-20. Parallel and Serial

*Differences and Similarities: Is There a Method to
Easily Separate Different Things? Is There a Method
to Group Similar Things?*

The figure depicts a way to use differences in size to automatically sort cutting waste from finished nuts. At machine shops, replacement gears used with lathes are sorted by their diameter. To do this, a rod is inserted into the hole in the middle. This is an example of using a shared attribute to group similar things.

Figure 14-21. Thread-cutting Machine

Examples of Idea Formulation

The Well

A thirsty man came to a well that had a hand pump to get a drink of water. He would pump vigorously, then try to catch the water from the spigot in his palms. Only a few droplets were coming out of the spigot, however, by the time he got his hands in position. The man did this several times before he left, discouraged.

Another man came to the well. Instead of repeating what the first man had done (that is, pump vigorously two or three times and then try to catch water from the spigot), he held the pump with one hand, sealed the spigot opening with the other, and drove the pump two or three times. Then he would release his hand and drink the water held back by his palm.

There are many ways to do something, and some ways work better than others!

Barnacles

> *When a battleship returns from a cruise, the hull of the ship is covered with barnacles, making the ship much slower in the water. A similar thing happens with people. Experience is important, but some experience can become "barnacles" — things we're attached to that get in our way. We must learn to separate these "barnacles" from the wisdom gained through experience. The older we get, the harder this becomes. People develop fixed ideas of how the navy, its fleet, or its tactics should always be.*
>
> *What is scary is not that the individual has fixed ideas, but that the person sitting comfortably in the commander's or the admiral's chair does not know that he has fixed ideas.* (Ryotaro Shiba, Saka no Ue no Kumo)

Goldfish

A partition with a hole just big enough for a goldfish to swim through is placed in a goldfish tank. When you place food on the side of the partition away from the goldfish, eventually it will learn to swim through the hole to the food. When you remove the partition after some time, the goldfish will still swim where the hole had been. People are like that goldfish — there are many things that people continue to do out of habit despite changes in the environment.

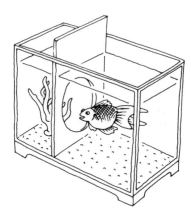

Figure 14-22.

Ideas Must Be Communicated

About 600 B.C., before the invention of the printing press, a Greek philosopher named Miletus discovered that rubbing amber would create static electricity, which could be used to lift wheat straw. It took 2500 more years to develop the radios and telephones we enjoy today. If a printing press had been available back in Miletus' time to spread the news of his discovery, modern civilization might have come about more quickly. The same thing applies to your good ideas. To have them recognized as good ideas, you must write them down and submit them as suggestions. An idea that is not expressed is almost valueless.

Hexagonal Pencils

Look at the pencil on your desk. It probably has a hexagonal cross-section. When pencils were first invented, they had a circular cross-section. Round pencils are still used in special applications, but most are hexagonal. Have you ever wondered why?

Round pencils are easy to hold in the hand, but they tend to roll when you set them down. If pencils had a triangular or square cross-section they wouldn't roll as much, but they would be harder to write with. The hexagonal shape is a compromise between a round shape that is easy to write with and an angular shape that keeps the pencil from rolling.

There are numerous examples such as this around us.

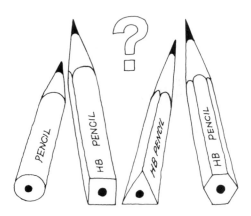

Figure 14-23.

STEP 4: IDEA MODIFICATION

There are many possible answers to problems that require improvement. The criteria to use for honing in on the best solution come from the benefits produced by various answers. More specifically, you must consider factors such as the feasibility of implementation and the cost, time, and labor required, balancing these factors against the benefits of implementation, the adaptability to other situations, and the expected life of the benefits.

If the net benefit is too small or absent, the idea will not be accepted. You may need to refine the idea by finding ways to reduce the cost, make better use of waste, or make the benefits last longer. You shouldn't expect every idea to be implemented. Many are "rough drafts" that must be discarded or polished further. However, ideas that are discarded serve as seeds for future ideas. You may simply need to broaden your perspective and deepen your knowledge and experience. The quality and the depth of your improvement activity depend on your sowing many seeds.

In Japanese painting known as *Iwaegu*, the individual layers of pigment are so light that the paper below is visible for the first few layers. However, by laying many coats on top of another, artists create works with a depth, lustre, and presence unmatched by more opaque oil paintings.

In a similar way, a person's wisdom and understanding represent an accumulation of layers of experience and insight deepened by variety and perspective. Good ideas are produced through numerous experiences of trial and error, while a passing idea is usually nothing more than that. Unless you have the courage to reevaluate and even discard the ideas you have, you will not enjoy the fruits of a really successful idea.

Factors Used in Evaluating Ideas

Knowing the factors used in evaluating your ideas is knowing what your company is looking for in suggestions. If you don't know what the company is looking for, you could make suggestions that completely miss the mark. You should evaluate your own ideas with these factors in mind before you submit them as suggestions. This will show what your idea lacks and what you should consider further.

The evaluation factors and the weights assigned to each of them vary from company to company, but most companies use some combination of the factors shown in the accompanying table.

Benefits to actual task (contribution to management)	1. Tangible benefits Benefits that can be measured financially, such as increased revenue or productivity, or reduced manpower, time, material, or processing requirements. 2. Intangible benefits Benefits that cannot be measured financially, such as reduced workload or improvement in quality, delivery time, safety, cleanliness, orderliness, morale, interpersonal relations, corporate image, or customer trust
Feasibility (difficulty of implementation)	The time and resources needed to implement the idea; the urgency of implementation (should it be implemented immediately or gradually?)
Adaptability	Whether the idea can be used in other work places or processes
Other effects	Whether implementing the suggestion will detrimentally affect other work places or processes
Continuity	Whether the benefits of the suggestion are long-lasting or transitory
Completeness	Whether the suggestion is concrete enough to implement immediately without modifications or additional work
Originality	Whether the idea is original and creative, an adaptation of an existing idea, or merely an imitation of a prior idea
Research effort	The amount of research, trial and error, and other efforts expended by the suggester. Is the suggestion just a passing thought or does it represent adversities overcome through courage and effort?
Suggestions pertaining to others' workplaces (negative value)	What is the relationship between the suggestion and the suggester's position? What effort was spent in the suggestion, judged from the position of the suggester.

Figure 14-24. Idea Evaluation Factors

STEP 5: IMPLEMENTING THE IMPROVEMENT IDEA

More and more companies are using the "implemented suggestion" system — ideas must be put into effect before credit or a reward will be given. This sometimes reflects an improvement in the suggestion-making skill of the employees, but it also may happen when the number of unimplemented "idea" suggestions becomes too large to be centrally managed by a single department.

These two factors are a driving force to get employees to actually implement their improvement ideas. Doing everything — from making suggestions, to implementing them, to confirming the benefits — completes the suggestion cycle, which is more satisfying for the suggesters.

If at all possible, employees should implement their own suggestions after getting proper approvals from management. The exact benefits of an improvement are never known until it is implemented, and employees can learn a lot while checking the actual results of their suggestions.

In an implementation system, the worker obtains the approval and advice of supervisors, and then implements his or her suggestion with the cooperation of colleagues and the technical staff. The new activity provides a chance for the suggester to develop new interpersonal relationships, skills, and experiences that would not have been possible while performing routine jobs. Placing a worker in a new setting gives that person a chance to grow as a human being.

Workers should appreciate that management undertakes significant risks in permitting implementation of improvement plans before examining them as suggestions. The fact that management permits ideas to be implemented on the simple approval and advice of supervisors shows a great trust in the employees' abilities and in their value for the company.

As a suggester, you must give careful consideration to the effects your improvement plan may have on other workers and on the earlier and later processes. It takes patience to achieve the intended benefits of an improvement plan.

Cautions Regarding Implementation of Improvement Plans

- *Obtain your supervisor's approval.*
- *Obtain or prepare the things you need for implementation.*
- *With group improvement plans, make individual responsibilities clear.*
- *Establish a daily schedule for the improvement plan.*
- *Notify everyone who might be affected by the improvement plan before you begin implementation.* Improvements entail changes in the status quo. People who are used to an old way may resist the new ways. Therefore, it is important to obtain the prior consent of those who will be affected by the improvement plan or to ask them to take part in the implementation.
- *Establish a trial period.* The implementation of an improvement plan must not adversely affect other departments or processes. The improvement plan should first be tried in a pilot project that is limited to your area and does not affect others.
- *Understand and deal with problems that occur during implementation.* No improvement is 100 percent effective on the first try. In most cases, new and unexpected problems will surface during implementation. Overcoming unexpected

Figure 14-25.

problems and completing implementation within the scheduled period are a part of implementing the improvement plan.

- *Seek the advice of your supervisors and the technical staff.* In most cases, professional knowledge and specific experience are required for solving the problems you encounter while implementing an improvement plan. Do not cling to the idea of "doing it on your own." If a problem seems overwhelming, always seek the advice or help of your supervisor and the technical or engineering staff.

STEP 6: FOLLOW-UP ON THE IMPROVEMENT PLAN

After an improvement plan is implemented, you must follow up on the results. We implement improvements with specific goals in mind, such as making jobs easier, improving efficiency, or reducing costs. It is important to check if your improvement plan is achieving the desired objectives, since it is possible for an improvement plan to have detrimental effects.

Following up on an improvement plan is, naturally, the obligation of the person who implemented it. The plan is not completely implemented until the effects of the improvement are checked. Moreover, understanding these effects is indispensable to understanding the overall value of the improvement plan.

If the results are not satisfactory, it may be necessary to go back to the beginning and start the improvement process over. This usually isn't necessary with small improvement plans that were well formulated in the beginning. However, achieving the desired results becomes more difficult as the complexity of the improvement plan increases.

After you are able to confirm that the desired effects are being achieved, you must communicate the improvement to avoid a regression to the old way of doing things. Unless changes in tasks or improvements in machines and tools are publicized, written in work standard sheets, and made familiar to all workers, the improved procedures or equipment can easily be forgotten, neglected, and gradually replaced by the past practices.

An improvement is not complete until every step, including follow-up, is implemented. Some of the steps outlined above may be superfluous when implementing simple improvements such as placing something on the left side of the worker that had previously been on the right. Even in such a case, however, the steps must be followed in a more abbreviated form. Those who only make idea suggestions and do not implement them should nevertheless become familiar with the steps described so that they can make a complete improvement when the time comes for them to do so.

Check the results

- Obtain the data after the implementation. Check whether the idea produced the desired effect.
- Compare the results with the pre-improvement figures.
- Is the comparison satisfactory?
- Is there room for improvement?
- Do you need to rework the improvement plan?

Make the improvement stick

- Gather data until the benefits stabilize. Make corrections if necessary.
- Revise the job procedure sheet to reflect the new method.
- Change the equipment, tools, and other surrounding conditions to fit the new procedure.
- Educate and train workers to familiarize them with the new procedure.

Challenge a new problem

Figure 14-26. Improvement Follow-up

FAMOUS QUOTATIONS ABOUT IDEAS

I have never done anything of worth by coincidence. None of my inventions have come as a result of coincidence. They were hard work. (Thomas Edison)

* * *

Man can put out about 1/20 of a horsepower. He has to rest at least 9 hours a day. He also has to eat and drink. As a power source, we are terrible. However, it is when man starts thinking of ideas that the difference between man and machine emerges. (Soichiro Honda)

* * *

Ideas are born amidst the noise of machines and work. (Kiyoshi Ichimura)

* * *

The innovative organization requires a learning atmosphere throughout the entire business. It creates and maintains continuous learning. No one is allowed to consider himself "finished" at any time. Learning is a continuing process for all members of the organization. (Peter Drucker, Management: Tasks, Responsibilities, Practices*)*

* * *

People show tremendous abilities when they are pushed to the very limit. People who are always the point man usually come up with good ideas. (Yajiro Ikari)

* * *

Creativity is the first edition of the mundane and the banal. (Maxim Gorki)

* * *

There is no joy other than the joy of creating. There is no man who is truly alive other than those who are creating. All others are just shadows on the earth with nothing to do with being alive. The joy of living, whether it is love or action, is the joy of creating. (Romain Rolland)

* * *

Failure allows a researcher to obtain valuable experience and expand his ideas to infinity. (Masafumi Inoki)

Chapter 15 is a selection from *The Canon Production System: Creative Involvement of the Total Workforce*, Japan Management Association and Connie Dyer, editors (Cambridge: Productivity Press, 1987)

15

Three Activities Aimed at a Livelier Workplace

VITALIZING THE WORKPLACE THROUGH THE "THREE SELFS"

The most popular and fundamental of the four Canon Principles emphasizes the threefold spirit of the self: self-motivation, self-respect, and self-reliance. This philosophy at Canon fosters an open, supportive environment along with a strong sense of duty, purpose, and responsibility.

The vitality of the workplace grows out of three morale-building activities based on the spirit of these "three selfs" — the *Five S campaign* (housekeeping for greater efficiency and reduction of waste), *small group activities*, and the *work improvement proposal system*. (Figure 15-1) Each of these activities lets workers experience the power of teamwork, creative endeavor, and success. Workers who have been buried in their work environment lose their passivity and become actively involved. They begin to think of ways to improve the work — it becomes interesting, enjoyable. And the vitality of the workplace increases rapidly.

This vitality is the most important force behind the success of the CPS effort, and it has fueled many creative improvements at individual factories. Executives and management at Canon understand the importance of team projects and small group activities

Editor's note: In 1975, Canon, Inc. lost money for the first time in its twenty-six year history. The Canon Production System (CPS) was developed in response to this circumstance. It has proved to be a success.

and take an active interest in them. Through their support, work-place vitalization activities have become a natural part of the daily routine at Canon.

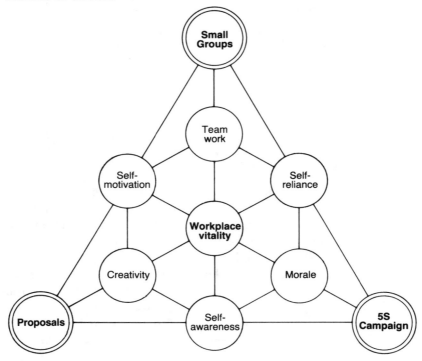

Figure 15-1. Three Activities that Vitalize the Workplace

THE FIVE S CAMPAIGN

It goes without saying that orderliness and organization are sensible as well as essential in the workplace. Improvement activities to promote these principles come under the general heading of Five S — five Japanese words that mean proper arrangement (*seiri*), orderliness (*seiton*), cleanliness (*seiketsu*), cleanup (*seiso*), and discipline (*shitsuke*). In some factories the English word "safety" adds a sixth S.

Some people complain that industrial housekeeping costs time and labor but produces no return. The function of Five S principles, however, is to reduce and ultimately prevent quality and productivity losses. They are essential to the elimination of waste in the work area and the factory as a whole.

Canon has benefited in two important ways through the Five S movement. First is the workers' change in consciousness — a readiness to follow the rules and "do what's been decided" that is now firmly entrenched throughout the workplace. For example, keeping parts and tools in their place was once a hard rule to enforce. It is never broken now; this reduces delays and wasted motion and helps visually control the workplace. The second benefit can be seen in the manufacturing process itself, in fewer accidents and equipment breakdowns, increased work efficiency, and lowered defect rates.

The Five S movement is promoted under the Canon slogan, "Use your legs and eyes; do regular checks and evaluations." For example, at Factories G and K, Five S Committees (chaired by the factory managers) conduct periodic inspections and photograph problem areas. The problems or suggestions for improvement are then reported on a Five S card with the photographs attached. The responsible work area must immediately develop a solution to the problem and submit a written plan to the Five S Committee.

Factory U has developed a self-grading Five S system. Each work area evaluates itself at set intervals (usually weekly), using a Five S checksheet. (Figure 15-2) These self-evaluations are reviewed by the foreman, section chief, and factory manager, then returned to the work area with comments or recommendations.

At Factories T and U, a work area that passes a certain level of inspection is designated a Five S Premier Work Center and awarded a Five S recognition plaque along with additional prizes. This work area then serves as a model for others in promoting the Five S movement. The model work areas must continue to pass regular inspections, however. They are expected to continue to look for ways to raise their level even higher.

SMALL GROUP ACTIVITIES

Small group activity programs flourish in every Canon factory, and everyone from line workers to plant managers participates in at least one group. (Figure 15-3) The names of group programs in each factory reflect their history or their primary focus.

Factory U

5 S Inspection Sheet		Evaluation Rank			Rank A: perfect score
					Rank B: 1-2 problems
		A	B	C	Rank C: 3 or more problems
	Item				Comments
Proper Arrangement	(Sort out unnecessary items)				
	Are things posted on bulletin board uniformly?				
	Have all unnecessary items been removed?				
	Is it clear why unauthorized items are present?				
	Are passageways and work areas clearly outlined?				
	Are hoses and cord properly arranged?				
Good Order	(A place for everything and everything in its place)				
	Is everything kept in its own place?				
	Are things put away after use?				
	Are work areas uncluttered?				
	Is everything fastened down that needs to be?				
	Are shelves, tables, and cleaning implements orderly?				
Cleanliness	(Prevent problems by keeping things clean.)				
	Is clothing neat and clean?				
	Are exhaust and ventilation adequate?				
	Are work areas clean?				
	Are machinery, equipment, fixtures, and drains kept clean?				
	Are the white and green lines clean and unbroken?				
Cleanup	(After-work maintenance and cleanup)				
	Is the area free of trash and dust?				
	Have all machines and equipment been cleaned?				
	Has the floor been cleaned?				
	Are cleanup responsibilities assigned?				
	Are trash cans empty?				
Discipline	(Maintaining good habits at Canon)				
	Is everyone dressed according to regulations?				
	Are smoking areas observed?				
	Are private belongings put away?				
	Does everyone refrain from eating and drinking in the workplace?				
	Does everyone avoid private conversations during work time?				

Rank totals [ ] [ ] [ ]

Figure 15-2. Five S Inspection Sheet

For example, the *ZD* groups in one plant got their start during the *Zero Defects* quality movement and kept the name. In another plant, *3G* activity refers to the three groups that must always work in close cooperation to ensure quality — the process in question and those on either side. Each group of three to eight or more workers has its own name or slogan to distinguish it from other groups, such as *Smile, Rainbow,* or *Sphinx.* (Figure 15-4)

Activity / Level	Self-regulated Groups		Project-centered Groups	
Workers	• To increase profits for the corporation and skill levels for the individual. • To instill a feeling that the work is worth doing.	ZD 3G N Plan KS		
Foremen			• To increase productivity and reduce defect rates using IE and QC methods. • For mutual instruction and exchange of techniques.	Mutual analysis and counsel method • IE Plan 310 * • Scramble 10 * • 7-up *
Section Chiefs			• To improve factory manufacturing operations and management system.	Mutual analysis and counsel method • WD Plan *
Division Chiefs Factory Manager			• To plan innovation and vitalization in the factory as a whole.	Mutual analysis and counsel method • PI Plan *

* Each of these activities promotes company productivity improvement targets.

Figure 15-3. Focus of Small Group Activities by Level

Self-regulated small groups carry out each aspect of their activity independently, from the selection of themes to actual problem solving. (Figures 15-5 and 15-6) Quality, productivity, and cost reduction are the most frequently chosen themes. (Figure 15-7) The groups meet formally for two to four hours a month

Department	Name of Group (No. of Group Members)		Target	Target Value	Work Period	Result
Direct Labor						
Assembly Dept. 1	"Rainbow"	15	Shorten the time of an assembly task	150 RU	3 months	Achieved
Machining Dept.	"Perfect"	7	Reduce defective rate	5.2% ⬥ 2.0%	6 months	Achieved (in 3 months)
Surface Treatment Department	"Smile"	11	Increase performance in models 500, 520	67% ⬥ 90%	3 months	Achieved
Indirect Labor						
Supplier Management Dept.	"Suzume"	6	· Make new work standard · Improve present work standard	one item three items	3 months	Achieved
Purchasing Dept.	"Silk Road"	4	Reduce mistakes in issuing slips	less than 1%	3 months	Achieved (mistakes reduced to 0.35% for the monthly issued amount of 1800 slips)
Engineering Dept.	"Sphinx"	12	Prepare data base of total cost for different types of processing	Drilling Grinding Assembly etc.	3 months	Achieved

Figure 15-4. Report of Small Group Activity in Factory T (Targets Achieved)

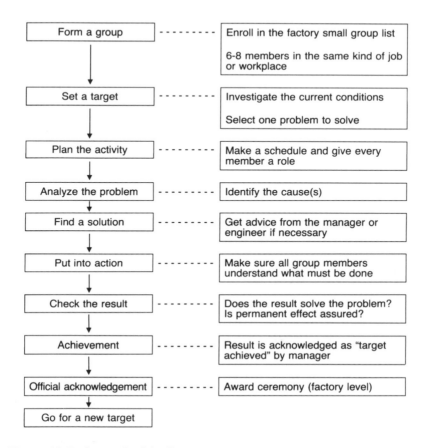

Figure 15-5. Group Activity Process

How to Set a Target

Identify current problems and select one to solve.

1. Is it a worthwhile problem to solve?

2. Can you expect support from your manager with the target you set?

3. Can the problem be solved through the effort of group members?

4. In tackling this problem, can you gain new experience and exercise your creativity?

Figure 15-6. Target-setting Guidelines

As of April 30, 1982

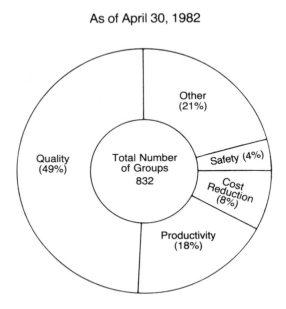

Figure 15-7. Theme for Small Group Activity

during regular working hours. The time they spend in meetings after work is also paid by the company. Group work is also supported by group activity offices in the factories and at company headquarters. These offices train groups and group leaders (see Figure 15-8), publish newsletters, and schedule open factory and company-wide meetings to present results and award prizes.

Groups achieving their targets receive a letter of commendation and a cash bonus from the factory manager. Groups with outstanding results are invited to present them at the All-Canon Small Group Activities Convention, held annually with affiliated companies. Since these conventions are important events, attended by both company executives and worker representatives, the honor of making an announcement is an excellent incentive to the groups.

Courses for "3G" Program

Managers, Foreman

• Methods of Project Support
  (group discussion)

• Significance of Small Group Activity
  (group discussion)

Group Leaders

• Group Leader Training Course (4 hrs.)
  (use *Handbook of 3G Activity*)

• How to Hold Group Meetings (4 hrs.)

• Work-Improvement Methods (4 hrs.)

• Quality Control Methods
  (histogram, pareto diagram, graphs
  and charts)

• Significance of Group Activity

Workers

• Fundamental 3G (1 hr.)

• Work-Improvement Methods (4 hrs.)

Figure 15-8. Small Group Training at Factory T

Typically, a self-regulated small group consists of the workers within a single work center. Some groups, however, are made up of individuals from different work centers or sections who do the same kind of work. These groups have been particularly effective at Canon. Members bring their shared understanding to the problem, and their improvements can be implemented consistently in several work centers at the same time.

Case Study 1 — Miscellaneous Workers Improvement at Factory T

At Factory T, one worker in each section of the manufacturing division usually handles the miscellaneous jobs, involving paperwork and errands. These workers participated in their own section's small group activities but felt out of place because no other member of the group did the same work. Furthermore, since the miscellaneous workers were typically women, they often felt isolated because other members of their group were all men. They did not lack motivation to tackle the problems in their own jobs, however. After consulting their supervisors, they formed their own six-member activity group.

The group's first step was to write their problems on cards, then classify and analyze them. They found that the biggest mutual problem area was paperwork management — copying, distributing, filing, etc. With their objective to "standardize paperwork and reexamine paper management," they set out to accomplish the following tasks:

- Determine what paperwork must be distributed and to whom.
- Standardize the format of documents used in all the sections.
- Create a unified system for classifying and managing paperwork.
- Establish the order in which paperwork is to be handled and clearly indicate where and for how long a document is to be filed.

This first project took the group eight months to complete — two months longer than they had planned. By the end of the project, however, the change in work procedures had produced significant improvements. (See Figure 15-9) Now 1.5 people could manage paperwork that formerly required 2.4 people; unnecessary duplication of copies was eliminated, resulting in a 20 percent reduction in filing binders; documents could be found quickly when they were needed.

Greater self-confidence was the activity's most important result, however. "We can do it, too," said the group members.

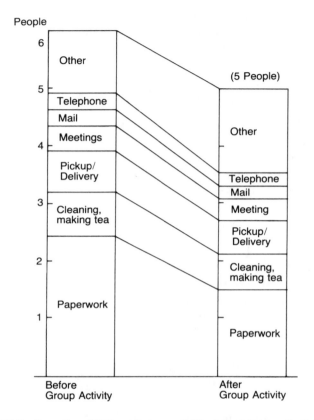

Figure 15-9. Results of "Miscellaneous" Workers' Group Activity

"We designed management procedures for the entire manufacturing division." Their enthusiasm continued, even after one of them was moved to another position, because of the labor savings the group had achieved. Their next project was to develop a work manual.

Mutual Analysis and Counsel Method

In addition to small groups at the worker level, Canon also encourages project-centered group activities at the foreman level and above. These groups have achieved excellent results that parallel the worker group activities in day-to-day operations.

In this type of group, a cross section of the plant's managers and supervisors reviews the problems in one department and investigates opportunities for improvement. On the basis of the advice and counsel received, the managers in that department then carry out the improvements.

Group members find they can:

- Look at the facts more objectively.
- Avoid falling into a rut, by looking at fresh approaches.
- Learn what works and what to avoid from the experience of other departments.
- Increase individual skills by sharing the very best ideas.
- Break down barriers to more effective communication and mutual evaluation in the future.

This method has proven so beneficial that it is now widely applied. For example, whenever company employees tour the workplace for inspection, they routinely write up their observations on a "mutual analysis and counsel sheet."

The following case illustrates how this method originated and how it works in practice.

Case Study 2 — Mutual Analysis and Counsel Method (IE Plan 310 at Factory F)

Ten years after the ZD movement began at Factory F, workers were still enthusiastically engaged in small group activities. Foremen and supervisors, however, were not involved in any organized improvement activity, and they saw this as a definite limitation. It occurred to them that if all levels engaged in small group activity, the level of vitality in the factory would be much higher and more significant improvements could be achieved.

To meet this need, project-centered group activities were initiated at the foreman level and above. Even division chiefs and the factory manager became involved.

IE Plan 310 was a project to increase productivity in one work area by 10 percent within three months. A foreman from the section and two others arranged to put aside their usual work in order to devote themselves full time to the project for the first three weeks. Their activities fell into five broad stages:

Step 1. Understand present conditions — Do loss analysis in the target work area and determine where productivity can be increased.

Step 2. Analyze present conditions — List factors currently holding back productivity as problems to be solved and rough out a plan for improvement.

Step 3. Design the improvement plan — Using previous analysis, brainstorm improvement ideas, evaluate them, and then draw up a detailed plan of action.

Step 4. Implementation — Communicate the plan to all departments involved and gain their cooperation, then implement the action plan.

Step 5. Confirmation — Do another loss analysis to quantify the results of all activities undertaken since the beginning of the project. (Figure 15-10)

After this activity began in May 1980, a new team was formed every month. Team learning and mutual instruction among supervisors and other managers substantially increased vitality among personnel at those levels. And this activity was eventually incorporated into Canon's IE in-service training for supervisors, as follow-up and reinforcement activity.

WORK IMPROVEMENT PROPOSAL SYSTEM

The work improvement proposal system has a long history at Canon. It has been promoted in the company systematically since 1952. Its purpose is to increase interest and involvement in the work effort and promote harmony and cooperation among workers.

Areas of work improvement include:

- Production efficiency
- Cost reduction (expenses)
- Quality improvement
- Safety and hygiene
- Work center environment
- Individual work procedures
- Nine-waste elimination

1. **Target Workplace:** Unit Assembly, Assembly Section

   1. Workers: 12 people
   2. Workers move from place to place according to a work plan, performing independent unit assembly operations that differ from unit to unit.
   3. There are both automatic machine and hand assembly operations.

2. **Loss Analysis**

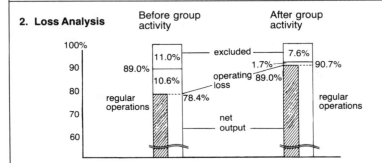

3. **Chief Measures Taken**

   1. **Shelf**
      1. Change construction
      2. Improve screw-tightening tool
      3. Discontinue pellet-check stage
      4. Improve work area

   2. **Spool gear**
      1. Shorten interval of automatic machine
      2. Rebuild 3St part feeder

   3. **142 ASA armature**
      1. Change layout
      2. Improve work area
      3. Shorten interval of air press

   4. **Overall**
      1. Take another look at work plan chart
      2. Thorough preparation before changeover

4. **Graph of Changes in Productivity**

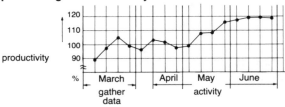

Figure 15-10. IE Plan 310 Activity — Sample Report

The Proposal Office was established to process suggestions from all personnel (except managers) — from development and design to manufacturing. When the CPS effort began in 1976, however, this office was relocated in the CPS Promotion Office so it could serve as one of the primary supports for the vitalization campaign.

Although CPS was aimed only at manufacturing, this move did not turn out to be problematic: after the transfer, proposal activity at Canon increased tenfold within the first two years and continued to rise, especially among line workers. (See Figure 15-11)

One factor in this increase was the new proposal memo system introduced in 1978. Under this system, an improvement idea written in the form of a simple memo is accepted in lieu of a formal proposal. This simplified format helped many individual workers experience the excitement of seeing their own creativity produce change.

Another important factor was the role of the supervisors and managers in encouraging the development and implementation of suggestions. Managers at Canon do not participate in the proposal system — their contribution is to give workers the instruction and guidance they need in order to come up with increasingly effective and creative ideas. The role of the manager in work improvement is to:

1. Show a positive attitude
2. Give hints to workers
3. Listen to workers' problems
4. Make improvement targets clear
5. Plan competitions and games
6. Put proposals into practice quickly
7. Give public recognition

Editor's note: In 1982, the total number of proposals at Canon was 326,989, higher than the level projected in the graph. By 1985, the number had almost tripled, to 893,301. The per person rate had climbed to 70.2. The highest total submitted by one person was 2,600. In 1984 Canon was thirteenth in the top 20 Japanese companies with the highest total numbers of employee suggestions. Matsushita Electric Industries was in first place with over 6.5 million.

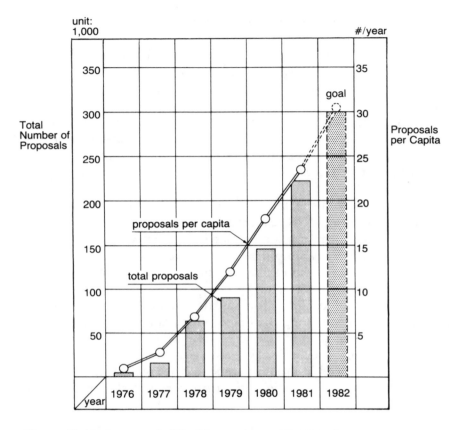

Figure 15-11. Increase in Work Improvement Proposals

In each factory proposals are judged by the section committee, and the grades of honorable mention through E Prize are assigned immediately. (Figure 15-12) All suggestions are recognized: even those that don't receive an honorable mention (acceptance award) are given a 50 yen participation certificate. (See Figure 15-13)

Proposals considered eligible for higher prizes (D through A) are formally re-submitted and judged by the district committee.

The implementation rate for suggestions is high — over 90 percent. In fact, most suggestions are not even submitted as proposals until after they have been implemented successfully.

What is Not a Proposal:

1. A wish or a demand.
   Example: I want a raise.

2. An abstract idea.
   Example: The company needs a new product.

3. A complaint.
   Example: The food at the cafeteria is bad.

4. Personal criticism.
   Example: I don't like A. He should be transferred.

5. Something that benefits only certain people.
   Example: We want an air-conditioner for our room.

After all, the rationale for the system is not simply to gain recognition, but to make successful improvement ideas work for the entire company.

Here is an example of a proposal to promote improvement: *Improvement Time* — every day from 11:30 to 12:00. The foreman can use this time only for activity related to improving the workplace. He may not attend meetings or answer the phone, and his colleagues should also avoid this period in arranging meetings. The foreman must use this time to think about problems in an organized way and draw up plans that will lead to truly effective improvements.

Once a year around ten of the year's A and B prize proposals are chosen to compete for the President's Prize for Work Improvement Proposals. The two with the highest ratings receive the Special President's Prize, and the authors are sent on an overseas study tour. (See Figure 15-14)

Editor's note: By 1985, the total savings to Canon from proposals rated above the level of "Fair" was over $202 million. The operating expense of the system was only $2.2 million, 96 percent of which was prize money.

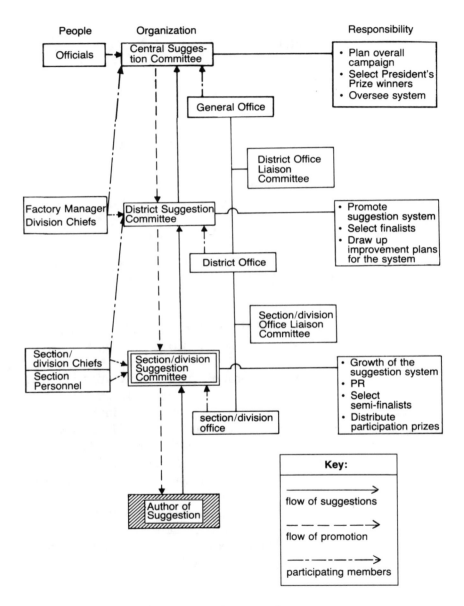

Figure 15-12. Work-improvement Proposal System

Proposal Rank	Prize
Special President's Award	Trip Abroad
A	¥ 50,000 ($250)
B	¥ 20,000 ($100)
C	¥ 10,000 ($50)
D	¥ 5,000 ($25)
E	¥ 3,000 ($15)
Good	¥ 1,500 ($7.50)
Fair	¥ 500 ($2.50)
Acceptance Award	¥ 150 ($.75)

Figure 15-13. Proposal Ranks and Prizes

One of the most notable features of the Canon suggestion system is the prize for lifetime accumulated points. Anyone submitting a proposal awarded an honorable mention or above receives from .33 to 5.0 points, depending on the grade received. These points are cumulated, and every year the 20 people with the highest totals receive the President's Prize for Accumulated Points, along with a gold medal and 300,000 yen ($1,500). The 30 people earning the highest points that particular year receive the President's Prize for Yearly Points, which carries an award of 100,000 yen ($750) and a silver medal. These annual prizes are a great incentive to authors of suggestions and a great source of pride to those who win.

THE AWARDS SYSTEM

One of the ideals of the CPS is to ensure that "evaluations are open; opportunity to win is equal." For this reason, personnel at every level from section chief down may compete for substantial prizes and announce their achievements regularly in a special forum.

The highest CPS award is the Premier Work Center Prize, given to sections practicing outstanding day-to-day management

Prize	Awarded to:	Achievement	Amount	Additional prize	No. Awards	Announced at:
Premier workplace	Section	• All-Canon model workplace • 30% improvement rate 3 years in a row	$1,000	Overseas study tour for section chief Eagle shield (gold)	1-2	CPS convention
Runner-up premier workplace	Section	• Factory model workplace • 30 % improvement rate 3 years in a row	$500	Eagle shield (silver)	10 +	
Excellence in waste elimination	Block, team	Excellent results in waste elimination	$250		50	
Prize for increasing CPS results	Foreman, asst. section chiefs, specialists	Successful application of waste elimination methods		Overseas study tour	3	CPS waste elimination convention CPS convention
Excellence in small group activities	Group	Excellent results through small group activities	$250		2	Canon small group activity convention
President's prize for accumulated points	Top 20 people	Highest total points for work improvement proposals	$1,500	Gold medal	20	
President's prize for yearly points	Top 30 people	Highest annual points for work improvement proposals	$500	Silver medal	30	
President's prize	Individual, group	Best of the year's proposals, B prize and up	$500		10 +	
Special president's prize	Individual, group	Top two president's prize winners		Overseas study tour for representative	2	CPS convention
Gold quality assurance prize (for cooperating factories)	Cooperating factory	Most outstanding quality record	$1,000	Eagle shield (gold)	2	Cooperating factories management training meeting
Silver quality assurance prize (for cooperating factories)	Cooperating factory	Outstanding quality record	$500	Eagle shield (silver)	3	

Figure 15-14. Awards and Honors

and achieving superior results in waste elimination. In each factory the CPS chairman personally inspects the sections recommended by the factory managers and interviews the section chiefs before making his decision. The winning section receives a money prize and a golden eagle shield (Photo 15-1), and the section chief is sent on an overseas study tour.

Photo 15-2. Golden Eagle Shield

The Prize for Excellence in Nine-Waste Elimination is given to work areas or teams achieving outstanding results in each of the nine types of waste. Other awards include the Prize for Increasing CPS Results, awarded to foremen and deputy section chiefs, and the previously mentioned Prize for Excellence in Small Group Activities. The President's Prize for Accumulated Points, the President's Prize for Yearly Points, the Special President's Prize, and the President's Prize are all related to work improvement proposals. Finally, individual factories have a variety of award programs of their own.

At Canon the award system is truly open. People who work hard to produce excellent results can expect to be highly praised and rewarded. Evaluation and selection are held to the strictest standards, however — in some years, no one is eligible for certain prizes. On the other hand, those who make the effort can and do win prizes over and over again.

ANNOUNCEMENT CONVENTIONS

Announcement conventions (Photo 15-2) serve three basic functions: to select outstanding personnel or work areas, announce the results of activities, and provide a forum for mutual instruction. (See Figure 15-15)

Photo 15-2. Announcement Convention

The CPS Waste Elimination Results Convention and the All-Canon Small Group Activity Convention fall into the first category. Every year local announcement meetings are held at every factory to decide who will represent the factory at the company wide conventions. At the convention these individuals are given the honor of making a 20-minute presentation on their improvement activities and vying for the Prize for Increasing CPS Results and the Prize for Excellence in Small Group Activities. The winners are then selected and announced by the CPS chairman and the Study Group Committee.

The CPS Convention is the largest forum for the second category, announcement of improvement results. Held with considerable fanfare every spring, this convention is attended by the

Announcement Convention	Individuals Making Announcements	
CPS Waste Elimination Convention	Foremen, asst. section chiefs, and staff	People contributing to successful workplace management through new waste elimination methods.
Canon Small Group Activity Convention	Small-group activity group leaders: (1 person from each factory)	Groups achieving out-standing results in small group activity
CPS Convention	Premier workplace prize: Section chief of winning section	Section chiefs
	Prize for increasing CPS results: 3 prize winners	Foreman, deputy section chiefs, staff
	Prize for excellence in small group activities: Leader of winning group	General workers
	Special President's prize for work improvement proposals: 1 prize winner	General workers

Figure 15-15. Announcement Conventions

president and other top company officials and sums up the results of the CPS activities for the previous year. All the section chiefs, foremen, ordinary workers, and staff who received awards during that year present their activities and achievements and are honored by the company as a whole.

Canon's announcement conventions bring together and reinforce all the vitalizing activities described in this chapter.

"Conventions where everyone can learn together" is an apt slogan to describe them, because they do more than serve as forums for reporting work activities and achievements. Those selected to speak can learn from having to reflect on their activities and summarize them for presentation. Those who listen have the opportunity to learn new management techniques and gain insight from the experience of other factories, sections, and individuals. And, more important, everyone learns *directly*, as part of a vivid personal experience. Finally, Canon benefits as a whole — in the higher levels of achievement for Canon factories and work areas, and for the individuals who work in them. For this reason, representatives come to listen not only from every Canon factory, but also from affiliated and overseas factories.

Keys to Fundamental Improvement

*Continuous improvement is the result of
continuous involvement.*

As long as improvement activity is viewed as "extra" effort, improvement results will only be "extra-ordinary," that is, periodic and inconsistent. It is not enough simply to maintain high levels; the goal must be to exceed them — always.

Canon established this "habit of improvement" by making improvement activity an inseparable part of everyone's daily work.

Opportunities for improvement are provided in a structured way through Five S and small group activities as well as company-wide waste elimination and productivity improvement drives. Incentives for individual and group efforts are provided through the work improvement proposal award and announcement systems. This wide range of activities satisfies individual as well as group concerns and helps achieve company targets at the same time.

Individual involvement at Canon is not maintained entirely by the appeal of group goals or satisfaction of group activity, however. At every level, opportunities exist for self-development and advancement through formal and informal skills training.

Chapters 16, 17, and 18 are selections from *Introduction to TPM: Total Productive Maintenance*, Seiichi Nakajima (Cambridge: Productivity Press, 1988)

16
TPM Is Profitable

Total productive maintenance (TPM) is productive maintenance carried out by all employees through small group activities. Like TQC, which is companywide total quality control, TPM is equipment maintenance performed on a companywide basis.

THE NEW DIRECTION IN PRODUCTION

TPM is the new direction in production. In this age, when robots produce robots and 24-hour automated production is a reality, the unmanned factory has become a realistic possibility. In discussing quality control, people often say that quality depends on process. Now, with increasing robotization and automation, it might be more appropriate to say that quality depends on equipment. Productivity, cost, inventory, safety and health, and production output — as well as quality — all depend on equipment.

Production equipment has become unimaginably sophisticated. We see equipment for automation, such as robots and unmanned production; we also see equipment for super-precise processing of micron-size objects and processing that requires speeds, pressures, and temperatures challenging current technology.

Increased automation and unmanned production will not do away with the need for human labor — only operations have been automated; maintenance still depends heavily on human input. Automated and technologically advanced equipment, however, require skills beyond the competence of the average maintenance supervisor or worker, and to use it effectively requires an appropriate maintenance organization. TPM, which organizes all employees from top management to production line workers, is a companywide equipment maintenance system that can support sophisticated production facilities.

The dual goal of TPM is zero breakdowns and zero defects. When breakdowns and defects are eliminated, equipment operation rates improve, costs are reduced, inventory can be minimized, and as a consequence, labor productivity increases. As Table 16-1 illustrates, one firm reduced the number of breakdowns to $\frac{1}{50}$ of the original number. Some companies show 17-26 percent increases in equipment operation rates while others show a 90 percent reduction in process defects. Labor productivity generally increased by 40-50 percent.

Of course, such results cannot be achieved overnight. Typically, it takes an average of three years from the introduction of TPM to achieve prize-winning results. Furthermore, in the early stages of TPM, the company must bear the additional expense of restoring equipment to its proper condition and educating personnel about the equipment. The actual cost depends on the quality of the equipment and the quality of maintenance. As productivity increases, however, these costs are quickly replaced by profits. For this reason TPM is often referred to as "profitable PM."

ACHIEVING ZERO BREAKDOWNS:
THE PARLOR FACTORY

At the Nishio pump factory of Aishin Seiki, which is called a "parlor factory," you must take off your shoes at the entrance.[1]

Inside, every section is so clean you may find it hard to believe that you are in a factory that processes metal cuttings. Thus, the nickname "parlor" is quite appropriate. The *zashiki* or "parlor" is the room where the Japanese entertain their guests, and it is usually kept immaculately clean. Although a closer look at the factory reveals cut metal processing for car pump parts, as well as oil and metal filing dust, there are neither oil splatters nor dust on the floor. The floor actually sparkles.

Since 1972, Aishin Seiki has received a prestigious award every five years: the Deming Prize in 1972, the Japan Quality

---

[1] In Japan, you never wear your shoes beyond the entrance to a home.

Category	Examples of TPM Effectiveness

P
(Productivity)
	• Labor productivity increased:
	  140% (Company M)
	  150% (Company F)
	• Value added per person increased:
	  147% (Company A)
	  117% increase (Company AS)
	• Rate of operation increased:
	  17% (68% → 85%) (Company T)
	• Breakdowns reduced:
	  98% (1,000 → 20 cases/mo.) (Company TK)

Q
(Quality)
	• Defects in process reduced:
	  90% (1.0% → 0.1%) (Company MS)
	• Defects reduced:
	  70% (0.23% → 0.08%) (Company T)
	• Claims from clients reduced:
	  50% (Company MS)
	  50% (Company F)
	  25% (Company NZ)

C
(Cost)
	• Reduction in manpower:
	  30% (Company TS)
	  30% (Company C)
	• Reduction in maintenance costs:
	  15% (Company TK)
	  30% (Company F)
	  30% (Company NZ)
	• Energy conserved:
	  30% (Company C)

D
(Delivery)
	• Stock reduced (by days):
	  50% (11 days → 5 days) (Company T)
	• Inventory turnover increased:
	  200% (3 → 6 times/mo.) (Company C)

S
(Safety/
Environment)
	• Zero accidents
	  (Company M)
	• Zero pollution
	  (every company)

M
(Morale)
	• Increase in improvement ideas submitted:
	  230% increase (36.8 → 83.6/person per year) (Company N)
	• Small group meetings increased:
	  200% (2 → 4 meetings/mo.) (Company C)

Table 16-1. Examples of TPM Effectiveness (Recipients of the PM Prize)

Control Prize in 1977, and the PM Prize in 1982. Aishin Seiki introduced TPM in 1979 with the idea that "no-man" manufacturing (automation) must begin with a "no-dust" workplace. The company's plan to reorganize the factory to improve operation management systems for each product created an opportunity to use the Nishio pump factory as a model "parlor factory".

In addition, a successful worker participation campaign under the slogan, "Let's create our own workplace with our own hands" initially contributed to a cleaner workplace. Workers sacrificed weekends and holidays to help in this effort. At Aishin Seiki, the standards for a clean workplace are based on the 6 *S*'s , the traditional 5 *S*'s (*seiri* — organization, *seiton* — tidiness, *seiso* — purity, *seiketsu* — cleanliness, and *shitsuke* — discipline), plus a sixth *S* *shikkari-yarou* or "let's try hard!" — which means that every person should show initiative and make a special effort.

Workers' efforts at Aishin Seiki eventually bore fruit. Since May 1982 there have been no equipment breakdowns; prior to TPM implementation they numbered more than 700 per month! Furthermore, the current level of quality is extraordinary — a mere 11 defects for every one million pumps produced! Indeed, the plant is now prepared for the unmanned production of the future.

17
TPM — Challenging Limits

Following World War II, the Japanese industrial sectors borrowed and modified management and manufacturing skills and techniques from the United States. Subsequently, products manufactured in Japan became known for their superior quality and were then exported to the Western industrial nations in large quantities, focusing world attention on Japanese-style management techniques.

FROM PM TO TPM

The same has happened in the field of equipment maintenance. More than thirty years have passed since Japan imported preventive maintenance (PM) from the United States. Later adoptions include productive maintenance (PM), maintenance prevention (MP), and reliability engineering. What we now refer to as TPM is, in fact, American-style productive maintenance, modified and enhanced to fit the Japanese industrial environment.

TPM is now well-accepted by the Japanese industrial sector, and is attracting the attention of Western industrial nations, China, and various southeast Asian countries.

FOUR DEVELOPMENTAL STAGES OF TPM

Preventive maintenance was introduced in the 1950's, with productive maintenance becoming well-established during the 1960's. The development of TPM began in the 1970's. The period prior to 1950 can be referred to as the "breakdown maintenance" period.

As illustrated in Table 17-1, the growth of PM in Japan can be divided into the following four developmental stages:

Stage 1: Breakdown Maintenance
Stage 2: Preventive Maintenance
Stage 3: Productive Maintenance
Stage 4: TPM

More recently, both predictive maintenance and equipment diagnostic techniques have attracted considerable attention. These techniques indicate the direction of future PM development.

		1976	1979
Stage 1	Breakdown maintenance	12.7%	6.7%
Stage 2	Preventive maintenance	37.3%	28.8%
Stage 3	Productive maintenance	39.4%	41.7%
Stage 4	TPM	10.6%	22.8%

Table 17-1. The Four Developmental Stages of PM and the Current Situation in Japan

In a company, TPM is achieved in stages corresponding to the stages of TPM development in Japan between 1950 and 1980. The information in Table 17-1 is based on data collected in 1976 and 1979 from 124 factories belonging to the JIPM. In three years, the number of factories actively practicing TPM more than doubled. Now, more than one fifth of these factories practice TPM.

Until the 1970's, Japan's PM consisted mainly of preventive maintenance, or time-based maintenance featuring periodic servicing and overhaul. During the 1980's preventive maintenance is rapidly being replaced by predictive maintenance, or condition-based maintenance. Predictive maintenance uses modern monitoring and analyzing techniques to diagnose the condition of equipment during operation — to identify the signs of deterioration or imminent failure.

DEFINITION AND DISTINCTIVE FEATURES OF TPM

TPM is often defined as "productive maintenance involving total participation." Frequently, management misconstrues this to mean workers only and assumes that PM activities are to be carried out autonomously on the floor. To be effective, however, TPM must be implemented on a companywide basis. Unfortunately, some firms abandon TPM because they fail to support workers fully or involve management.

A complete definition of TPM includes the following five elements:

1. TPM aims to maximize equipment effectiveness (overall effectiveness).
2. TPM establishes a thorough system of PM for the equipment's entire life span.
3. TPM is implemented by various departments (engineering, operations, maintenance).
4. TPM involves every single employee, from top management to workers on the floor.
5. TPM is based on the promotion of PM through *motivation management*: autonomous small group activities.

The word "total" in "total productive maintenance" has three meanings that describe the principal features of TPM:

1. *Total effectiveness* (referred to in point 1 above) indicates TPM's pursuit of economic efficiency or profitability.
2. *Total maintenance system* (point 2) includes maintenance prevention (MP) and corrective maintenance (CM) as well as preventive maintenance.
3. *Total participation of all employees* (points 3, 4, and 5) includes autonomous maintenance by operators through small group activities.

The first principal feature of TPM, "total effectiveness" or "profitable PM," is also emphasized in predictive and productive maintenance. The second feature, a "total maintenance system," is another concept first introduced during the productive maintenance era. It establishes a maintenance plan for the equipment's entire lifespan and includes maintenance prevention (MP: maintenance-free design), which is pursued during the equipment design stages. Once equipment is assembled, a total maintenance system requires preventive maintenance (PM: preventive medicine for equipment) and corrective maintenance (CM: repairing or modifying equipment to prevent breakdowns and facilitate ease of maintenance). The last feature, "autonomous maintenance by operators" (small group activities), is unique to TPM.

	TPM features	Productive Maintenance features	Preventive Maintenance features
Economic efficiency (profitable PM)	○	○	○
Total system (MP-PM-MI)*	○	○	
Autonomous maintenance by operators (small group activities)	○		

TPM = Productive Maintenance + small-group activities

*MP = maintenance prevention
PM = preventive maintenance
MI = maintainability improvement

Figure 17-1. Relationship Between TPM, Productive Maintenance, and Preventive Maintenance

In American-style PM, the maintenance department is generally responsible for carrying out PM. This reflects the concept of division of labor, an important feature of American labor unions. Japanese-style PM, or TPM, on the other hand, relies on everyone's participation, particularly autonomous maintenance by operators.

If a company is already practicing productive maintenance, TPM can be adopted easily by adding autonomous maintenance by operators to the existing system. If a company has not yet implemented preventive or productive maintenance, however, a sudden shift from breakdown maintenance to TPM will be extremely difficult, although not impossible.

STRIVING FOR OVERALL
EQUIPMENT EFFECTIVENESS

The object of production improvement activities is to increase productivity by minimizing input and maximizing output. More than sheer quantity, "output" includes improving quality, reducing costs, and meeting delivery dates while increasing morale and improving safety and health conditions, and the working environment in general.

The relationship between input and output in production activities can be illustrated in a matrix (Figure 17-2). *Input* consists of labor, machine, and materials, while *output* is comprised of production (P), quality (Q), cost (C), delivery (D), safety, health and environment (S), and morale (M).

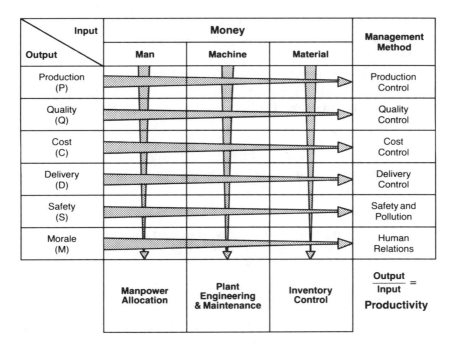

Figure 17-2. Relationship Between Input and Output in Production Activities

Correlating these factors in terms of equipment maintenance demonstrates clearly that all aspects of PQCDSM are related to output. With increasing robotization and automation, the more the production process shifts from workers to machines, the larger the role played by the equipment itself in controlling output, or PQCDSM. Productivity, quality, cost, and delivery, as well as safety and health, environment, and morale all depend on the condition of equipment.

TPM strives to maximize output (PQCDSM) by maintaining ideal operating conditions and running equipment effectively. A piece of equipment that suffers a breakdown, experiences periodic speed losses, or lacks precision and produces defects is not operating effectively.

The life cycle cost (LCC) (the cost incurred during the equipment's lifespan) required to maintain equipment at its optimal level is limited. TPM strives to achieve overall equipment effectiveness by *maximizing* output while *minimizing* input, *i.e.*, the life cycle cost (LCC).

To achieve overall equipment effectiveness, TPM works to eliminate the "six big losses" that are formidable obstacles to equipment effectiveness. They are:

Down time

- Equipment failure — from breakdowns
- Setup and adjustment — from exchange of die in injection molding machines, etc.

Speed losses

- Idling and minor stoppages — due to the abnormal operation of sensors, blockage of work on chutes, etc.
- Reduced speed — due to discrepancies between designed and actual speed of equipment

Defect

- Process defects — due to scraps and quality defects to be repaired
- Reduced yield — from machine startup to stable production

ZD AND TPM: DEFECT PREVENTION SYSTEMS

The ZD (zero defects) movement came to Japan from the United States in 1965, when ZD campaigns were widespread there. In 1979, Philip Crosby, the creator of ZD, published the best-selling *Quality is Free*, (New York: McGraw-Hill), in which he defined quality as "conformity to requirements" and called for the companywide implementation of ZD or "quality management." His four principles of quality management are listed in Table 17-2. The goal of zero defects is to create a means of promoting prevention — an essential element in the pursuit of quality.

---

1. The definition of quality is conformance to requirements
2. The system of quality is prevention
3. The performance standard is zero defects
4. The measurement of quality is the price of nonconformance

From Philip B. Crosby, *Quality Without Tears* (New York: McGraw-Hill Book Co., 1984)

Table 17-2. The Four Absolutes of Quality Management

Zero defects and productive maintenance have a common philosophy. While zero defects strives to prevent defects, productive maintenance in Japan has emphasized the importance of preventing breakdowns for over 30 years. Since equipment failure is a type of defect, both ZD and PM, in effect, are preventive systems aimed at eliminating defects.

THE TOYOTA PRODUCTION SYSTEM AND TPM

The Toyota production system is well-known both in Japan and abroad. It has been argued that Japanese automobile manufacturers achieve their superior productivity through the practice of ZD by auto and parts manufacturers.

Unlike a traditional quality effort based on defect discovery, Japanese-style ZD is based on defect prevention. In Japan, the operators themselves are the inspectors responsible for quality assurance.

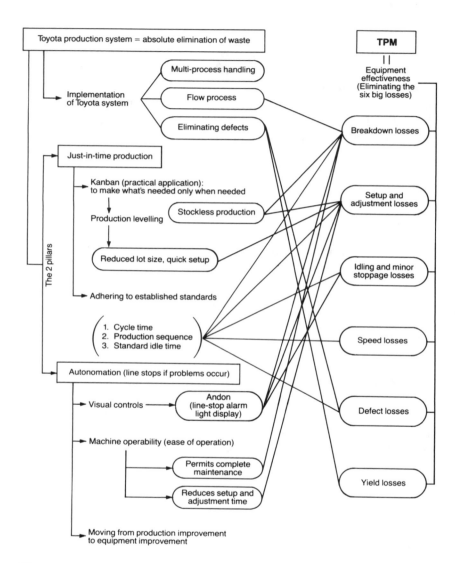

Figure 17-3. Toyota Production System and TPM

ZD is considered a significant factor in the success of a just-in-time production system as well. Indeed, if there were defects among supplied parts, just-in-time production as well as zero inventory production would be impossible. Thanks to ZD, parts inventories in Japan are usually held from two hours to two days, compared to Western averages of up to 10 days.

Figure 17-3 illustrates the relationship between TPM and the principal features of the Toyota production system. According to its creator, Taiichi Ohno, the Toyota production system is based on the absolute elimination of waste, namely the elimination of defects and inventories in just-in-time production to produce "the necessary objects, when needed, in the amounts needed." The Toyota production system strives to attain zero defect and zero inventory levels, which, in essence, is ZD.

As illustrated on the right side of the figure, the purpose of TPM is to eliminate the six big losses. This corresponds to the absolute elimination of waste in the Toyota production system.

In striving for zero breakdowns, TPM promotes defect-free production, just-in-time production, and automation. It is safe to say that without TPM, the Toyota production system could not function. The fact that Toyota-related companies are rapidly implementing TPM confirms its importance in the Toyota production system.

18

Maximizing Equipment Effectiveness

If we are told that equipment effectiveness at Plant X is more than 85 percent, we might reasonably assume that the equipment is being operated efficiently and effectively. But what method of calculation was used to determine the rate of equipment effectiveness and on what data were the calculations based? Many companies use the term "rate of equipment effectiveness, but their methods of calculation vary widely."

EQUIPMENT USAGE AT ONLY HALF ITS EFFECTIVENESS

Often, what is referred to as the rate of equipment effectiveness is actually the operating rate or *availability*.

Measuring Availability

The *operating rate* is based on a ratio of operation time, excluding downtime, to loading time. The mathematical formula for this is:

$$\text{Availability} = \frac{\text{operation time}}{\text{loading time}} = \frac{\text{loading time} - \text{downtime}}{\text{loading time}}$$

In this case, *loading time*, the amount of time spent loading the system per day (or month), is derived by subtracting the planned loading time from the running time per day (or month).

Planned downtime refers to the amount of downtime officially scheduled in the production plan, which includes downtime for scheduled maintenance and management activities (such as morning meetings). For example, assume the working shift per day is eight hours, or 480 minutes. If the planned downtime per day is 20 minutes, then the loading time per day will be 460 minutes.

The *operation time* is derived by subtracting equipment downtime (non-operation time) from loading time; in other words, it refers to the time during which the equipment is actually operating. Equipment downtime involves equipment stoppage losses resulting from failures, setup/adjustment procedures, exchange of dies, etc. For example, again assume a loading time per day of 460 minutes. If downtime per day were composed of breakdowns (20 minutes), setup (20 minutes) and adjustment (20 minutes), or a total of 60 minutes, the operation time per day would be 400 minutes. In this case, the availability ("rate of operation time") would be calculated as follows:

$$\text{Availability} = \frac{400 \text{ minutes}}{460 \text{ minutes} \times 100} = 87\%$$

Accurate Data Is Essential

If the raw data collected in the workplace were accurate, 87 percent availability would be a reliable figure; however, the accuracy of records on actual equipment operation varies depending on the company. Often, such figures are not even recorded. Some managers feel that the time workers spend recording data is wasted and should be used for operational procedures. Minimal operation records must be kept, however, and the recording procedures should be simple and expedient.

Assume, as in the example above, that the planned downtime is 20 minutes, and the recorded downtime 60 minutes, supposedly caused by breakdowns — 20 minutes, setup — 20 minutes, and adjustments — 20 minutes. It is difficult to determine the accuracy of these recorded times. Obviously, there is no need to measure times to the second, but in practice, records often vary from the actual elapsed time by as much as ten minutes. Some companies do not even record equipment failure downtime unless it exceeds thirty minutes. This is an unsound practice. Operation times based on such crude data, in which failure downtime of ten or twenty minutes goes unrecorded, can only lead to crude management as well.

If we want to practice "profitable TPM" and pursue optimal equipment effectiveness, the following two factors are crucial. First, we must keep accurate equipment operation records so that the appropriate management and controls can be provided (with narrower targets); and second, we must devise a precise scale for measuring the equipment operation conditions.

A Broader Range of Factors Must Be Considered

Equipment operation conditions are not reflected accurately when they are based solely on the availability (operation time ratio) figure mentioned above. Of the six big equipment losses, only downtime losses are calculated to determine availability. Other equipment losses such as speed and defect losses are not accounted for. To represent actual equipment operating conditions accurately, all six equipment losses must be included in the calculations.

As shown in Figure 18-1, TPM includes all six of the big equipment losses in its calculations. It measures overall equipment effectiveness by multiplying availability and performance efficiency by the rate of quality products. This measure of overall equipment effectiveness combines the factors of time, speed, and quality of the equipment operation and measures how these factors can increase added value.

Performance Efficiency

Performance efficiency is the product of the operating speed rate and the net operating rate. The *operating speed rate* of equipment refers to the discrepancy between the ideal speed (based on equipment capacity as designed) and its actual operating speed. The mathematical formula for the operating speed rate is:

$$\text{Operating speed rate} = \frac{\text{theoretical cycle time}}{\text{actual cycle time}}$$

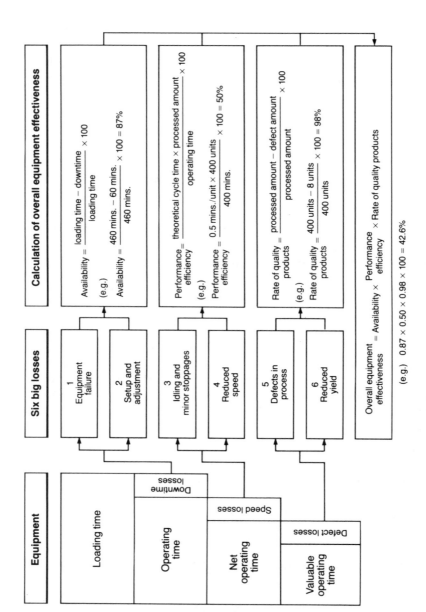

Figure 18-1. Overall Equipment Effectiveness and Goals

For example, if the theoretical (or standard) cycle time per item is 0.5 minutes and the actual cycle time per item is 0.8 minutes, the calculations would go as follows:

$$\text{Operating speed rate} = \frac{0.5 \text{ minutes}}{0.8 \text{ minutes} \times 100} = 62.5\%$$

The *net operating rate* measures the maintenance of a given speed over a given period. This figure cannot tell us, however, whether the actual speed is faster or slower than the design standard speed. It measures whether an operation remains stable despite periods during which the equipment is operated at a lower speed. It calculates losses resulting from minor recorded stoppages, as well as those that go unrecorded on the daily logs, such as small problems and adjustment losses:

$$\text{Net operating rate} = \frac{\text{actual processing time}}{\text{operation time}} =$$

$$\frac{\text{processed amount} \times \text{actual cycle time}}{\text{operation time}}$$

For example, if the number of processed items per day is 400, the actual cycle time per item is 0.8 minutes and the operation time is 400 minutes:

$$\text{Net operation rate} = \frac{400 \text{ items} \times 0.8 \text{ minutes}}{400 \text{ minutes} \times 100 = 80\%}$$

$(1 - \text{net operation rate})$, which is 20% = losses caused by minor stoppages

Let us calculate the performance efficiency:

$$\text{Performance efficiency} =$$
$$\text{net operation rate} \times \text{operating speed rate} =$$

$$\frac{\text{processed amount} \times \text{actual cycle time}}{\text{operation time} \times \text{ideal cycle time} \div \text{actual cycle time}} =$$

$$\frac{\text{processed amount} \times \text{ideal cycle time}}{\text{operation time}} =$$

$$\frac{400 \text{ (items)} \times 0.5 \text{ minutes}}{400 \text{ minutes} \times 100 = 50\%}$$

(or $0.625 \times 0.80 \times 100 = 50\%$)

If the rate of quality products is 98 percent, then the overall equipment effectiveness is as follows (see also Table 18-1):

Overall equipment effectiveness =
Availability × performance efficiency × rate of quality products =
0.87 × 0.50 × 0.98 × 100 = 42.6%

Even though the availability is 87 percent, the overall equipment effectiveness, when actually calculated, is not even 50 percent, but an astonishingly low 42.6 percent. The data used in these examples are representative of the average company. In essence, the numbers reveal that equipment was being used at only half its effectiveness.

A: Working hours per day = 60 minutes × 8 hours = 480 minutes
B: Planned downtime per day (downtime accounted for in the production schedule for scheduled maintenance, or for management purposes such as morning meetings) = 20 minutes
C: Loading time per day = A − B = 460 minutes
D: Stoppage losses per day (breakdowns — 20 minutes; setup — 20 minutes; adjustment — 20 minutes) = 60 minutes
E: Operating time per day = C − D = 400 minutes
G: Output per day = 400 items
H: Rate of quality products: 98%
I: Ideal cycle time: 0.5 minutes/item
J: Actual cycle time = 0.8 minutes/item

Therefore,
F: Actual processing time = J × G = 0.8 × 400
T: Availability = E/C × 100 = 400/460 × 100 = 87%
M: Operating speed rate = I/J × 100 = 0.5/0.8 × 100 = 62.5%
N: Net operating rate = F/E × 100 = (0.8 × 400)/400 × 100 = 80%
L: Performance efficiency = M × N × 100 = 0.625 × 0.800 × 100 = 50%

Overall equipment effectiveness = T × L × H × 100 = 0.87 × 0.50 × 0.98 × 100 = 42.6%

Table 18-1. Overall Equipment Effectiveness Calculations

Based on our experience, the ideal conditions are:

- Availability . . . greater than 90%
- Performance efficiency . . . greater than 95%
- Rate of quality products . . . greater than 99%

Therefore, the ideal overall equipment effectiveness should be:

Overall equipment effectiveness:

$$0.90 \times 0.95 \times 0.99 \times 100 = \;>85\%$$

This figure is not just a remote goal. All the PM prize-winning companies have an equipment effectiveness greater than 85 percent.

Table 18-2 presents overall equipment effectiveness calculations made at a representative plant. Following this example, calculate the overall equipment effectiveness of your own company. Be prepared for a figure that is considerably lower than you expected. The lower the present overall equipment effectiveness, however, the more untapped potential your company possesses.

For example, if the present overall equipment effectiveness at your firm were 50 percent and you used TPM to raise it to 85 percent, the difference would be a 35 percent increase. A ratio of 35 to 50 percent would represent a 70 percent increase in overall equipment effectiveness.

An increase in overall equipment effectiveness produces an increase in productivity. We have presented examples of PM prize-winning firms increasing their productivity by 50 percent, but even a 70 percent increase in productivity is not unattainable.

BREAKDOWNS AND MINOR
STOPPAGES IMPEDE AUTOMATION

Murata Kikai is well known as a model factory for the flexible manufacturing system (FMS). Its advanced level of automation is impressive.

Seven machining (MC) centers, unmanned carts, automatic pallet changers, automated warehouses, and so on, are controlled by computers. Only two workers were needed during the day to palletize machined parts and transport them to the automated warehouses. The rest of the work is performed 24-hours a day by continuous automated processing.

The work, which is pre-set on pallets, is ordered by the computer to be transported from the automated warehouse by unmanned carts to the automatic pallet changer in the machining

Process	A Working hours (h)	B Planned downtime (h)	C Loading time (h) A − B	D Downtime loss (h)	E Operating time C − D	F Actual processing time (h) J × G	T Availability E/C × 100 (%)	G Quantity processed		H Quality rate G₁/G
								Output (number of quality products) G_1	Total (including losses and rework) G	G_1/G
Internal Finish	17.75	2.3	15.45	—	15.45	10.6	100	4,000	4,018	99.6
	18.58	0.6	17.98	—	17.98	12.8	100	4,800	4,818	99.6
	16.83	0.7	16.13	—	16.13	11.65	100	4,400	4,418	99.6
Total	(59.66)	(3.7)	(55.96)	—	(56.06)	(39.05)	(100)	(14,800)	(14,863)	(99.55)
External Finish	6.5	0.1	6.4	—	6.4	4.62	100	1,187	1,190	99.7
	17.75	0.7	17.5	0.5	16.55	13.8	97.1	3,513	3,542	99.2
	17.75	0.8	16.95	—	16.95	12.86	100	3,297	3,309	99.6
	16.0	1.1	14.9	—	14.9	12.25	100	3,030	3,150	96.2
Total	(58.0)	(1.7)	(56.3)	(0.5)	(54.8)	(43.62)	(99.27)	(11,027)	(11,191)	(98.67)
External Finish	6.5	0.1	6.4	0.2	6.2	3.17	96.9	1,187	1,202	98.8
	17.75	0.7	17.05	—	17.05	9.48	100	3,513	3,593	99.8
	17.75	0.8	16.95	—	16.95	8.95	100	3,297	3,392	97.2
	16.0	1.1	14.9	—	14.9	8.1	100	3,030	3,060	99.0
Total	(58.0)	(1.7)	(56.3)	(0.2)	(55.1)	(29.7)	(99.22)	(11,027)	(11,247)	(98.2)

Process	I Standard cycle time (s) M/C	J Actual cycle time (s) M/C	L Operation performance ratio M×N (%)	M Operation speed ratio J/J (%)	N Net operation ratio F/E (%)	Number of minor stoppages	Number of exchanges of diamond grindstone	Overall equipment effectiveness T×L×H
Internal Finish	9.5	9.8	66.4	96.9	68.6	2	2	66.1
	9.5	9.8	68.9	96.9	71.2	4	2	68.6
	9.5	9.8	69.9	96.9	72.2	—	2	69.6
Total	(9.5)	(9.78)	(66.9)	(97.07)	(69.7)	(8)	(7)	66.5
External Finish	14	16.6	60.6	84.3	72.2	1	3	60.4
	14	16.65	70.3	84.1	83.4	—	8	67.6
	14	16.45	64.5	85.1	75.9	—	6	64.2
	14	16.15	71.2	86.7	82.2	—	6	68.1
Total	(14)	(16.45)	(66.3)	(85.05)	(78.42)	(1)	(23)	65.6
External Finish	9.5	10.4	46.4	91.3	51.1	—	1	43.6
	9.5	10.5	50.0	90.1	55.6	—	4	49.9
	9.5	10.5	47.5	90.1	52.8	—	3	45.5
	9.5	10.4	49.6	91.3	54.4	—	3	45.1
Total	(9.5)	(10.45)	(48.4)	(90.7)	(53.47)	—	(11)	48.4

Table 18-2. Calculations Chart for Overall Equipment Effectiveness

center. After being processed in the machining center, the work is once again transported to the warehouse by unmanned carts and stored. Currently, the processed cast-iron product requires four manufacturing processes. One lot averages 30-50 items, and approximately 1,300 different types can be produced. For this reason, the factory is a model workplace for the flexible manufacturing system.

This FMS has not yet achieved full automation. Its one shortcoming lies in the area of maintenance. When breakdowns and minor stoppages occur during the night, the entire automated system shuts down. Although operation procedures involving processing, setup, removal, and conveyance have all been successfully automated, maintenance is still difficult to automate.

Murata Kikai's method of increasing labor productivity by performing setup procedures during the day and using automated production at night has been adopted in various industries; however, unless breakdowns and minor stoppages are completely eliminated, further increases in labor productivity will not be realized.

Neither large breakdowns nor minor stoppages can be ignored. Minor stoppages happen for a variety of reasons. Equipment will stop when work clogs at the top of a chute, when a limit switch slips out of position, or when a sensor is alerted because a quality defect has occurred. As in the Aishin Seiki "parlor factory" that eliminated breakdowns, "no-man manufacturing" (automation) starts with "no-dust" workplaces. We often refer to the 5 S's of equipment maintenance, because we can only eliminate equipment failures and minor stoppages and achieve full automation by performing thorough daily maintenance through cleaning, lubricating, bolting, and so on, and through inspections to create a clean, dust-free workplace.

STOP ACCELERATING THE DETERIORATION OF EQUIPMENT

We like to say that equipment maintenance means maintaining the health of equipment. Preventive medicine has reduced the incidence of disease and increased the human life span significantly. Similarly, preventive maintenance is preventive medicine and health maintenance for equipment.

Figure 18-2 compares preventive medicine with preventive maintenance. In preventive medicine, emphasis is placed on the prevention of illness, so that disease will not be contracted at all. Proper diet and basic hygiene (*e.g.*, washing hands, gargling) help prevent disease. In addition, periodic health checkups performed by specialists promote early detection and treatment.

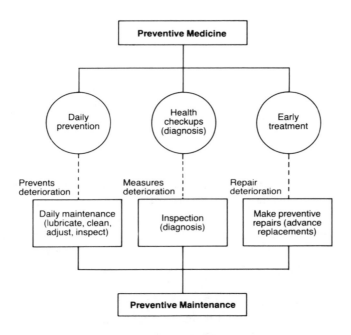

Figure 18-2. Preventive Medicine for Equipment = Preventive Maintenance

Daily equipment maintenance serves the same purpose. By diligently lubricating, cleaning, and performing adjustments (such as bolting) and inspections, deterioration can be prevented and potential equipment failures ("disease") averted. Just as people are responsible for their own health, the person using a piece of equipment should be responsible for its health. In other words, daily maintenance is the responsibility of the equipment operator. This is the basic premise behind autonomous maintenance by operators. Furthermore, maintenance personnel, who in effect are "equipment doctors," are responsible for *periodic inspections* (equipment audits functioning as health checkups) and *preventive repairs* (advance replacements functioning as early treatment).

Thus, preventive maintenance decreases the number of breakdowns (equipment disease) and inevitably increases equipment life span.

The practicality of preventive medicine is easy to grasp. The cost of daily prevention and periodic checkups is minimal compared to expenses incurred when health care is neglected and when illness leads to hospitalization.

Similarly, it is cheaper to repair the equipment on a preventive basis than to wait until it has completely deteriorated. At that stage the cost of restoring equipment is exorbitant. Oddly enough, however, many companies choose not to practice preventive maintenance or practice it only halfheartedly, even though they understand its importance. Perhaps they are like people who knowingly sacrifice their health and shorten their life spans by overworking and eating and drinking immoderately.

Factories that fail to implement preventive maintenance are, in essence, accelerating the deterioration of their equipment. They are as unlike the "parlor factory" as night is from day. In such factories, powdered dust and chips fly in all directions and lubricants and oil drip while the equipment and floor are littered with dirt, dust, oil, and raw materials.

When dust and dirt adhere to moving parts and rubbing surfaces of the machinery, the surfaces are scratched, causing deterioration. And, when lubrication is neglected, excessive friction or burning can result, wasting energy.

A general inspection often reveals that more than half the nuts and bolts are loose. When loosening and deterioration go unattended, they can cause excessive shaking, which encourages abnormal friction and triggers further deterioration. Moreover, when plumbing maintenance is inadequate, leaks may develop resulting in excessive waste of precious materials and energy. In factories where such neglect is rampant, sudden failures and minor stoppages are inevitable and common.

Some factory managers have a defeatist attitude: They say, "We can't prevent breakdowns and minor stoppages." Their factories are already in a critical state; breakdowns and minor stoppages have reduced overall equipment effectiveness and reduced productivity. Pressed by the production schedule, these factories do not have the flexibility to implement preventive maintenance. Breakdowns and minor stoppages continue, and conditions go from bad to worse.

At some point, however, unfavorable conditions like these must be stopped. Bad habits and defeatist attitudes can be deeply ingrained in the minds of all the employees — from top management to workers on the floor; they then become part of the company's basic disposition. Middle managers and front line personnel alone cannot change the disposition of the company. Moreover, lukewarm determination will not be enough to change long-standing bad habits. Only when top management is seriously committed to TPM can those habits be discarded and an unfavorable environment altered. Only then is fundamental improvement in a company's disposition possible.

PREVENTIVE MAINTENANCE ALONE CANNOT ELIMINATE BREAKDOWNS

About ten years ago, management at Company N reported that although they had been practicing preventive maintenance for many years, the number of equipment failures had not decreased significantly. They were advised that preventive maintenance alone cannot eliminate breakdowns and encouraged to implement TPM. Taking this action eventually proved successful — they went on to win the PM Prize.

Why can't preventive maintenance by itself eliminate breakdowns?

According to the principles of reliability engineering, the causes of equipment failure change with the passage of time. In Figure 18-3, breakdowns, or the failure rate, appear on the vertical axis. The failure rate curve is also referred to as the "life span characteristic curve", or the "bathtub" curve (for its characteristic shape). When equipment is new, there is a high failure rate (early failure period), which eventually drops and levels off. Then the failure rate stabilizes at a certain level for a long period of time (accidental failure period). Finally, as equipment approaches the end of its useful life, the failure rate increases once again (wear-out failure period).

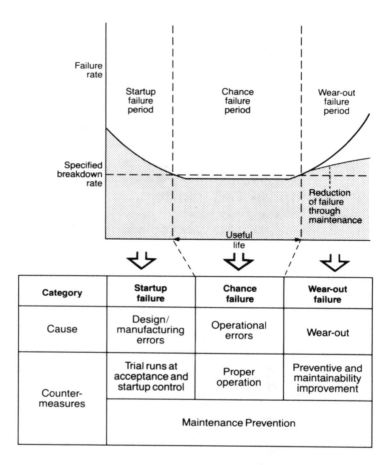

Figure 18-3. Lifespan Characteristics and Breakdown Countermeasures

At the Hamamatsu factory of the Japan National Railways, Shinkansen (bullet train) cars are serviced. According to the staff there, the failure rate for bullet train cars exactly mirrors the life span characteristic curve. The Tokaido Shinkansen began its service in 1964, the year the Olympics were held in Tokyo. At that time, newspapers frequently ran articles such as: "The Shinkansen Fails Again." Breakdowns occurring at that time corresponded to the early period failure.

Early period failures, accidental failures, and wear-out failures each have different causes, as illustrated in Figure 18-3. Therefore, to achieve successful results each type of breakdown must be treated by different countermeasures.

Causes of early period failure are design and manufacturing errors. To combat them, the design department must conduct test runs at the earliest stage. Furthermore, startup or corrective maintenance must be pursued to discover and treat weaknesses in design and manufacturing.

Accidental failures are caused primarily by operation errors, so the most effective countermeasure is to ensure that operators use equipment properly.

Wear-out failures are due to the limited natural life span of equipment parts. Equipment life can be extended by preventive maintenance and by corrective maintenance (through changes in design). This will reduce the wear-out failure rate.

Maintenance prevention is an effective countermeasure for all three types of breakdowns. A "maintenance-free" equipment design must be incorporated at the planning/design stage to prevent early period, accidental, and wear-out failures.

When the life cycle of equipment is considered in this manner, it becomes obvious that preventive maintenance alone cannot eliminate breakdowns. The success of TPM depends upon the cooperation of all departments. Maintenance as well as design/planning and operations departments should be involved in the elimination of breakdowns.

FIVE COUNTERMEASURES
FOR ZERO BREAKDOWNS

Ideally, breakdowns can be eliminated entirely through maintenance prevention (MP), or the adoption of "maintenance-free" design. The condition of most factory equipment, however, is far from this ideal.

The first step toward improvement is to eliminate failures in equipment currently being operated. The experiences gained from this endeavor can then be fed back to design better equipment. Gradually the equipment will approach the ideal.

According to the Japanese Industrial Standards (JIS), "a failure results in loss of a standard function in a certain object (*e.g.*, system, machine, part)." This "loss of a standard function" indicates that machine failures are not limited to unexpected breakdowns that lead to a complete stoppage. Even when equipment is running, deterioration can cause various losses, such as the loss of a standard function, longer and more difficult setup/adjustments, frequent idling and minor stoppages, and reduction in processing speed and cycle time. Such losses must be treated as failures.

Unexpected breakdowns with complete stoppage are called "function-loss failures" while those involving equipment deterioration despite continued operation are called "function-reduction failures."

Breakdowns represent the tip of the iceberg. We tend to become overly concerned with breakdowns and serious defects because they are so obvious, and there certainly are cases in which a single defect causes a breakdown. Small defects, however, such as dirt, dust, friction, loosening, scratches, and warping — which may seem insignificant on their own — are the real problem.

These small defects can suddenly become large. Sometimes they overlap to create a stronger effect, triggering both function-loss and function-reduction failures. As the saying goes, "even one match can cause a fire," so it is important to stamp out defects while they are small. This is the fundamental concept behind preventive maintenance.

Defects that go undetected and untreated are called "hidden defects." If they remain untreated, they will trigger breakdowns. Therefore, it is important to expose hidden defects and restore optimal conditions.

To eliminate failures we must expose hidden defects and treat equipment before it breaks down. The following five concrete countermeasures help eliminate failures:

1. Maintaining well-regulated basic conditions (cleaning, lubricating, and bolting)
2. Adhering to proper operating procedures
3. Restoring deterioration
4. Improving weaknesses in design
5. Improving operation and maintenance skills

Figure 18-4 illustrates the relationships between these five countermeasures. Breakdowns often occur because people fail to implement simple measures. As this figure illustrates, breakdowns can be eliminated by carrying out simple procedures in a simple manner.

To ensure that simple procedures are performed thoroughly, both the operations and maintenance departments must understand each other's role and cooperate, like the wheels of a car. They must be willing to adjust their points of view and behavior and fulfill their respective duties. Everyone involved with equipment operation or maintenance must work to eliminate failures. (Figure 18-5 shows the division of labor between the operations and maintenance departments in pursuing the goal of zero breakdowns.)

UNLICENSED OPERATION OF AUTOMATED EQUIPMENT

Consider two types of companies: The first type of company possesses a high degree of technical ability. Equipment and dies are designed and manufactured within the company and workers are trained to handle their equipment properly. The other type of company subcontracts the production of its equipment and dies and attaches no importance to equipment technology. It operates its automated equipment nonchalantly, without technical know-how, like a automobile driver without a license.

Anjo Denki is a subsidiary of Nippondenso with approximately 600 employees. It produces electrical relays specifically for cars. The president of the firm is an expert engineer capable of designing his own equipment. He praises the West German corporate emphasis on technology and manages his company in a similar manner. He is a strong advocate of TPM and the integration of TPM and TQC. In 1978, his company won the PM prize in Category 2, and in 1981, the prize in Category 1.

By implementing TPM, Anjo Denki significantly increased its overall equipment effectiveness in such areas as its automated assembly line — even its parent company, Nippondenso, was impressed with the progress. It is company policy to train all of its employees to deal with the equipment. Young production engineers

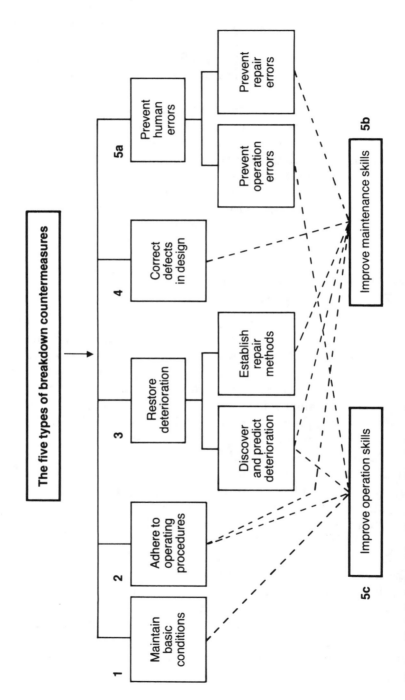

Figure 18-4. Relationships Between Breakdown Countermeasures

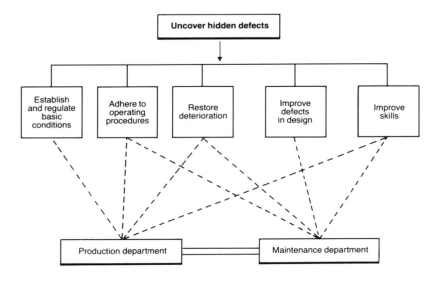

Figure 18-5. Responsibilities of the Operations and Maintenance Departments

are being trained to develop automatons; operators in the mechanical division, which manufactures dies and special equipment, are studying for the technical qualification exams in engineering to increase their competence; and many regular and part-time employees in the workplace have learned the basics of equipment maintenance and practice autonomous maintenance, taking to heart the principle that all individuals are responsible for their equipment.

From now on, development of efficient equipment will be the key to survival. For example, Yoshida Kōgyō (YKK) develops its own equipment and also dominates the world zipper market.

Like Anjo Denki, most of the companies awarded the PM Prize for TPM implementation possess the technical ability to develop and produce their own equipment and dies. One small company that won the PM Prize in 1981 was particularly impressive. Even though it had fewer than fifty employees, its two veteran engineers developed all the equipment, tools, and dies.

We strongly encourage in-house design and manufacture of equipment and dies, because it helps polish and perfect production techniques and skills. Moreover, keeping up with technological progress is essential to survival.

Companies choosing to ignore TPM are the complete opposite of those described above. They subcontract the design and manufacture of equipment and dies and only a few qualified technicians are on hand to ensure effective equipment operation. But dependence on outside manufacturers for equipment and dies wastes a potential advantage. In addition, a company that has not developed its own equipment, tools, and dies, will also lack the level of technical ability necessary for effective maintenance. Finally, since the life cycle of equipment and dies cannot be controlled within the company, its ability to provide maintenance prevention and corrective maintenance is low.

The rationale behind subcontracting equipment, tools, and dies is to focus energy and resources on production itself rather than on indirectly related processes such as design and development. However, this indifference and sometimes contempt for equipment technology indicates a lack of understanding of its importance in manufacturing today.

Equipment is becoming increasingly sophisticated. Computers as well as hydraulic and electric controls are being used. Companies neglecting technology give their new employees who just graduated from technical high schools only brief training before sending them to the production floor. Obviously, new employees who barely understand the structure and functions of their sophisticated, automated equipment will have difficulty operating it. Defects in process, equipment breakdowns, and accidents are inevitable. Such inadequate use of sophisticated equipment certainly represents a kind of "unlicensed operation" that is a far cry from the level of operations found in companies practicing TPM.

ERRORS IN EQUIPMENT INVESTMENT

Japanese cars are extremely fuel-efficient and their low breakdown rate keeps repair costs down to a minimum. Thus, Japanese cars are more economical than the average American car despite the higher price tag.

In 1983, the author met with a U.S. LCC consultant who, like the author, was a member of the Society of Logistics Engineers (SOLE). Since the life cycle cost (LCC) of Japanese cars is exceptional, the consultant hoped to establish a U.S.-Japan exchange of ideas on this subject.

Certainly since the oil crisis, Japanese car manufacturers have striven to attain high fuel-efficiency and reliability. Furthermore, they have sought to win the international price war by eliminating waste and implementing value engineering (VE). As a result, Japan has surpassed Western nations to achieve the lowest total life cycle costs in terms of purchase price, fuel, and upkeep.

Based on this, the consultant assumed that information on LCC would be widespread in Japanese industry. He was surprised to learn that hardly any Japanese auto manufacturers practice the so-called "Design To LCC" (DTLCC), in which a company commits to pursue economic life cycle cost as early as the design stage. Although the "pursuit of economic LCC" is understood as a concept in Japan and has been put into practice to a limited extent, Japanese manufacturers still lack the "LCC design" procedures that are being developed and actually applied in the U.S.

For other durable consumer goods, such as household appliances and cameras, Japan has the lowest life cycle costs as well. Consumers are the ultimate beneficiaries of a company's pursuit of economic LCC. And, since to increase sales manufacturers are obliged to give consumers what they want, they should pursue economic LCC aggressively. No consumer would object to this.

Why is it, then, that when we talk about the pursuit of economic life cycle in relation to the productive or capital goods of factory production equipment, the discussion becomes vague and ambiguous? With respect to equipment investment, just as with durable consumer goods, an economic LCC will benefit the consumer.

Many companies miscalculate their profits and losses when considering equipment investment. The following example, provided by Professor Senju Shizuo of Keio University, compares the economic effectiveness of two types of paints and illustrates traditional attitudes towards LCC.

To cover a certain area, Paint A would cost $5,000 and last three years. Paint B would cost $15,000 (three times the cost of Paint A) and last six years. Which is more economical?

As illustrated in Figure 18-6, Paint A would require labor costs of $20,000, resulting in a total figure of $25,000 (including the $5,000 for the paint). Since the life span of the paint is three years, another $25,000 would be needed three years later.

Comparison of two types of paints

	Cost of paint	Lifespan	Ratio
Paint A	$5,000	3 years	$1,666/year
Paint B	$15,000	6 years	$2,500/year

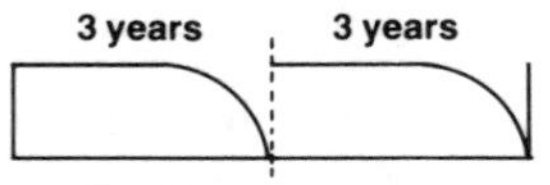

3 years   **3 years**

Cost of paint	$5,000	$5,000
Labor costs	$20,000	$20,000

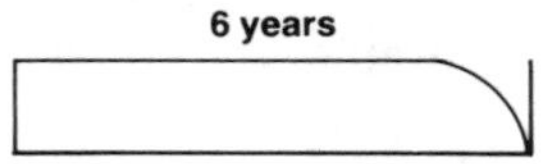

6 years

Cost of paint	$15,000
Labor costs	$20,000

(from Senju Shizuo, Session 1, Third Terotechnology Symposium, 1979)

Figure 18-6. Pursuit of Economic Life Cycle Cost

Paint B, on the other hand, would require $15,000 for paint and $20,000 for labor (same as for Paint A). The total figure for Paint B, therefore, would be only $35,000 over a six year period.

Comparing the total costs for six years, including labor, Paint B is far more economical — $15,000 less than paint A.

It would be a mistake to purchase paint A based on price alone, saying that paint A costs $5,000 for a life span of three years, or $1,666 per year, while paint B costs $15,000 for a life span of six years, or $2,500 per year. Purchasing the paint is not the only goal of the transaction. If you actually want to have the area painted over a given period of time, clearly, the overall calculations of profits and losses must be based on the total costs for paints A and B, including labor.

The same is true for equipment investment, as the following example will illustrate: Companies A and B have submitted estimates for equipment. As shown in Table 18-3, company A's estimate is $50,000 and company B's is $35,000. Many companies would compare the two firm's estimates and sign a contract with company B, because "B is cheaper than A."

	A	B
Purchasing price of equipment	$100,000	$70,000
Annual sustaining cost	$30,000	$60,000
Life	5 years	
Interest rate	10%	
Annual value method	$56,380	$78,466
Present value method	$213,730	$297,460

(Figures for annual and present values based on economic engineering.)

Table 18-3. A Comparison of Equipment Life Cycle Costs

As the paint example shows, however, it is a mistake to make such a decision based on purchase price alone. It would be more profitable to compare life cycle costs. In other words, we should consider the total costs over a five-year period, including annual maintenance ($15,000 for Company A, $30,000 for Company B) and a 10 percent calculated interest rate.

When comparing long-term economic effectiveness in this manner, we must consider the time value of money. Cost conversions based on factors such as calculated interest must be measured, using tools of engineering economics. There are three methods of comparison available: (1) All monetary earnings and expenses are converted into current values, referred to as the present value method. (2) The final value method is applied at the end of the period of comparison. (3) The annual value method is used to estimate annual expenses.

Here, we shall use the annual and present value methods in comparing the two companies, both of which result in lower figures for Company A, as shown in Table 18-3. In other words, when the life cycle costs of the two firms are compared over a five-year period, Company A is clearly the better choice.

The U.S. Department of Defense has been approving its contracts for the procurement of large-scale projects based on LCC since 1976. The U.S. Department of Defense used to calculate profitability based simply on a comparison of procurement prices. Over time, however, a rapidly increasing percentage of the defense budget had to be allotted for operation and maintenance costs, rather than for the procurement of new projects. To increase the Department's purchasing power while keeping costs down, procurements were made on an estimated budget based on LCC.

Other examples of the growing use of LCC calculations are businesses that rent or lease construction equipment, computers, and even copying machines. The rental or leasing fees for such equipment are calculated using the annual value method formula, which is based on LCC and includes maintenance costs as well as other service charges.

Through the activities of the American Society for Logistics Engineering, information on life cycle cost is being disseminated internationally — no country can afford to ignore LCC.

THE FIVE TPM DEVELOPMENT ACTIVITIES

The practical details and procedures for using TPM to maximize equipment effectiveness must be tailored to the individual company. Each company must develop its own action plan, because needs and problems vary, depending on the company, type of industry, production methods, and equipment types and conditions.

When members of the Japan Institute of Plant Maintenance consult for a Japanese company, they propose a TPM development schedule designed to meet the company's predisposition, needs, and problems, based on preliminary diagnosis and investigation. There are, however, some basic conditions for the development of TPM that apply in most situations.

Generally, the successful implementation of TPM requires:

1. Elimination of the six big losses to improve equipment effectiveness
2. An autonomous maintenance program
3. A scheduled maintenance program for the maintenance department
4. Increased skills of operations and maintenance personnel
5. An initial equipment management program

These are the basic TPM development activities. These developmental activities constitute the minimal requirements for the development of TPM.

Chapters 19 and 20 are selections from *Zero Quality Control: Source Inspection and the Poka-Yoke System*, Shigeo Shingo (Cambridge: Productivity Press, 1986)

19

Inspections

THE SIGNIFICANCE OF INSPECTIONS

We have explained that production activities form a network of processes and operations. What, then, is the significance of inspections?

Inspections Supplement Processes

As we have seen, production is constructed of a network of processes and operations. Processes, we said, can be further broken down into four categories: work, inspection, transportation, and delay. We also said that inspections consist of comparisons with standards, but this is merely a description of the act of inspection. Within a process, inspections are characterized by the following functions:

- Inspections reveal and prevent defects in the course of work.
- Inspections reveal and prevent defects in the course of transportation.
- Inspections reveal and prevent defects in the course of delays.

In this way, inspections may be said to supplement work, transportation, and delays. Strictly speaking, the inspection function can be thought of as secondary to production, with inspections themselves playing only a passive, wasteful role.

Although from an operations point of view it is necessary to conduct maximally efficient inspection operations, the fact that inspections are of little value on the process side means that even the most efficient inspection operations are nothing more than efficiently wasteful. It follows that we need, first of all, to examine why we are conducting inspections at all. Even more, we need to carry out higher-order investigations aimed at finding methods of work, transportation, and delays that obviate the need for inspections.

Although inspections are supplementary to work, transport, and delays, from this point I am going to focus on the functions of inspections with respect to work, or processing.

On Defects and Inspections

Isolated Defects and Serial Defects

Isolated defects are essentially those that occur only once. An example would be a single part that is defective because one particular unit of raw material was flawed.

Serial defects, in contrast, occur repeatedly. For example, many pieces might lack holes because a broken punch was not detected right away.

Sensory Inspections and Physical Inspections

Sensory inspections are inspections performed by means of the human senses, e.g., judgments of plating adequacy or inspections of paint saturation. It tends to be difficult to set criteria for inspections of this kind, because different people will make different judgments and even the same person might make different judgments on different days.

Physical inspections involve the use of measuring devices, such as calipers or micrometers.

Subjective Inspections and Objective Inspections

Subjective inspections are made by the same person who performed the work. This method always suffers from the dangers of compromise and inattention.

Objective inspections, on the other hand, are made by some-one other than the operator who performed the work. This method provides for more rigorous inspections — with fewer lapses of attention — than does the subjective method.

Process-Internal Inspections and Process-External Inspections

Inspections carried out at the same process where the work was performed are process-internal inspections, and inspections carried out at a different process are process-external inspections. Because process-internal inspections permit rapid transmission of information, or feedback, in the event a defect occurs, they are more efficient in reducing defects.

Statistical Inspections and Nonstatistical Inspections

In carrying out inspections — especially sampling inspections — the number of samples may be chosen either in accordance with statistical theory or not. Obviously, it is more rational to determine the number of samples on the basis of statistical theory.

100 Percent Inspections and Sampling Inspections

An inspection of every processed item is a 100 percent inspection, and the method of extrapolating from an appropriate number of samples constitutes sampling. Inspection labor costs can be considerably reduced where it is permissible to conduct sampling inspections. It is sometimes claimed that 100 percent inspections generally take a great deal of trouble and increase the risk of oversights.

Feedback and Action

When a defect occurs, information to that effect sent back to the work process is known as inspection feedback. Such feedback is most effective when it is given promptly, for it permits counter-measures to be devised and methods altered at the work process where the defect occurred. This devising of countermeasures is known as action.

Measurement and Judgment

Measurement refers to the determination of numerical values through the use of measuring devices such as calipers or micrometers after work has been completed. A decision to accept or reject the item is then made on the basis of these numerical results. Since inspections essentially involve distinguishing acceptable from unacceptable goods, however, it is not always necessary to make numerical measurements. Sometimes a simple gauge-like judgment tool is adequate for determining whether an item is acceptable. When inspections focus on judgments rather than measurements, automated inspections can make use of extremely simple and inexpensive devices.

Quantity Inspections and Quality Inspections

Checks to ascertain that needed quantities suffer from neither excesses nor shortages are quantity inspections, while quality inspections include checks such as the following:

- Is the part machined to within permissible limits?
- Has the surface been ground to within permissible limits?
- Is the degree of hardness obtained in heat treatment suitable?
- Are any parts missing from the assembly? Are all parts present the right ones?
- Are there any scratches? Is the part clean?

Quality inspections may even involve judgments made with the aid of numerical measuring devices as long as what is being checked is product quality.

INSPECTIONS DON'T REDUCE DEFECTS

A plant manager at A Industries complained during one of my visits that he simply could not find any way to reduce defects. "What have you tried?" I asked.

He told me that an inspector at the very end of the process in question separated the good products from the defective ones, but that about 100 units out of every 1,000 were defective. At that point, the plant manager ordered an increase in the number of inspectors. The next day, the number of defective units dropped to 80 and the second day it fell to 60. He felt somewhat relieved to be on the right track, but on the fourth day the number of defective items rose again, this time to 120 (*Figure 19-1*). "What on earth am I supposed to do to cut defects?" he asked.

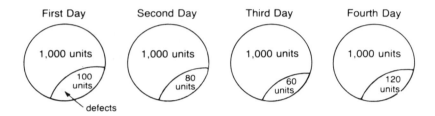

Figure 19-1. Inspections and Defects

This is what I told the plant manager:

"Two inspectors may be able to catch defects that might slip by one inspector, and using the two inspectors may, indeed, eliminate such oversights and keep you from mixing defective items in with the good ones you send to customers.

"That issue, however, is unrelated to the question of reducing defects.

"In any event, there isn't much point in inspecting goods at the end of the process. Since defects are generated during the process, all you are doing is discovering those defects. Adding inspection workers is pointless, because there's no way you're going to reduce defects without using processing methods that prevent defects from occurring in the first place.

"It follows, then, that when a defect shows up, you've got to send information to that effect back to the work stage so that processing can be corrected. "At any rate, it's an unalterable fact that processing produces defects and all that inspections can do is find those defects. That's why approaching the problem only at the inspection stage is meaningless."

20

Approaching the Zero QC Method

PRELIMINARY STAGE: THE OLD METHOD

I was taught that an inspection within a process is the act of comparison with a standard, principally to eliminate defective goods. When 100 percent inspections took too much trouble, I used appropriate sampling inspections. I imagined that the occurrence of a certain level of defects was inevitable in any work done by humans, and thought that we should pay attention so as to not produce defective items as we work. At the same time, I vaguely assumed that we could reduce defects by making inspections more and more rigorous. In short, I thought that judgment inspections were the only kind of inspections there were.

STAGE 1: ENCOUNTER WITH THE STATISTICAL QUALITY CONTROL (SQC) METHOD

In 1951, when I was in charge of education for the Japan Management Association, a Mr. A from Nippon Electric Company came to my office and asked me if I had heard about quality control. I replied that I understood the term to mean efforts to inspect products, make high-quality goods, and eliminate defects.

"That's not good enough," he told me. "It's not quality control unless you use statistics." He then proceeded to explain the American-style statistical quality control (SQC) method to me. He told me about experimental planning methods, determination of significant differences, factor charts, histograms, and control charts for informative inspections. For the next several hours, I listened to him explain such things as standard limits and control limits, control charts and 3 SD limits, X.R control charts, P control charts, and sampling inspections based on statistical science.

What particularly impressed me was the revolutionary idea of informative inspections that could reduce defects in the future. With this approach, control charts would be drawn up and, whenever values appeared outside of the control limits, information to that effect would be fed back to the process involved and work methods would be improved. I was further struck by the truly revolutionary technique of determining whether a situation was normal or not through classification according to 3 SD control limits. At the most basic level, I was enormously impressed by the theoretical backing provided by the science of inductive statistics. It seemed to me, too, that the theory-based techniques of experimental planning methods and the determination of significant differences were extremely effective.

Mr. A told me he had total confidence in this theoretical sampling inspection system, in which sampling inspections that used to depend solely on intuition were put on a scientific, statistical footing.

His final words left a powerful and lasting impression. "From now on," he stressed, "if it doesn't use statistics, it's not quality control." For a long time afterwards, I believed that quality control systems that used the science of statistics were the ultimate in quality control methods. I believed, furthermore, that informative inspections constituted a revolutionary control system for raising quality, and inductive statistics provided the most rational technique available. I invited Dr. Eisaburo Nishibori to the Japan Management Association and devoted myself to studying the statistical quality control (SQC) method.

STAGE 2: ENCOUNTER WITH POKA-YOKE METHODS

In 1961, I visited Yamada Electric in Nagoya. There, the plant manager told me the following story.

"One of the operations we do involves the assembly of an extremely simple push-button device that we deliver to our parent company, Matsushita Electric, in Kyushu. The device is composed of two buttons, an *on* button and an *off* button, under each of which we have to enclose a small spring. Sometimes, though, one of our workers forgets to put in a spring. When Matsushita Electric discovers a switch without a spring, we have to send an inspector all the way to Kyushu to check every switch that was delivered.

"This is a real pain in the neck, so whenever it happens, we tell workers to be particularly careful and for a while things improve a bit. The same thing happens again before long, though, and these chronic defects are getting to be a real nuisance. Matsushita bawls us out every time for making mistakes in such a simple operation, and recently I had to go to Kyushu myself to apologize. Is there anything we can do to keep these defects from occurring?"

I immediately went into the plant to observe the assembly of the switches.

The operation was an extremely simple one. A worker would insert two small springs and then install the buttons. As I watched, however, a worker neglected to put in a spring before installing the button. The head of the manufacturing department saw this, too. In a panic, he scolded the worker for forgetting the spring and then had the switch reassembled.

I thought about what I had seen for a moment and then turned to Mr. Y, the manufacturing department chief.

"What," I asked him, "does it mean for a human being to 'forget' something?"

Mr. Y looked puzzled and replied, "To 'forget' means . . . well . . . it just means to forget, doesn't it?"

When I asked him to explain, he was unable to answer and finally fell silent. After a brief pause, I suggested to him that there were really two kinds of forgetting. The first involves simply forgetting something. Since people are not perfect, they will, on rare occasions, inadvertently forget things. It is not that they forget things intentionally; they just happen, inadvertently, to forget now and then.

"Haven't you ever, in your whole life, forgotten anything?" I asked Mr. Y.

"Sure I have," he replied. "I forget things now and then. My wife always chews me out about it."

I observed that, that being the case, he was probably in a poor position to complain to his wife that his workers were forgetting things.

The other type of forgetting, I told him, involves forgetting that one has forgotten. We are all familiar with this kind of forgetting. It is the reason, for example, that we make checklists for ourselves. If people had the omnipotence of gods, they would be able to remember everything and they would not need checklists.

"When I go to play golf," I said, "I carry a checklist with me in a notebook. When I am about to leave, I mostly depend on my memory when I'm getting together the equipment I need. Afterwards, though, I look at my checklist and when I notice, for example, that I have forgotten my gloves, I immediately get my gloves and put them in my bag. That way, I have all my equipment with me when I get to the golf course.

"The same thing applies to this operation. Rather than thinking that workers ought to assemble the switches perfectly every time, you should recognize that, being human, they will, on rare occasions, forget things. To guard against that," I suggested, "Why not take the idea of a checklist and incorporate it into the operation?" The next question was how this could be done, so I had them put the following suggestions into effect (*Figure 20-1*):

- A small dish was brought and, at the very beginning of the operation, two springs were taken out of a parts box containing hundreds of springs and placed on the dish.
- Switch assembly took place next; then springs were inserted and buttons installed.
- If any spring remained on the dish after assembly, the worker realized that spring had been left out, and the assembly was then corrected.

This change in the operation completely eliminated the problem of missing springs and the parent company made no more complaints on the subject.

Since springs in the earlier operation had been taken out of a parts box containing hundreds of other springs, there had been no way of knowing whether a spring had been removed or not. The new operation made it possible to know that a part had been forgotten and so eliminated the problem of missing springs.

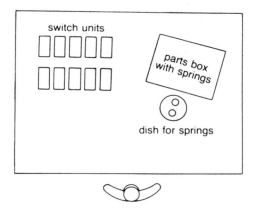

Figure 20-1. Ensuring Spring Insertion

Whenever I hear supervisors warning workers to pay more attention or to be sure not to forget anything, I cannot help thinking that the workers are being asked to carry out operations as if they possessed divine infallibility. Rather than that approach, we should recognize that people are, after all, only human and as such, they will, on rare occasions, inadvertently forget things. It is more effective to incorporate a checklist — i.e., a poka-yoke — into the operation so that if a worker forgets something, the device will signal that fact, thereby preventing defects from occurring. This, I think, is the quickest road leading to attainment of zero defects.

This poka-yoke concept is actually based on the same idea as "foolproofing," an approach devised mainly for preserving the safety of operations. In the early days, I used the term "foolproofing" (in Japanese, *bakayoke*), but around 1963, when Arakawa Auto Body adopted a "foolproofing" device to prevent seat parts from being spot-welded backwards, one of the company's part-time employees burst into tears when her department head explained that a "fool-proofing" mechanism had been installed because workers sometimes mixed up left- and right-hand parts. "Have I really been such a fool?" she sobbed. She ended up staying home the following day and the department head went to see her there.

He tried all sorts of explanations. "It's not that you're a fool," he told her. "We put the device in because anybody can make inadvertent mistakes." Finally, he managed to persuade her.

When the department head told me this story, it was clear to me that "foolproofing" was a poorly chosen term. But what name would be suitable? After some thought, I gave the name poka-yoke (mistake-proofing) to these devices because they serve to prevent (or "proof;" in Japanese, *yoke*) the sort of inadvertent mistakes (*poka* in Japanese) that anyone can make.

Since the word poka-yoke (pronounced POH-kah YOH-kay) has been used untranslated in the English version of my book, *A Study of the Toyota Production System*[1], and appears in the French, Swedish, and Italian-language editions, it is now current throughout the world.

In the years following the development of the idea, poka-yoke devices were used widely. Because the adoption of appropriate poka-yoke devices results in the total elimination of defects, I began to have some doubts about the conventional view of exclusive reliance on SQC methods.

I think the source of this doubt lay in the fact that the poka-yoke approach uses 100 percent inspections to guard against inadvertent mistakes. I had come to assume that if we admit the existence of inadvertent mistakes, then 100 percent inspections are superior to sampling inspections based on statistical theory. Nevertheless, my belief that SQC provided the best quality control methods available remained largely unshaken. At the time, I thought that the total elimination of defects had been an effect of 100 percent inspections. If, instead, I had noted the significance of checking actual working conditions, the concept of "source inspections" would surely have been developed sooner.

It is clear to me now that my belief that SQC methods were unsurpassed impeded development in the direction of source inspections.

---

[1] This book, one of the first available in this country on Just-in-Time, has been retranslated and is available from Productivity Press.

STAGE 3: ENCOUNTERS WITH
SUCCESSIVE AND SELF-CHECKS

Application of the poka-yoke concept in numerous plants brought success that exceeded my expectations. Unfortunately, however, although poka-yoke devices were fine in situations permitting the use of physical detection methods, there are a surprising number of things that can only be checked by means of sensory detection methods. The poka-yoke approach cannot be applied in such cases.

Despite the fact that SQC methods had achieved markedly better results than conventional judgment inspection methods, I still felt there was something missing. In particular, I wondered why it was that, appropriately applied, the poka-yoke method was capable of eliminating defects entirely while SQC methods could only lower defect rates. I concluded that, although the SQC system was characterized by informative inspections, the answer to the question lay in the fact that the detection of abnormalities was performed selectively and corrective action took place slowly. If that was the case, I thought, then more rapid action would be provided by *self-checks*. It seemed to me that the answer lay in having the processing operation worker carry out both checks and action.

Given the long-standing emphasis on the objectivity of inspections, however, this concept was flawed by the idea that, if the worker involved carried out his or her own inspections, he or she might be apt to compromise on quality, or might inadvertently let defects slip by. This is why stress had always been laid on the need to guarantee the independence of inspections — on the idea that inspections had to be performed by disinterested inspectors.

Since this inevitably slowed down corrective action, it occurred to me that the need for objective inspections did not require that inspections be carried out — as is common — at the end of the work process. Why not have the closest person perform inspections? The "closest person," i.e., the operator at the next process, could just as well take on the job of inspector. This would have the benefit that information about any abnormality discovered could be relayed immediately to the worker at the previous process. This is how the *successive check system* was devised. This method garnered considerable success in subsequent experimental applications at a number of plants (*Figure 20-2*).

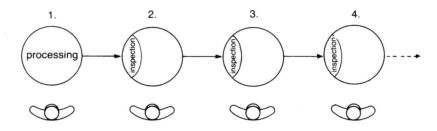

Figure 20-2. Successive Checks

In 1963, I went as a consultant to Matsushita Electric's Moriguchi Television Division. Mr. Kishida, the head of the division, told me that his plant had adopted a SQC system because of a 15 percent process defect rate. The SQC methods, along with the enthusiastic use of control charts and QC Circle activities, had brought the defect rate down to 6.5 percent, but afterward it had just stayed there. Mr. Kishida was still not satisfied and he asked me if there were some other methods he might use.

After a good deal of thought, I proposed that he try a successive check system. I explained the method to him and the new system was rapidly put into place. One month later, the interprocess defect rate fell to 1.5 percent. Three months later, that rate had dropped to 0.65 percent, and the defect rate at the last process had gone as low as 0.016 percent.

Emboldened by the success of the successive check system, I realized that a *self-check system* would allow even faster corrective action to take place. Self-checking, though, was said to be flawed by workers' tendencies to make compromises and inadvertently overlook problems.

Those issues related to sensory inspections, however, and it dawned on me that, in cases where poka-yoke devices could be used, a self-check system was even better than a successive check system. With this in mind, I actively developed poka-yoke devices and worked to expand the use of successive check systems. In instances where it was technically or economically unfeasible to apply poka-yoke methods to self-check systems, we tried hard to incorporate poka-yoke functions into successive check systems.

This way of using self-check systems and successive check systems proved to be markedly more successful than SQC systems using control charts.

Yet these self-check systems and successive check systems remained approaches based on the idea of informative inspections, and in that sense were founded on the same concepts as were SQC-based control chart systems. The reason that they were far more successful in reducing defects resided in large part, I think, in the fact that the detection of abnormalities was carried out by means of 100 percent inspections rather than sampling inspections, and when abnormalities occurred, corrective action was taken extremely rapidly. Considerations such as these were already outside the scope of inductive statistics, and I felt my confidence in statistically based SQC systems collapsing rapidly. Yet I was still spellbound by my preconceived notion that quality control methods backed by scientific statistical theory were superior. I still could not completely escape this idea.

STAGE 4: SAMPLING INSPECTIONS DO NOTHING BUT MAKE INSPECTION PROCEDURES MORE RATIONAL

In 1964, Mr. Tokizane, managing director at the headquarters of Matsushita Electric's Television Division, told me that he didn't want a single television made by his company to be defective. "I feel that way," he said, "because an individual customer generally buys only one television set. If that one set is defective, then that customer may assume that all Matsushita television sets are lemons. I won't allow defects in even one set, and so I'm in the plant nearly every day keeping an eye on workers."

I replied that I thought his attitude seemed reasonable, but then something about the use of statistically based sampling inspections had suddenly occurred to me: no matter how scientific a basis sampling inspections may have, the entire method rests on the notion that a certain level of defects is inevitable, whether it be one television set in 10,000 or one in 100,000.

Yet here was Mr. Tokizane, saying that he could not allow even one defective television set — even if it were one in 10,000 or one in 100,000. The idea that sampling inspections were extremely rational measures backed by the science of inductive statistics contradicted Mr. Tokizane's perfectly justifiable assertion that he would not allow a single defective television set in his company.

Unable to resolve this conflict, I fell to thinking as I headed home from Osaka by train. My confusion continued until we reached the outskirts of Tokyo, when suddenly it hit me: the statistical basis of sampling inspections meant only that such inspections made inspection techniques more rational; it did *not* make quality assurance more rational. Sampling inspections, in other words, may represent a rationalization of methods, but in no way do they represent a rationalization of goals.

The superiority of 100 percent inspections clearly dawned on me as I realized that they, and not sampling inspections, had to be used if one wished to put quality assurance on a more rational basis.

The justification for using sampling inspections was that 100 percent inspections would take too much trouble and cost too much. Why not, then, use 100 percent inspection techniques like poka-yoke ones — techniques that require little in the way of trouble or expense? This realization for the first time released me from the spell of sampling inspections and the inductive statistics behind them.

STAGE 5: ENCOUNTER WITH SOURCE INSPECTIONS

As explained above, I had been concentrating on the use of 100 percent inspections and on speeding up feedback and action. My thinking had never gone beyond the concept of informative inspections, and although I had given considerable thought to reducing defects, I had not adopted the more radical position of wanting to eliminate defects entirely.

As I went about applying poka-yoke methods, however, I noticed that the installation of suitable poka-yoke devices had the effect of reducing defects to zero. Was there some approach, I wondered, in which carrying out suitable inspections would make it possible to eliminate defects altogether?

Then it hit me. Why not just perform inspections at the sources of defects? Thus, around 1967, I arrived at the concept of *source inspections*. It had dawned on me that the occurrence of a defect was the *result* of some condition or action, and that it would be possible to eliminate defects entirely by pursuing the cause. The causes of defects lie in worker errors, and defects are the results of neglecting those errors. It follows that mistakes will not turn into defects if worker errors are discovered and eliminated beforehand.

I began advocating source inspections based on this fundamental notion and, in terms of actual techniques, installed a variety of poka-yoke systems that proved to be enormously successful.

In 1971, I joined the Japan Management Association's first overseas study group in visits to various plants in Europe. During that trip, we toured the facilities of Wotan, a molding machine manufacturer in Dusseldorf, West Germany.

During a question-and-answer period following the tour, a Mr. K of the M Spring Company — one of our group who always asked lively questions — stood up and asked the people at Wotan if they carried out quality control.

"Of course we do," the manufacturing division chief representing the company replied. "But," continued Mr. K, "in touring your plant I didn't see a single control chart."

"Control chart? What on earth is that?"

Mr. K then triumphantly proceeded to explain control charts while the Wotan representative listened in silence. When Mr. K had finished, the Wotan executive responded:

"That's a very interesting idea, but don't you think it's fundamentally wrong-headed?" Mr. K bristled. "Fundamentally wrong-headed?! What are you talking about?"

"The idea you just described deals with defects after they occur," the Wotan representative explained. "The basic idea behind our approach to quality control is to prevent defects from occurring in the first place."

"How in the world do you do that?" Mr. K asked.

Our host said that, rather than checking quality after a task had been completed, they checked whether operating methods were suitable before the job started.

As I listened to the Wotan representative, I recalled a scene I had just witnessed in the machine shop. When the operator in charge of a radial boring machine had put drills in place and was ready to begin, he motioned to a roving quality control officer, who came over to the machine and, using a chart as a guide, checked both drill positions and the positions of stoppers used to determine hole depths. Only when he gave the OK sign did the operator start the machine. As I listened to the division chief's words, I realized that it was this type of operation he was talking about.

The Wotan representative then asked Mr. K what the process defect rate at his company was.

"Only about 2.5 percent," said Mr. K proudly.

"I see," our host replied. "but the process defect rate at my company isn't any higher than 0.3 percent."

That took the wind out of Mr. K's sails and he was silent for the rest of the question-and-answer period.

I realized that the idea of checking operating conditions before the operations rather than after them was precisely the same as my concept of source inspections. I remember taking courage from this realization and thinking that this attested to the superiority of the source inspection concept. It was at that point, in fact, that my philosophy with regard to source inspections took definite shape.

At the same time, I repeatedly heard people say that the SQC system "builds quality into the process." But where was the evidence?

My claim was that a process is a flow in which raw materials are converted into finished products, and that any errors in process standards would naturally generate defects.

It is in this way that we finally arrive at a Zero QC system aimed at zero defects.

STAGE 6: THE ACHIEVEMENT OF A MONTH WITH ZERO DEFECTS

In 1977, I hurried to the Shizuoka plant of Matsushita Electric's Washing Machine Division when I heard that the facility had achieved a continuous record of one month with zero defects in a drainpipe assembly line operation involving 23 workers.

When I got there, I found that this significant goal had been attained by the use of source inspections, self-checks, and successive checks, and by the installation of effective poka-yoke devices — ingenious and relatively inexpensive mechanisms that everyone had cooperated in coming up with. These devices were installed according to the characteristics of the processes involved. This success resulted from the extraordinary efforts of supervisors working under Mr. Izumi, the department head, as well, of course, as those of the foreman, Mr. Muneo Iwabori, who directed actual work on the shop floor.

Before Matsushita's accomplishment, I had secretly been afraid that it might be impossible for a drainpipe assembly line employing so many workers and handling 30,000 units each month to actually go through an entire month with zero defects. Seeing this achievement gave me an unprecedented jolt, therefore, and I drew boundless confidence and courage from the realization that, given the proper conceptual approach and appropriate techniques, and given suitable leadership and general enthusiasm and cooperation, people can in fact achieve things that have been thought to be impossible.

The Matsushita Washing Division's Shizuoka plant continued zero defect production for over six months, and I confidently appealed to a number of other plants with the assertion that they, too, could achieve zero defects for the space of one month. Lo and behold, these plants began to achieve zero defect production for one month, and even for several months running. To myself, I thought how difficult such success would be to achieve with SQC methods based on inductive statistics.

STAGE 7: BASIC CONCEPTS FOR A ZERO QC SYSTEM

A Zero Quality Control system is built on the following basic ideas:

1. Use source inspections, i.e., inspections for preventing defects, to eliminate defects entirely. This does not mean

dealing with the results of defect generation, it means applying control functions at the stage where defects originate.

2. Always use 100 percent inspections rather than sampling inspections.
3. Minimize the time it takes to carry out corrective action when abnormalities appear.
4. Human workers are not infallible. Recognize that people are human and set up effective poka-yoke devices accordingly.

A RESPONSE TO INDUCTIVE STATISTICS

When I first heard about inductive statistics in 1951, I firmly believed it to be the best technique around, and it took me 26 years to break completely free of its spell.

Considered from an independent vantage point, several observations can be made with respect to inductive statistics:

- Inductive statistics remains an excellent technique.
- Active use should be made of statistics in the sense that the technique is extremely effective in the planning phase of management.
- Nevertheless, statistics is not always effective in control and execution phases. In fact, it can surely be said that an infatuation with statistics has impeded the progress of the management function itself.
- A major feature of SQC systems is the capacity for information inspections, and it is extremely important to pursue this function to the limit.
- In any case, inductive statistics is an excellent technique for making methods more rational; it does not necessarily have anything to do with rationalizing the attainment of goals.

Index

Books from Productivity, Inc.

Productivity, Inc. publishes books that empower individuals and companies to achieve excellence in quality, productivity, and the creative involvement of all employees. Through steadfast efforts to support the vision and strategy of continuous improvement, Productivity, Inc. delivers today's leading-edge tools and techniques gathered directly from industry leaders around the world. Call toll-free 1-800-394-6868 for our free catalog.

20 Keys to Workplace Improvement (Revised Edition)
Iwao Kobayashi

The 20 Keys system does more than just bring together twenty of the world's top manufacturing improvement approaches—it integrates these individual methods into a closely interrelated system for revolutionizing every aspect of your manufacturing organization. This revised edition of Kobayashi's bestseller amplifies the synergistic power of raising the levels of all these critical areas simultaneously. The new edition presents upgraded criteria for the five-level scoring system in most of the 20 Keys, supporting your progress toward becoming not only best in your industry but best in the world.
ISBN 1-56327-109-5/ 302 pages / $50.00 / Order 20KREV- B171

Becoming Lean
Inside Stories of U.S. Manufacturers
Jeffrey Liker

Most other books on lean management focus on technical methods and offer a picture of what a lean system should look like. Some provide snapshots of before and after. This is the first book to provide technical descriptions of successful solutions and performance improvements. The first book to include powerful first-hand accounts of the complete process of change, its impact on the entire organization, and the rewards and benefits of becoming lean. At the heart of this book you will find the stories of American manufacturers who have successfully implemented lean methods. Authors offer personalized accounts of their organization's lean transformation, including struggles and successes, frustrations and surprises. Now you have a unique opportunity to go inside their implementation process to see what worked, what didn't, and why. Many of these executives and managers who led the charge to becoming lean in their organizations tell their stories here for the first time!
ISBN 1-56327-173-7 / 350 pages / $35.00 / Order LEAN-B171

Productivity, Inc., Dept. BK, P.O. Box 13390, Portland, OR 97213-0390
Telephone: 1-800-394-6868   Fax: 1-800-394-6286

Handbook for Productivity Measurement and Improvement
William F. Christopher and Carl G. Thor, eds.

An unparalleled resource! In over 100 chapters, nearly 80 front-runners in the quality movement reveal the evolving theory and specific practices of world class organizations. Spanning a wide variety of industries and business sectors, they discuss quality and productivity in manufacturing, service industries, profit centers, administration, nonprofit and government institutions, health care and education. Contributors include Robert C. Camp, Peter F. Drucker, Jay W. Forrester, Joseph M. Juran, Robert S. Kaplan, John W. Kendrick, Yasuhiro Monden, and Lester C. Thurow.
ISBN 1-56327-007-2 / 1344 pages / $90.00 / Order HPM- B171

Implementing a Lean Management System
Thomas L. Jackson with Karen R. Jones

Does your company think and act ahead of technological change, ahead of the customer, and ahead of the competition? Thinking strategically requires a company to face these questions with a clear future image of itself. *Implementing a Lean Management System* lays out a comprehensive management system for aligning the firm's vision of the future with market realities. Based on hoshin management, the Japanese strategic planning method used by top managers for driving TQM throughout an organization, Lean Management is about deploying vision, strategy, and policy to all levels of daily activity. It is an eminently practical methodology emerging out of the implementation of continuous improvement methods and employee involvement.
ISBN 1-56327-085-4 / 182 pages / $65.00 / Order ILMS- B171

Manufacturing Strategy
How to Formulate and Implement a Winning Plan
John Miltenburg

This book offers a step-by-step method for creating a strategic manufacturing plan. The key tool is a multidimensional worksheet that links the competitive analysis to manufacturing outputs, the seven basic production systems, the levels of capability and the levers for moving to a higher level. The author presents each element of the worksheet and shows you how to link them to create an integrated strategy and implementation plan. By identifying the appropriate production system for your business, you can determine what output you can expect from manufacturing, how to improve outputs, and how to change to more optimal production systems as your business needs changes.
ISBN 1-56327-071-4 / 391 pages / $45.00 / Order MANST- B171

Productivity, Inc., Dept. BK, P.O. Box 13390, Portland, OR 97213-0390
Telephone: 1-800-394-6868   Fax: 1-800-394-6286

JIT Factory Revolution
A Pictorial Guide to Factory Design of the Future
Hiroyuki Hirano

The first encyclopedic picture-book of Just-In-Time, using photos and diagrams to show exactly how JIT looks and functions in production and assembly plants. Unprecedented behind-the-scenes look at multiprocess handling, cell technology, quick changeovers, kanban, andon, and other visual control systems. See why a picture is worth a thousand words.
ISBN 0-915299-44-5 / 218 pages / $50.00 / Order JITFAC- B171

A Revolution in Manufacturing
The SMED System
Shigeo Shingo

The heart of JIT is quick changeover methods. Dr. Shingo, inventor of the Single-Minute Exchange of Die (SMED) system for Toyota, shows you how to reduce your changeovers by an average of 98 percent! By applying Shingo's techniques, you'll see rapid improvements (lead time reduced from weeks to days, lower inventory and warehousing costs) that will improve quality, productivity, and profits.
ISBN 0-915299-03-8 / 383 pages / $75.00 / Order SMED- B171

5S for Operators
5 Pillars of the Visual Workplace
Productivity Press Developement Team

Operator books are based on the principles of adult learning to meet the reading needs of a shopfloor audience. Written at the appropriate reading level, these books are heavily illustrated with photos and drawings. The text is set up with one concept for every two to four pages so that it can be easily read in chunks; headers and assists in the margin make the significance of each section stand out. Each chapter summarizes main concepts and tools at the beginning and lists application questions at the end. This particular book presents the main concepts and tools from Hirano's *5 Pillars of the Visual Workplace*. Hirano discusses how the 5S theory fosters efficiency, maintenance, and continuous improvement in all areas of the company, from the plant floor to the sales office. It explains why the 5S's are important and gives the who, what, where, and how of 5S implementation.
ISBN 1-56327-123-0 /136 pages, illustrated / $25.00 / Order 5SOP-B171

Productivity, Inc., Dept. BK, P.O. Box 13390, Portland, OR 97213-0390
Telephone: 1-800-394-6868   Fax: 1-800-394-6286

Building Organizational Fitness
Management Methodology for Transformation and Strategic Advantage
Ryuji Fukuda

The most urgent task for companies today is to take a hard look at the future. To remain competitive, management must nurture a strong capability for self-development and a strong corporate culture, both of which form part of the foundation for improvement. But simply understanding management techniques doesn't mean you know how to use them. You need the tools and technologies for implementation. In *Building Organizational Fitness,* Fukuda extends the power of his managerial engineering methodology into the context of the top management strategic planning role.
ISBN 1-56327-144-3 / 250 pages / $65.00 / Order BFIT-B171

Do it Right the Second Time
Benchmarking Best Practices in the Quality Change Process
Peter Merrill

Is your organization looking back on its quality process and saying "it failed"? Are you concerned that TQM is just another fad, only to be replaced by the next improvement move-ment? Don't jump ship just yet. Everyone experiences failures in their quality improvement process. Successful organizations are different because they learn from their failure: They do it right the second time. In this plain-speaking, easy-to-read book, Peter Merrill helps companies take what they learned from their first attempts at implementing a quality program, rethink the plan, and move forward. He takes you sequentially through the activi-ties required to lead a lasting change from vision to final realization. Each brief chapter covers a specific topic in a framework which leads you directly to the issues that concern your organization.
ISBN 1-56327-175-3 / 225 pages / $27.00 / Order RSEC-B171

Kaizen Teian 1
Developing Systems for Continuous Improvement
Through Employee Suggestions
Japan Human Relations Association (ed.)

Especially relevant for middle and upper managers, this book focuses on the role of managers as catalysts in spurring employee ideas and facilitating their implementation. It explains how to run a proposal program on a day-to-day basis and outlines the policies that support a "bottom-up" system of innovation and defines the three main objectives of kaizen teian: to build participation, develop individual skills, and achieve higher profits.
ISBN 1-56327-186-9 / 217 pages / $30.00 (paperback) / Order KT1P-B171

Productivity, Inc., Dept. BK, P.O. Box 13390, Portland, OR 97213-0390
Telephone: 1-800-394-6868   Fax: 1-800-394-6286

Integrating Kanban with MRPII
Automating a Pull System for Enhanced JIT Inventory Management
Raymond S. Louis

Manufacturing organizations continuously strive to match the supply of products to market demand. Now for the first time, the automated kanban system is introduced utilizing MRPII. This book describes an automated kanban system that integrates MRPII, kanban bar codes and a simple version of electronic data interchange into a breakthrough system that substantially lowers inventory and significantly eliminates non-value adding activities. This new system automatically recalculates and triggers replenishment, integrates suppliers into the manufacturing loop, and uses bar codes to enhance speed and accuracy of the receipt process. From this book, you will learn how to enhance the flexibility of your manufacturing organization and dramatically improve your competitive position.
ISBN 1-56327-182-6 / 200 pages / $45.00 / Order INTKAN-B171

Kaizen for Quick Changeover
Going Beyond SMED
Kenichi Sekine and Keisuke Arai

Especially useful for manufacturing managers and engineers, this book describes exactly how to achieve faster changeover. Picking up where Shingo's SMED book left off, you'll learn how to streamline the process even further to reduce changeover time and optimize staffing at the same time.
ISBN 0-915299-38-0 / 315 pages / $75.00 / Order KAIZEN-B171

Kanban and Just-In-Time at Toyota
Management Begins at the Workplace
Japan Management Association /Translated by David J. Lu

Toyota's world-renowned success proves that with kanban, the Just-In-Time production system (JIT) makes most other manufacturing practices obsolete. This simple but powerful classic is based on seminars given by JIT creator Taiichi Ohno to introduce Toyota's own supplier companies to JIT. It shows how to implement the world's most efficient production system. A clear and complete introduction.
ISBN 0-915299-48-8 / 211 pages / $40.00 / Order KAN-B171

Productivity, Inc., Dept. BK, P.O. Box 13390, Portland, OR 97213-0390
Telephone: 1-800-394-6868   Fax: 1-800-394-6286

40 Top Tools for Manufacturers
A Guide for Implementing Powerful Improvement Activities
Walter Michalski

We know how important it is for you to have the right tool when you need it. And if you're a team leader or facilitator in a manufacturing environment, you've probably been searching a long time for a collection of implementation tools tailored specifically to your needs. Well, look no further. Based on the same principles and user-friendly design of Tool Navigator: The Master Guide for Teams, here is a group of 40 dynamic tools to help you and your teams implement powerful manufacturing process improvement. Use this essential resource to select, sequence, and apply major TQM tools, methods, and processes.
ISBN 1-56327-197-4 / 160 pages / $25.00 / Order NAV2-B171

A New American TQM
Four Practical Revolutions in Management
Shoji Shiba, Alan Graham, and David Walden

For TQM to succeed in America, you need to create an American-style "learning organization" with the full commitment and understanding of senior managers and executives. Written expressly for this audience, *A New American TQM* offers a comprehensive and detailed explanation of TQM and how to implement it, based on courses taught at MIT's Sloan School of Management and the Center for Quality Management, a consortium of American companies. Full of case studies and amply illustrated, the book examines major quality tools and how they are being used by the most progressive American companies today.
ISBN 1-56327-032-3 / 598 pages / $50.00 / Order NATQM-B171

Tool Navigator
The Master Guide for Teams
Walter J. Michalski

Are you constantly searching for just the right tool to help your team efforts? Do you find yourself not sure which to use next? Here's the largest tool compendium of facilitation and problem solving tools you'll find. Each tool is presented in a two to three page spread which describes the tool, its use, how to implement it, and an example. Charts provide a matrix to help you choose the right tool for your needs. Plus, you can combine tools to help your team navigate through any problem solving or improvement process. Use these tools for all seasons: team building, idea generating, data collecting, analyzing/trending, evaluating/selecting, decision making, planning/presenting, and more!
ISBN 1-56327-178-8 / 550 pages / $150.00 / Order NAVI1-B171

Productivity, Inc., Dept. BK, P.O. Box 13390, Portland, OR 97213-0390
Telephone: 1-800-394-6868   Fax: 1-800-394-6286

Toyota Management System
Linking the Seven Key Functional Areas
Yasuhiro Monden

Here's the first comprehensive and systematic explanation of the management system that drives the world's leading auto maker. The development of JIT production at Toyota and the company's achievement of unprecedented levels of productivity were made possible by its supportive, integrated management system. This new book reveals for the first time exactly how that management system works. It looks carefully at each of Toyota's seven management subsystems and how they work as an integrated whole.
ISBN 1-563267-139-7 / 245 pages / $30.00 (paperback) / Order TMS7P-B1711

TPM Case Studies
Factory Management Series
Nikkan Kogyo Shimbun (ed.)

Total Productive Maintenance (TPM) combines the best features of productive and predictive maintenance with innovative management strategies and total employee involvement. This collection of foundational articles and classic implementation case studies culled from NKS Factory Management Journal details how TPM has helped prize-winning companies in Japan achieve remarkable results. It includes in-depth explorations of the approach to loss reduction and plantwide implementation; a classic essay on the relationship between JIT and TPM by Seiichi Nakajima, the "father" of TPM; and numerous detailed examples of equipment modifications addressing specific types of losses.
ISBN 1-56327-066-8 / 200 pages / $30.00 / Order TPMCS-B171

Quick Response Manufacturing
A Companywide Approach to Reducing Lead Times
Rajan Suri

Quick Response Manufacturing (QRM) is an expansion of time-based competition (TBC) strategies which use speed for a competitive advantage. Essentially, QRM stems from a single principle: to reduce lead times. But unlike other time-based competition strategies, QRM is an approach for the entire organization, from the front desk to the shop floor, from purchasing to sales. In order to truly succeed with speed-based competition, you must adopt the approach throughout the organization.
ISBN 1-56327-201-6/ 560 pages / $50.00 / Order QRM-B171

Productivity, Inc., Dept. BK, P.O. Box 13390, Portland, OR 97213-0390
Telephone: 1-800-394-6868   Fax: 1-800-394-6286

TPM in Process Industries
Tokutaro Suzuki (ed.)

Process industries have a particularly urgent need for collaborative equipment management systems like TPM that can absolutely guarantee safe, stable operation. In TPM in Process Industries, top consultants from JIPM (Japan Institute of Plant Maintenance) document approaches to implementing TPM in process industries. They focus on the process environment and equipment issues such as process loss structure and calculation, autonomous maintenance, equipment and process improvement, and quality maintenance. Must reading for any manager in the process industry.
ISBN 1-56327-036-6 / 400 pages / $85.00 / Order TPMPI-B171

Zero Quality Control
Source Inspection and the Poka-Yoke System
Shigeo Shingo

Dr. Shingo reveals his unique defect prevention system, which combines source inspection and poka-yoke (mistake-proofing) devices that provide instant feedback on errors before they can become defects. The result: 100 percent inspection that eliminates the need for SQC and produces defect-free products without fail. Includes 112 examples, most costing under $100. Two-part video program also available; call for details.
ISBN 0-915299-07-0 / 328 pages / $75.00 / Order ZQC-B171

Productivity, Inc., Dept. BK, P.O. Box 13390, Portland, OR 97213-0390
Telephone: 1-800-394-6868   Fax: 1-800-394-6286

TO ORDER: Write, phone, or fax Productivity, Inc., Dept. BK, P.O. Box 13390, Portland, OR 97213-0390, phone 1-800-394-6868, fax 1-800-394-6286. Outside the U.S. phone (503) 235-0600; fax (503) 235-0909
Send check or charge to your credit card (American Express, Visa, MasterCard accepted).

U.S. ORDERS: Add $5 shipping for first book, $2 each additional for UPS surface delivery. Add $5 for each AV program containing 1 or 2 tapes;
add $12 for each AV program containing 3 or more tapes. We offer attractive quantity discounts for bulk purchases of individual titles; call for more information.

ORDER BY E-MAIL: Order 24 hours a day from anywhere in the world. Use either address: To order: service@productivityinc.com
To view the online catalog and/or order: http://www.productivityinc.com

QUANTITY DISCOUNTS: For information on quantity discounts, please contact our sales department.

INTERNATIONAL ORDERS: Write, phone, or fax for quote and indicate shipping method desired. For international callers, telephone number is 503-235-0600 and fax number is 503-235-0909. Prepayment in U.S. dollars must accompany your order (checks must be drawn on U.S. banks). When quote is returned with payment, your order will be shipped promptly by the method requested.

NOTE: Prices are in U.S. dollars and are subject to change without notice.

ABOUT THE SHOPFLOOR SERIES

Put powerful and proven improvement tools in the hands of your entire workforce!

Progressive shopfloor improvement techniques are imperative for manufacturers who want to stay competitive and to achieve world class excellence. And it's the comprehensive education of all shopfloor workers that ensures full participation and success when implementing new programs. The Shopfloor Series books make practical information accessible to everyone by presenting major concepts and tools in simple, clear language and at a reading level that has been adjusted for operators by skilled instructional designers. One main idea is presented every two to four pages so that the book can be picked up and put down easily. Each chapter begins with an overview and ends with a summary section. Helpful illustrations are used throughout.

Books currently in the Shopfloor Series include:

5S for Operators
5 Pillars of the Visual Workplace
The Productivity Press Development Team
ISBN 1-56327-123-0 /
incl. applic. questions / 133 pages
Order 5SOP-B171 / $25.00

Quick Changeover for Operators
The SMED System
The Productivity Press Development Team
ISBN 1-56327-125-7 /
incl. applic. questions / 93 pages
Order QCOOP-B171 / $25.00

Mistake-Proofing for Operators
The Productivity Press Development Team
ISBN 1-56327-127-3 / 93 pages
Order ZQCOP-B171/ $25.00

TPM for Supervisors
The Productivity Press Development Team
ISBN 1-56327-161-3 / 96 pages
Order TPMSUP-B171 / $25.00

TPM Team Guide
Kunio Shirose
ISBN 1-56327-079-X / 175 pages
Order TGUIDE-B171 / $25.00

TPM for Every Operator
Japan Institute of Plant Maintenance
ISBN 1-56327-080-3 / 136 pages
Order TPMEO-B171 / $25.00

Autonomous Maintenance
Japan Institute of Plant Maintenance
ISBN 1-56327-082-X / 138 pages
Order AUTMOP-B171 / $25.00

Focused Equipment Improvement
for TPM Teams
Japan Institute of Plant Maintenance
ISBN 1-56327-081-1 / 138 pages
Order FEIOP-B171/ $25.00

Just-In-Time for Operators
The Productivity Press Development Team
ISBN 1-56327-133-8 / 96 pages
Order JITOP-B171 / $25.00